University of London Historical Studies

IX

UNIVERSITY OF LONDON HISTORICAL STUDIES

REGALIAN RIGHT IN
MEDIEVAL ENGLAND

REGALIAN RIGHT IN MEDIEVAL ENGLAND

BY

MARGARET HOWELL

UNIVERSITY OF LONDON
THE ATHLONE PRESS
1962

Published by
THE ATHLONE PRESS
UNIVERSITY OF LONDON
at 2 Gower Street, London WC1

Distributed by Constable & Co. Ltd
12 *Orange Street, London* WC2

Canada
University of Toronto Press

U.S.A.
Oxford University Press Inc
New York

Printed in Great Britain by
WESTERN PRINTING SERVICES LTD
BRISTOL

PREFACE

THE first aim of this book was to attempt a systematic study based on unprinted public records of the exercise of regalian right in England in the thirteenth century, and this is still the core of the work. In the course of the Introduction I have explained how this investigation forced me to try to track the subject further back, into a period where the evidence was much more fragmentary. This research into beginnings accounts for the first part of the book, where I have tried to piece together the main outline of the development of regalian right from the Norman Conquest to the reign of King John. By the fourteenth and fifteenth centuries, the significance of regalian right has narrowed sharply, and centres almost entirely in the king's right of patronage *sede vacante*. I have attempted to cover the period when this change of emphasis takes place, in the early fourteenth century, and to examine its nature, but I have not followed the story beyond this turning point, when the evidence begins to produce returns of such diminishing interest. The pattern of historical development combined with availability of evidence makes the thirteenth century the natural focal point for a study of regalian right in medieval England.

This book is derived from a thesis which was approved in January 1955 for the degree of Doctor of Philosophy in the University of London. I wish to thank the governing bodies of Royal Holloway College and Westfield College for the award of research studentships which enabled me to prepare the thesis and the members of their History departments for unfailing help and kindness. I am glad to acknowledge the kindness of Mrs. Joan Varley and Miss Dorothy Williamson who facilitated access to unpublished documents connected with the bishopric of Lincoln: and the help given me by the officer of the Athlone Press in the preparation of the manuscript for the press. I should like to thank Miss Sylvia Overton for substantial help in the compiling of the index. To Professor R. R. Darlington, who read the book in manuscript and again in proof, I am deeply indebted for valuable advice and correction. Finally, I owe to two of my teachers all the gratitude that can be due from a pupil: to Miss Beryl Smalley who first awakened my interest in medieval history; and to Professor Sir Goronwy Edwards, who supervised my work for the thesis, guided me through the problems of developing it into this book, and read the proofs.

Milham Ford School, Oxford   M.E.H.
    June 1960

CONTENTS

LIST OF ABBREVIATIONS

Accounts of the Executors of Gravesend and Bitton	*Account of the Executors of Richard Bishop of London, 1303, and of the Executors of Thomas Bishop of Exeter, 1310,* ed. W. H. Hale and H. T. Ellacombe (Camden Society, New Series, x, 1874).
Benedict of Peterborough	Benedict of Peterborough, *Gesta Regis Henrici Secundi* (Rolls Series, 1861).
B.M.	British Museum.
Cal. Chan. Warrants	*Calendar of Chancery Warrants, 1214–1326* (P.R.O., 1927).
Cal. Charter R.	*Calendar of Charter Rolls, 1226–1300* (2 vols., P.R.O., 1903–6).
Cal. Close R.	*Calendar of Close Rolls, 1272–1330* (10 vols., P.R.O., 1892–1908).
Cal. Fine R.	*Calendar of Fine Rolls, 1272–1356* (6 vols., P.R.O., 1911–21).
Cal. Inq. Misc.	*Calendar of Inquisitions Miscellaneous, Chancery, 1219–1349* (3 vols., P.R.O., 1916).
Cal. Liberate R.	*Calendar of Liberate Rolls, 1226–51* (3 vols., P.R.O., 1916–37).
Cal. Pat. R.	*Calendar of Patent Rolls, 1232–1327* (13 vols., P.R.O., 1893–1913).
Chancellor's R. (C.R. in appendices)	Chancellor's Roll (P.R.O.).
Chron. Abingdon	*Chronicon Monasterii de Abingdon,* ed. J. Stevenson (Rolls Series, 1858).
Chron. Majora	Matthew Paris, *Chronica Majora,* ed. H. R. Luard (Rolls Series, 1872–83).
Close R.	*Close Rolls, 1227–72* (14 vols., P.R.O., 1902–38).
Dalderby Memorand.	Memoranda volume of the Register of John Dalderby (Archives of the Bishopric of Lincoln, Bishops' Registers No. iii).

Davis, *Regesta*	*Regesta Regum Anglo Normannorum, 1066–1154*, ed. H. W. C. Davis (1913).
Deeley, 'Papal Provision'	A. Deeley, 'Papal Provision and Royal Rights of Patronage in the Early Fourteenth Century', *Eng. Hist. Review* XLIII (1928), pp. 497–527.
Durham MS. 5520	Manuscript 5520 in the Durham Cathedral Archives, as transcribed in the appendix to the thesis of the late W. K. Evers, 'Disputes about Episcopal Elections in the Reign of Henry III etc.' (Maitland Library, Oxford).
Eadmer, *Hist. Novorum*	Eadmer, *Historia Novorum in Anglia etc.*, ed. M. Rule (Rolls Series, 1884).
Eccles.	P.R.O., Ecclesiastical Documents.
Edwards, *English Secular Cathedrals*	K. Edwards, *The English Secular Cathedrals in the Middle Ages* (1949).
Eng. Hist. Review	*English Historical Review*
Exannual R.	Exannual Roll (P.R.O.).
Fine R.	Fine Roll (P.R.O.).
Gesta Abbatum Mon. S. Albani	*Gesta Abbatum Monasterii Sancti Albani*, ed. H. T. Riley (Rolls Series, 1882–5).
Handbook	*Handbook of British Chronology*, ed. F. M. Powicke (1939).
Hist. Dunelm. Script. Tres	*Historiae Dunelmensis Scriptores Tres*, ed. J. Raine (Surtees Society IX, 1839): Chronicles of Geoffrey of Coldingham and Robert Graystanes.
Hist. Eliensis	*Historia Eliensis* in *Liber Eliensis* I, ed. D. J. Stewart (Anglia Christiana Societas, 1848).
Hoyt, *The Royal Demesne*	R. S. Hoyt, *The Royal Demesne in English Constitutional History, 1066–1272* (1950).
Hugh Candidus	*The Chronicle of Hugh Candidus, a Monk of Peterborough*, ed. W. T. Mellows (1949).
Jocelin of Brakelond	Jocelin of Brakelond, *Cronica*, ed. H. E. Butler (1949).
K.R. Mem. R.	King's Remembrancer's Memoranda Roll (P.R.O.).

Knowles, *Monastic Order* D. Knowles, *The Monastic Order in England* (2nd edition, 1949).

Liber Niger *Liber Niger Monasterii Sancti Petri de Burgo* (Appendix to the *Chronicon Petroburgense*, ed. T. Stapleton (Camden Society XLVIII, 1849), pp. 157–83).

Liberate R. Liberate Roll (P.R.O.).

Lincoln Lincoln Cathedral Dean and Chapter Archives.

L.T.R. Mem. R. Lord Treasurer's Remembrancer's Memoranda Roll (P.R.O.).

Luchaire, *Institutions Monarchiques* A. Luchaire, *Histoire des Institutions Monarchiques de la France sous les Premiers Capétiens*, 987–1180 (2nd edition, 1891).

Materials *Materials for the History of Thomas Becket*, ed. J. C. Robertson (Rolls Series, 1875–85)

Miller, *Abbey and Bishopric of Ely* E. Miller, *The Abbey and Bishopric of Ely* (1951).

Min. Acc. Ministers' Accounts (Bishops' Temporalities) (P.R.O.).

Mitchell, *Studies in Taxation* S. K. Mitchell, *Studies in Taxation under John and Henry III* (1914).

Ordericus Ordericus Vitalis, *Historia Ecclesiastica*, ed. A. Le Prevost (Société de l'Histoire de France, 1838–55).

Pat. R. *Patent Rolls, 1216–32* (2 vols., P.R.O., 1901–3).

Pipe R. (P.R. in appendices) Pipe Roll (P.R.O.).

Poole, *Domesday to Magna Carta* A. L. Poole, *From Domesday Book to Magna Carta* (1951).

P.R.O. Public Record Office.

Ralph de Diceto Ralph de Diceto, *Opera Historica*, ed. W. Stubbs (Rolls Series, 1876).

Ramsay, *Revenues of the Kings of England* J. H. Ramsay, *A History of the Revenues of the Kings of England, 1066–1399* (1925).

Red Book of Worcester *The Red Book of Worcester*, ed. M. Hollings (Worcestershire Historical Society, 1934–9)

Reg. W. Giffard	*The Register of Walter Giffard etc., 1266–79,* ed. W. Brown (Surtees Society CIX, 1904).
Reg. R. Kellawe	*The Register of Richard de Kellawe etc., 1314–16,* II, ed. T. D. Hardy (Rolls Series, 1874).
Reg. H. Newark	*The Registers of John de Romeyn etc., Part II and of Henry Newark etc., 1296–9,* ed. W. Brown (Surtees Society CXXVIII, 1916).
Reg. J. Pontissaria	*Registrum Johannis de Pontissaria etc., 1282–1304,* ed. C. Deedes (Canterbury and York Society, 1915–24).
Reg. R. Winchelsey	*Registrum Roberti Winchelsey, 1294–1313,* ed. R. Graham (Canterbury and York Society, 1917–42).
Reg. Worcs. Sede Vacante	*The Register of the Diocese of Worcester during the Vacancy of the See, 1301–1435,* ed. J. W. Willis Bund (Worcestershire Historical Society, 1893–7).
Rot. de Liberate ac de Misis et Prestitis	*Rotuli de Liberate ac de Misis et Prestitis Regnante Johanne* (Record Commission, 1844).
Rotuli Hundredorum	*Rotuli Hundredorum* (2 vols., Record Commission, 1812–18).
Rot. Litt. Claus.	*Rotuli Litterarum Clausarum 1204–27* (2 vols., Record Commission, 1833–44).
Rot. Litt. Pat.	*Rotuli Litterarum Patentium, 1201–16* (Record Commission, 1835).
Southern, 'Ranulf'	R. W. Southern, 'Ranulf Flambard and Early Anglo-Norman Administration', *Transactions of the Royal Historical Society,* Fourth Series, XVI (1933), pp. 95–128.
Statutes of the Realm	*Statutes of the Realm, 1235–1509* (2 vols., 1810–16).
Stubbs, *Lectures on Early Eng. Hist.*	W. Stubbs, *Lectures on Early English History* (1906).
s.v.	*sede vacante.*
Symeon of Durham	Symeon of Durham, *Opera Omnia,* ed. T. Arnold (Rolls Series, 1882–5).

Taxatio Ecclesiastica	*Taxatio Ecclesiastica Angliae et Walliae Auctortitate P. Nicholai IV* (Record Commission, 1802).
Tout, *Chapters in Admin. Hist.*	T. F. Tout, *Chapters in the Administrative History of Mediaeval England* (1920–33).
Wharton, *Anglia Sacra*	*Anglia Sacra etc.*, ed. H. Wharton (1691).
Wilkins, *Concilia*	*Concilia Magnae Britanniae et Hiberniae etc.*, I and II, ed. D. Wilkins (1737).
William of Malmesbury, *Gesta Regum* and *Historia Novella*	William of Malmesbury, *De Gestis Regum Anglorum, Historia Novella, etc.*, ed. W. Stubbs (Rolls Series, 1887–9).
William of Newburgh	William of Newburgh, *Historia Rerum Anglicarum*, ed. R. Howlett, in *Chronicles of the Reigns of Stephen, Henry II and Richard I*, I and II (Rolls Series, 1884–5).

Introduction

REGALIAN right in its fully developed form was the claim made by the crown to appropriate the revenues, or a part of the revenues, of a vacant bishopric to its own use,[1] and to present to those ecclesiastical benefices which *sede plena* were in the gift of the bishop.

In England the right seems to have been a post-Conquest development,[2] and between the Conquest and the end of the reign of King John it seizes the attention of the general historian of the period on at least three occasions. The practice is thought to have been started by William Rufus 'persuasione Flambardi', in the vacancy at Canterbury which followed the death of Lanfranc, a precedent which was ruthlessly followed in the case of other vacancies during this reign and the next.[3] Stephen renounced the right, but Henry II reverted to the custom of his grandfather with such gusto that 'even William Rufus can scarcely have made a better income out of the revenue of the church than did Henry II'.[4] The story reaches its fitting climax in the reign of John, that king of ill repute, who certainly made a far larger profit out of vacant sees than any previous ruler. This simple dramatic account of what has usually been regarded as the significant part of the history of regalian right in England, based fairly closely on the accounts of those contemporary chroniclers who mention the practice in order to condemn it, virtually ends with the end of the reign of John.

Clearly the first task of any specialized study of the *jus regale* as such must be to retrace the ground as far as the end of John's

[1] One cannot say with confidence that the royal claim extended only to the 'temporalities' until the thirteenth century. See below, pp. 37–9.

[2] This is a point on which Anglo-Norman chroniclers are agreed and I have not been able to find evidence to the contrary. For a consideration of the evidence see below, pp. 5–11.

[3] See below, p. 5, n. 3.

[4] A. L. Poole, *From Domesday Book to Magna Carta* (Oxford, 1951), p. 220.

reign. The evidence is scattered and fragmentary, and it demands many suspensions of judgement, but it is worth bringing
together in order to see how far it corroborates the accepted
impression, and how far it may suggest any modifications or
changes of emphasis. The second task must be to look beyond
the end of John's reign to find out whether the practice of regalian right in the thirteenth century does in fact cease to be
historically significant.

A preliminary answer to this second question may be given
immediately. In 1214 John granted his charter to the church,[1]
a kind of ecclesiastical counterpiece to Magna Carta itself. The
king conceded free episcopal elections to cathedral chapters
and promised that there should be no delays in the royal licence
to elect, nor in the royal assent to the election. This seemed to
point to much shorter vacancies for the future. Had vacancies in
fact become much shorter, then that further clause in this
charter, by which John reserved to himself and his heirs the
exercise of regalian right, might have been of slight importance.
But this was not the case. Whatever the hopes of Stephen
Langton[2] and Innocent III, the episcopal vacancies of the
reigns of Henry III and Edward I were not short. Rufus gained
much opprobrium for keeping the see of Canterbury open for
four years, but Henry III, pious though he was, kept Winchester
void for over six.[3] Even if this was exceptional, as it was, there
were at least nine other vacancies in the reign of Henry III,
excluding those in the Welsh sees, when the king retained the
temporalities in his hand for over two years.[4] In Edward I's

---

[1] *Select Charters*, ed. W. Stubbs (9th edition, Oxford, 1913), pp. 282–4.

[2] See W. S. McKechnie, *Magna Carta* (2nd edition, Glasgow, 1914), p. 212.
He suggests that Stephen Langton perhaps thought it unnecessary to press the king
for a renunciation of the custody of vacancies since they might now be expected to
be short.

[3] 9 June 1238–10 Sep. 1244.

[4] The temporalities of Canterbury were in the king's hand 3 Aug. 1231 to a
date probably later than 1 Feb. 1234 (the date of a writ addressed to the keeper
of the archbishopric, *Close R., 1231–34*, p. 374); and again from 16 Nov. 1240
to a date later than 24 Nov. 1243 (Fine R. 41, m.11), and again from 18 July 1270
to 12 Dec. 1272 (*Cal. Pat. R., 1272–81*, p. 2). Those of Durham were in hand from
1 May 1226 to 22 July 1228 (*ibid., 1225–32*, p. 196); and again from 15 Apr. 1237
to 12 Feb. 1241 (*Close R., 1237–42*, p. 272); those of Winchester from 24 Dec. 1258
(the date of the appointment of Nicholas de Haudlo as keeper; *Cal. Pat. R. 1258–66*,
p. 7) to 24 Aug. 1262 (*ibid.*, pp. 729–30). All these were very wealthy sees. The other

reign there were five vacancies in which the king held the temporalities for over eighteen months,[1] and in both reigns vacancies of more than six months were common.

These vacancies were a source of rich profit to the English crown in the thirteenth and early fourteenth centuries. The issues of the vacant bishoprics were essentially casual revenue, subject to many factors of chance, and it is when a king is in urgent need of money that the importance of casual revenue is at its height. A medieval government, very broadly speaking, used its regular income for subsistence; and it is in the spending of its casual revenue, the windfalls, that its policy and interests may be revealed. Henry III and Edward I were both at times very needy monarchs; they valued their casual revenue highly.

The church still remained at issue with the king over the exercise of regalian right, after 1214, but it no longer wasted its strength in attacking the right itself; instead, much effort and much thought were spent in the attempt to regulate the exercise of the claim and to mitigate its effects. The struggle was fought on a more sophisticated plane than before, but it was perhaps more constructive in its outcome too.

If we regard John's charter of 1214, not as the end of the historical importance of regalian right in England, but as the beginning of a second phase in the history of the right we may be approaching the right perspective. This second phase only lasted for roughly a century. By the reign of Edward II

---

long vacancies were at Chichester, in hand 1 Feb. 1244 to 20 July 1246 (*Close R.*, *1242–47*, p. 442); at Lichfield, 8 Dec. 1241 to 25 Mar. 1246 (*Cal. Pat. R.*, *1232–47*, p. 476), and at London, 29 Sep. 1241 to 16 Mar. 1244 (*ibid.*, p. 421). The initial dates of the vacancies here given are the dates of the bishops' deaths as noted in the *Handbook of British Chronology*, ed. F. M. Powicke (London, 1939), pp. 133–206. Since the evidence for the minority of Henry III is obscure, only those vacancies occurring from 1226 onwards (that is, the year before Henry declared his majority) have been included in this calculation.

[1] The temporalities of Canterbury were in the king's hand 8 Dec. 1292 to 4 Feb. 1295 (*Cal. Pat. R.*, *1292–1301*, p. 129); those of Carlisle from Sep. 1278 to 10 July 1280 (*ibid.*, *1272–81*, p. 386); those of Ely from 25 Mar. 1298 to 10 Oct. 1299 (*ibid.*, *1292–1301*, p. 441); those of Winchester from 12 Feb. 1280 to 11 Aug. 1282 (*ibid.*, *1281–92*, p. 33); those of York from 22 Sep. 1304 to 31 Mar. 1306 (*ibid.*, *1301–07*, p. 421). Salisbury also was vacant for more than eighteen months at the beginning of the reign but in this case the temporalities were in the hands of the dean and chapter for a fine of 3,000 marks.

vacancies were shorter, and as a source of revenue, although not as a source of patronage, their importance was now clearly on the wane. Meanwhile the period between the early thirteenth century and the early fourteenth century deserves exploration.

CHAPTER I

The Beginnings of
Regalian Right in England

THE chronicler Eadmer records that William Rufus was the
first king of England to begin the practice of appropriating to the royal treasury the revenues of vacant
bishoprics and abbeys, a practice which he 'in no way acquired
from the tradition of his father's reign'.[1] The statement seems
to find widespread support among the Anglo-Norman chroniclers[2] and widespread acceptance among English historians.[3]

An explanation of the practice was supplied by Stubbs.
Rufus and his wily favourite Ranulf Flambard were thought
mainly responsible for having worked out an ingenious adaptation of feudal principles to vacant ecclesiastical fiefs. Lay fiefs
in wardship were a rich source of revenue to the crown, and

[1] 'Et quidem ipse primus hanc luctuosam oppressionem ecclesiis Dei induxit
nullatenus eam ex paterna traditione accipiens' (Eadmer, *Historia Novorum*, ed.
M. Rule (Rolls Series, London, 1884), p. 27).

[2] *Chronicon Monasterii de Abingdon*, ed. J. Stevenson (Rolls Series, London, 1858),
II, 42. William of Malmesbury, *De Gestis Regum Anglorum*, ed. W. Stubbs (Rolls
Series, London, 1887–89), II, 369. Ordericus Vitalis, *Historia Ecclesiastica*, ed. A. Le
Prevost (Société de l'Histoire de France, Paris, 1838–55), III, 313.

[3] 'The entire absence of complaints during the Conqueror's reign is of itself
strong evidence that he did not annex the revenues during a vacancy, and the
explicit statements of the reliable Abingdon chronicle and of William of Malmesbury, as also of Orderic, that the custom of applying to religious houses the procedure of lay fees was introduced by Rufus at the suggestion of Ranulf Flambard,
may be accepted as giving the truth' (D. Knowles, *The Monastic Order in England*
(2nd edition, Cambridge, 1949), p. 613). See also A. L. Poole, *Domesday to Magna
Carta*, p. 169; W. E. Lunt, *Financial Relations of the Papacy with England to 1327*
(Cambridge, Massachusetts, 1939), p. 51 n. 2, and J. H. Ramsay, *A History of the
Revenues of the Kings of England* (Oxford, 1925), I, 2.

Note, however, the rather greater caution of E. A. Freeman (*The Reign of
William Rufus* (Oxford, 1882), I, 336), who does not commit himself to the absolute
originality of any of Flambard's feudal 'inventions'. His comment is: 'That all this
in its fully developed and systematic form was the work of Randolf Flambard, I
hope I may now assume.' See however A. Friedberg, *De Finium inter Ecclesiam et
Civitatem Regundorum Judicio* (Leipzig, 1861), pp. 220–1, where it is said that the
practice began with the Conqueror.

vacant sees and abbeys could be so too, if their position were
equated with that of the lay fiefs.[1] That explanation of the
origin of regalian right in England is still often accepted without
any radical modification.[2] As the lawgiver of feudalism, Ranulf
Flambard has been almost driven from the field, since the main
characteristics of English feudal practice have been traced to
the Conqueror's reign and often to Norman precedents, but as
far as Rufus's ecclesiastical policy is concerned Flambard's
colourful reputation remains essentially unchallenged; here he
still flourishes in all his villainy and inventiveness.

That William Rufus did exercise what later came to be
known as regalian right in vacant English bishoprics, and also
in vacant abbeys, is not in doubt. When a prelate died, Rufus's
first step was to send clerks to make a comprehensive description of the property of the bishopric or abbey. Eadmer records
that at Canterbury '. . . cuncta . . . intus et extra per clientes
suos describi praecepit'.[3] The king then appointed a keeper to
administer the see or abbey during the vacancy, and arranged
for the appropriation of the revenues of the fief to the crown.
In the case of an abbey the keeper might be a monk who would
answer to the king for the fruits of the vacancy. The monk
Motbertus was appointed to administer Abingdon in 1097:

. . . curam rerum infra extrave ministrabat, non ecclesiae provectibus
sed regii marsupii mercibus.[4]

---

[1] 'The analogy of lay fiefs was applied to churches with as much minuteness as
was possible.' (W. Stubbs, *The Constitutional History of England* (5th edition, Oxford,
1926), I, 324.)

[2] A. L. Poole, *loc. cit.*, p. 169: 'The means by which William II wrung money
from the church was an ingenious adaptation of feudal principles to the special
conditions pertaining to ecclesiastical fiefs.'

D. Knowles, *loc. cit.*, p. 613: 'The move was dictated by motives of avarice, whatever feudal analogies might be urged.'

Mr. R. W. Southern, in discussing the revision of the traditional view of Flambard is nevertheless cautious on this point ('Ranulf Flambard and Early Anglo-
Norman Administration', *Transactions Royal Hist. Soc.*, Fourth Series, XVI (1933),
pp. 96–7 and p. 103). Mr. Southern does not state whether the practice of appropriating the revenues of a vacancy, as distinct from prolonging it, was new or not,
but he remarks that Flambard's ecclesiastical exactions 'were involving quite
illegal extensions of the royal power'.

[3] Eadmer, *Hist. Novorum*, p. 26. William of Malmesbury corroborates this; *Gesta
Regum*, II, 369.

[4] *Chron. Abingdon*, II. 42.

A vacant bishopric might be supervised by a different type of custodian. The see of Worcester, for example, in the vacancy of 1095–6 may have been administered by the local sheriff, Urse d'Abetot, and a certain Bernard, who has been tentatively identified with William I's chaplain, Bernard son of Ospac.[1] These men were royal officials. At Canterbury in the vacancy between Lanfranc and Anselm, the custody of the see was sold and resold to the highest bidder, a practice encouraging every kind of abuse and which may go far to account for the bitterness of Eadmer's accusations against Rufus. Monks daily subjected to the insults and greed of these profiteers would have a grim story to tell of this vacancy.[2] According to the Winchester chronicler, Ranulf Flambard himself had in 1097 the custody of as many as sixteen vacant bishoprics and abbeys.[3] In some of these cases he may have been a kind of 'super keeper' with subordinates to act for him within the individual see or abbey.

The question of abuse and oppression may be set aside for the moment. What is indisputably clear is that Rufus did hold vacant ecclesiastical fiefs in his hand and exploited their resources for the crown. The chroniclers state that Rufus's practice was unprecedented, and that he acted 'persuasione Flambardi'.[4] Flambard was the villain of the monastic chronicles, and villainy is more shocking when it is without precedent. For this reason the alleged novelty of the practice of Rufus and Flambard deserves careful scrutiny. Something evidently was new, but was everything new? Did Rufus indeed owe nothing at all to the tradition of his father's reign?

The Conqueror's general practice on the death of a bishop or an abbot is described by Ordericus. First the king ordered a description of the property:

. . . sollicitus princeps prudentes legatos ad orbatam domum mittebat omnesque res Ecclesiae ne a profanis tutoribus dissiparentur describi faciebat.[5]

[1] *Regesta Regum Anglo-Normannorum, 1066–1100*, ed. H. W. C. Davis (Oxford, 1913), pp. 98–9, no. 387 and p. 144.
[2] *Hist. Novorum*, pp. 26–7.
[3] *Annales Monasterii de Wintonia*, ed. H. R. Luard, in *Annales Monastici*, II (Rolls Series, London, 1865), p. 39.
[4] Ordericus, III, 313.
[5] *Ibid.*, II, 200.

With the omission of the phrase 'ne a profanis tutoribus dis-siparentur' this description would apply equally well to Rufus's first act at Canterbury, on the death of Lanfranc.[1] The act was the same, but the motive different. Whereas Rufus's aim was the acquiring of accurate information about the episcopal property as a basis for profitable exploitation that of the Conqueror was the prevention of theft by the sacrilegious.

The *Historia Eliensis* corroborates Orderic's statement on this custom of description by a specific illustration.[2] On the death of Abbot Theodwin in 1075, an inventory of the treasure of the church of Ely was drawn up by three of the king's servants and arrangements were made for the care of the vacant abbey. Over the appointment of a custodian Theodwin himself had already taken the initiative:

> Godefridum monachum ejusdem loci, et sibi per cuncta fidelis-simum, procuratorem pro se dereliquit. Hic regis praecepto [or *concessu*][3] et fratrum obtentu[4] ipsius ecclesiae VII fere annis fidelis procurator remansit. . . .

The dying abbot had left Godfrey as custodian, but it was by the will of the brethren and, equally important, either *praecepto* or at least *concessu regis*, that Godfrey continued as keeper for seven years.

The custody of the vacant abbey of Ely was thus a matter of royal concern even in the reign of William I. There are parallels discernible between the practice of the Conqueror in this vacancy and the practice characteristic of Rufus, first in the description of the treasure and secondly in the appointment of a monk of the house to act as guardian during the vacancy. There is a difference too. The monk Motbertus at Abingdon in 1097 paid the revenue of the vacant abbey to William Rufus. At Ely in 1075, the monk Godfrey ruled 'quamsi abbas' and there is no mention of appropriation of revenue to the royal treasury.

Yet, even in the hands of a normally scrupulous prince, the opportunities of vacancy might lead to occasional abuse. In

---

[1] See above, p. 6.

[2] *Historia Eliensis*, ed. D. J. Stewart, in *Liber Eliensis*, 1 (Anglia Christiana Soc., London, 1848), pp. 249–51. The dates of the deaths of the abbots in this passage of the *Historia Eliensis* are incorrect.

[3] In one MS. the reading is *concessu; ibid.*, p. 250.

[4] The phrase 'et fratrum obtentu' is omitted in one MS.; *ibid.*

1077 William I was informed of the death of Frederick, abbot of St. Albans:

Rex igitur Willelmus, de morte Abbatis Fretherici certificatus, Coenobium Sancti Albani vacans in manu sua tenuit, et, extirpatis sylvis et depauperatis hominibus, oppressit: et, nisi correptionibus Lanfranci refrenaretur, irrestaurabiliter destruxisset.[1]

The statement, especially in its reference to Lanfranc, is circumstantial. In the same connection the action of William I on the death of Abbot Thurstan at Ely in 1072 is worth noting:[2]

Rex igitur citius cognito praedicti abbatis decessu ad Ely misit, et quicquid optimum in ornamentis et variis rebus ibi fuisse didiscerat, in thesaurum suum jusserat asportari.[3]

These two instances may well have been exceptional and caused by some political or personal animosity. Yet if these chroniclers are correct they show that even the Conqueror's behaviour was not invariably unimpeachable.

The evidence concerning the Conqueror's general practice is admittedly scanty, but it compels certain cautious conclusions. In this reign a vacant see or abbey fell under royal care, perhaps one may even go as far as to say royal control. There is, however, no evidence for the systematic appropriation of vacancy revenue to the royal treasury, although the fate of Ely in 1072 and of St. Albans in 1077 may suggest that the property of a vacant church was already not always immune.

Wherein then, did the novelty of Rufus's practice lie? The most succinct and perhaps most reliable statement of Rufus's innovation is that given by the chronicler of Abingdon, the house which was administered for Rufus by the monk Motbertus:

Ea tempestate, infanda usurpata est in Anglia consuetudo, ut si quae praelatorum persona ecclesiarum vita decederet, mox honor ecclesiasticus fisco deputaretur regio.[4]

---

[1] *Gesta Abbatum Monasterii Sancti Albani,* ed. H. T. Riley (Rolls Series, London, 1867), I, 51.

[2] This is the Ely vacancy preceding that of 1075 referred to above, p. 8.

[3] *Hist. Eliensis,* p. 248. This sounds like an exercise of the *jus spolii,* unless it is the treasure of the church rather than that of the late abbot which is plundered. In either case it is the tone of the act which is significant.

[4] *Chron. Abingdon,* II, 42.

The word *consuetudo* may be important. In his *customary* exploitation of vacancies as a source of royal income, Rufus may well
have been guilty of a policy not shared by his father. But the
practice of 'keeping' a vacant see or abbey was common to
both: here Rufus stood well within the *paterna traditio*. In short,
his policy is seen much more convincingly as the abuse of his
father's policy than as a bright and devilish invention which
occurred to the mind of Ranulf Flambard. Flambard's real
contribution to the development of regalian right in England
was his efficiency in transforming what was in origin a royal
trust into a most profitable royal right. There is no ground for
assuming that the practice of royal custody of vacant sees or
abbeys was the invention of Rufus and Flambard any more than
it was likely to have been the invention of the Conqueror.

The question now arises whether this particular royal right
derived anything from Anglo-Saxon custom. According to
Orderic a vacant abbey in the Anglo-Saxon period was in the
care of the bishop of the diocese, and the metropolitan acted as
custodian of vacant bishoprics.[1] The revenues were given to
deserving ecclesiastical causes: 'pauperibus vel structuris basili-
carum, vel aliis bonis operibus'. There is an interesting passage
in the *Historia Eliensis* which perhaps supplements this picture a
little. It concerns an Ely vacancy shortly before the Conquest:

> Post decessum vero abbatis Wlfrici, Stigardus [sic] Doroberniae
> archiepiscopus, abbatiam de Ely, sed et episcopatus atque abbatias
> sibi assumpsit plurimas et gratia utriusque domini sui, Ædwardi
> scilicet et Haroldi regum, eas propriis pastoribus viduatas, quamdiu
> voluit in sua manu tenuit, et quibus voluit personis conferebat. Nam
> Wintoniensem, Clastoniensem, S. Albani et S. Augustini et Elyen-
> sem, ante Turstanum abbatem abbatias in manu sua receperat et
> velut proprias possidebat. Ipso quoque suggerente, Haroldus, qui
> regnum sceptri tenebat, ipsum Turstanum ab eodem Stigando bene-
> dici fecit.[2]

[1] 'Antequam Normanni Angliam obtinuissent, mos erat ut, dum rectores
ecclesiarum obirent, episcopus coenobiorum, quae in sua diocesi erant, res sollicite
describeret, et sub ditione sua, donec abbates legitime ordinarentur, custodiret.
Similiter archiepiscopus episcopi res, antistite defuncto, servabat, . . .' (Ordericus,
III, 313).

[2] *Hist. Eliensis*, pp. 219–20. There is a marginal note to this passage in the edition
cited, 'The pluralities of Archbishop Stigand', and it has generally been stated that
Stigand in fact held the abbey of Ely in plurality (e.g. Freeman, *Norman Conquest*,

As Stigand in this case clearly administered the estates of the vacant abbey of Ely for his own benefit the picture given by Orderic seems idealized in respect of this particular vacancy. But it may well be true that the custody of a vacant bishopric or abbey was customarily in the hands of ecclesiastics in England before the Conquest.[1] Orderic may be almost if not entirely correct in assigning no part to the Anglo-Saxon kings in a vacancy.[2]

What apparently cannot be traced to the custom of Edward the Confessor may be traced with much greater probability to the custom of the dukes of Normandy before the conquest of England. Orderic's statement that the Conqueror sent his officers to make an inventory of the treasure of the vacant church is specifically applied to William's practice in Normandy as well as in England,[3] and at least one historian of Norman institutions goes so far as to describe the Conqueror's practice as the exercise of regalian right.[4] It would seem, then, that William I's treatment of vacancies in England was simply an extension to his new kingdom of a right which he had been accustomed to exercise in his duchy on the continent.[5]

III, 69 and *Dictionary of National Biography*, reissue, London, 1908–9, XVIII, 1256). But this does not seem the most natural interpretation of this passage, which merely states that Stigand held this abbey and others in his hand for as long as he wished and then bestowed them on what persons he wished. In the case of Ely he used his influence to get the king to bestow the abbey on Thurstan. To say that Stigand's tenure of the lands of Ely was 'pluralism' in the accepted sense of the word scarcely seems warranted. Freeman has an interesting cautionary note on the rest of Stigand's 'pluralities' in an Appendix (*Norman Conquest*, III, 638).

[1] Ely was in the diocese of Dorchester. One would have expected therefore, according to Orderic's scheme, that Bishop Wulfwig would have had the custody of Ely, rather than Stigand.

[2] It should be noted, however, that Stigand controlled these abbeys 'gratia utriusque domini sui'.

[3] 'Hanc nimirum observationem quinquaginta sex annis custodivit, quibus regimen in ducatu Normanniae seu regno Angliae tenuit; . . .' (Ordericus, II, 200–1).

[4] 'On a vu ci-dessus que Guillaume le Conquérant ne se privait pas d'exercer à la mort des évêques le droit de régale; . . .' (L. Valin, *Le Duc de Normandie et sa cour, 912–1204* (Paris, 1909), p. 78).

[5] For a detailed consideration of the exercise of regalian right on the continent before the eleventh century see particularly E. Lesne, *Histoire de la propriété ecclésiastique en France* (Lille and Paris, 1910 etc., in progress), I and II and 'Les origines du droit de régale', *Nouvelle Revue Historique de Droit Français et Etranger*, XLV (1921), pp. 5–52.

From the evidence relating to earlier continental practice one fact at least becomes clear. Rufus and Flambard, in taking custody of vacant bishoprics and abbeys, stood in an established tradition, not, it would seem, an Anglo-Saxon tradition, but a Norman and ultimately a Carolingian tradition. So, of course, did William the Conqueror. Moreover, the practice was one from which both church and state could derive benefit, but the benefit had often been very heavily weighted on the side of the state when the lay ruler was unscrupulous. So it was to be in England too. The difference between the practice of William I and that of William II in respect of vacant sees and abbeys was the difference of use and abuse. William I, although sometimes falling short of the highest Hildebrandine standards was a strong reliable defender of the church who was generally scrupulous in the exercise of his responsibilities. William Rufus had his eye on profit.

The question remains as to whether in extent and in degree William Rufus's methods were such as to justify the general impression of enormity which the chroniclers have created. The oppression in question may be broadly classified into two kinds. First, Rufus is accused of despoiling ecclesiastical property in a vacancy. Among the general complaints of spoliation there are two charges which are more specific than the rest. On the death of Abbot Paul in 1093, St. Alban's abbey saw its groves hewn down and its men impoverished by the extortion of money 'causis cavillatoriis adinventis'.[1] In the vacancy at Canterbury in 1089–93 there had been an even more serious abuse, the alienation of some of the property of the see. Anselm's refusal to ratify these royal grants of the archiepiscopal possessions was one of the points at issue between himself and Rufus.[2] Alienation of property, capital depreciation and impoverishment of the tenants were serious crimes, especially if Rufus indulged in them often.

The type of oppression which has been much more emphasized, partly perhaps because it roused the wrath of the monastic chroniclers so violently, was Rufus's maltreatment of the monks

---

[1] *Gesta Abbatum Mon. S. Albani*, I, 65.

[2] William of Malmesbury, *De Gestis Pontificum Anglorum*, ed. N. E. S. A. Hamilton (Rolls Series, London, 1870), p. 83.

of a vacant house. The most detailed evidence comes from Canterbury. Here according to Eadmer, the royal keepers 'nefandissimi hominum' strode through the cloisters 'torvo ac minaci vultu'. The monks were subjected to every indignity and perhaps worst of all they were limited to a fixed allowance of food, fixed presumably in an arbitrary way by either the king or the keepers.[1] The force of this grievance can be fully appreciated only in the light of the economic arrangements which obtained at Canterbury *sede plena*. In this cathedral monastery, as in some others, the monks seem to have had a fairly full measure of control over certain manors or other property specifically set aside by the archbishop to provide for their maintenance.[2] To be placed on a fixed allowance, therefore, might constitute a double grievance. In the first place it might be felt that the allowance was insufficient, and quite apart from that the monks would regard the arrangement as an infringement of their rights over what they had come to regard almost as their own property.

Eadmer's testimony is valuable evidence for what happened at Canterbury in this vacancy between Lanfranc and Anselm. But he goes further and states that this was one instance of a general oppression affecting many other English churches.[3] Ordericus supports Eadmer in this:

... rex ... tam in abbatiis coenobitas, quam in episcopiis episcopales decanos et canonicos cuilibet satellitum suorum subegit. Parcam autem ad victum suum distributionem rerum eis delegebat, et reliquos redditus suae ditioni mancipabat.[4]

Did Rufus then as a general rule maltreat the monks of cathedral churches and abbeys? In proceeding towards an answer to this question there are a few pieces of evidence concerned with specific vacancies which deserve careful consideration. The first is a later passage in the chronicle of Ordericus:

[1] (Rex) ... 'taxatoque victu monachorum inibi Deo famulantium, reliqua sub censum, atque in suum dominium redigi jussit' (*Hist. Novorum*, p. 26).

[2] For the division of property at Canterbury see B. W. Kissan, 'Lanfranc's Alleged Division of Lands between Archbishop and Community', *Eng. Hist. Review*, LIV (1939), pp. 285–93. The author concludes that the division was certainly pre-Conquest.

[3] *Loc. cit.*, pp. 26–7.

[4] Ordericus, III, 312.

Sic etiam defuncto Baldwino abbate sancti regis et martyris Edmundi, et Simeone Eliensi aliisque Patribus de saeculo migrantibus mortali, per Angliam regales ministri coenobia cum omnibus ad eadem pertinentibus invadebant, et monachis victum et vestitum cum parcitate erogabant, caetera vero regiis thesauriis ingerebant.[1]

For the case of Bury St. Edmunds we have no further evidence. For events at Ely about the time of Abbot Symeon's death there is an extensive account in the *Historia Eliensis*, and Mr. R. W. Southern has suggested that this is indeed a specific illustration which lends considerable weight to the chroniclers' general complaint that monks in a vacancy were kept on an arbitrarily fixed ration.[2] It should be noticed, however, that the events at Ely took place not in a vacancy, but *abbatia plena*. The weak Abbot Symeon, unable to defend the property of his own monastery, appealed to the king for assistance and in response to this appeal the king sent to the abbey a commission of royal justices with Flambard at their head to inquire into the matter. Soon after their arrival Flambard quarrelled with the monks and seized some of their treasure. Later, at the king's request there was drawn up a list of amounts in money and in kind which were to be allotted for the specific needs of the monks in food and clothing.[3] There was nothing necessarily sinister in this arrangement in itself, for there seems to be no evidence that it was intended to replace some system by which the monks had control over property especially set aside for their maintenance.[4] It is true that in some cathedral monasteries, as at Canterbury and Worcester, a system of separation of conventual property had already developed, but such an arrangement

---

[1] *Ibid.*, iv, 10.

[2] 'Ranulf Flambard', p. 104. Mr. Southern summarises the story from the *Hist. Eliensis*, pp. 277–8.

[3] 'Haec igitur sunt quae idem Ranulfus et Symeon abbas ex jussu regis Willelmi constituerunt, uno quoque anno dari ad opus fratrum ad vestimenta eorum septuaginta libras. Ad coquinam eorum sexaginta libras; ad sagimen ducentos porcos . . .' the list continues (*Hist. Eliensis*, p. 278).

Mr. Southern says that Flambard 'pensioned off each monk with an amount of food and clothing fixed by himself', but this passage seems rather to imply that a block grant was made to the whole convent.

[4] It was in Henry I's reign that Bishop Hervey (1109–31) specified a definite division of property between the monastery of Ely and its head. Hervey's grant is worded, 'Ego . . . res monachorum a rebus episcopalibus separatim ordinavi . . .', B.M., Harleian MS. 43.H.4.

was not yet common in autonomous abbeys. Moreover, it is interesting to note that some such arrangement as that drawn up by Flambard and Symeon at Ely was sometimes adopted in the early twelfth century as the actual basis of a system of separation of conventual property.[1] Whatever the administrative arrangements within an abbey for the control of monastic property, whether they involved 'separation' or not, the specific requirements of the monks in terms of food and clothing had to be assessed as the first step. This assessment was the logical basis of any provision for their daily needs. Perhaps the real grievance of the Ely monks on this particular occasion was less that the allowance was arbitrarily fixed than that it was, so the chronicler complains, 'brevis'.[2] But in any case, an arrangement made *abbatia plena*, with the abbot's consent, and perhaps intended to be permanent cannot be used too confidently as evidence for typical procedure in a vacancy.[3]

A further specific piece of evidence on this question relates to

---

[1] The division of property between abbot and convent at Ramsey has as its starting-point the weekly needs of the monks. The allocation of the revenue of certain manors to supply those needs is the second step (*Cartularium Monasterii de Rameseia*, ed. W. H. Hart and P. A. Lyons (Rolls Series, London, 1884–93), III, 230–4). For a very similar arrangement see J. Armitage Robinson, *Gilbert Crispin, Abbot of Westminster* (Cambridge, 1911), pp. 41–5. The document there printed (p. 41) sets out in detail the needs of the monks (in food by the week and in clothing by the year) and again specified manors are allocated to supply the necessary revenue. It has been suggested (*loc. cit.*) that this document may represent the provisions made for a vacancy. If so it seems likely that it is a description of existing conditions *abbatia plena* (like the *Liber Niger*, appendix to the *Chronicon Petroburgense*, ed. T. Stapelton (Camden Soc. XLVII, London, 1849), pp. 157–83) made to assist the keepers in vacancy administration.

[2] It is interesting to notice that the £70 assigned to the clothing of the Ely monks (see above, p. 14, n. 2) corresponds exactly with the £70 allowed for the clothing of the monks of Westminster (*Gilbert Crispin*, p. 41). The monks of Peterborough had £40 allocated to their clothing according to the *Liber Niger*, p. 166.

[3] It may be noted in connection with this incident at Ely that the English kings in the thirteenth and fourteenth centuries frequently took under their protection houses which had fallen into debt, often at the express wish of the house itself. On these occasions the keepers appointed by the king seem to have intervened to quite a considerable extent in the internal economy of the house (K. L. Wood Legh, *Studies in Church Life in England under Edward III* (Cambridge, 1934), pp. 1–9, 31 and 34–5). Evesham was taken into the king's hand in this way (*Cal. Pat. R., 1258–66*, p. 58; 29 Oct. 1259), and the following brief writ concerning the priory of Mersea is perhaps worth quoting: 'Commitment during pleasure to William de Sutton of the priory of Mereseye, saving to the prior and monks their reasonable sustenance' (*Cal. Fine R., 1272–1307*, p. 340; 6 July 1294).

the see of Durham. There was a vacancy here from 1096 to 1099. But from the Durham chronicler we hear nothing of *taxatus victus* or of any other oppression. Far from it:

(Rex). . . a monachis vero nil accipiens immo largus et bene-ficus, nil oppressionis et injuriae illis a quoquam irrogari permisit.[1]

Similarly in a Worcester vacancy of Rufus's reign the rights of the monks appear to have been protected. Bishop Wulfstan died in 1095 and there is extant the text of a writ addressed by Rufus to the earl of Warwick and the sheriffs of Worcestershire and Warwickshire. It includes this command:

All property appropriated to the maintenance of the monks is to be in the hands of the prior.[2]

Clearly it was not the king's intention that the monks of Worcester should be kept on a sparse fixed allowance. On the contrary they were to be allowed full control of the property traditionally set aside for their maintenance. A royal writ is fair evidence of royal policy, although, as in the case of the chronicles, it is safer not to generalize; the evidence is valid for the instance to which it refers.

To sum up, it seems apparent that specific evidence for or against a general practice of assigning the monks of a vacant house a fixed allowance of necessaries is scanty. What is quite clear is that there was no uniformity of treatment, that Eadmer's testimony for Canterbury must be confined to that see and that Orderic's generalization cannot be accepted as wholly valid. In cathedral churches, at least, William Rufus did not always restrict the monks to an arbitrarily fixed ration. The property of the monks of Worcester was left inviolate, and the king has a very clear record for his treatment of the monks at Durham.

Before concluding this account of the policy of Rufus in respect to episcopal vacancies mention must be made of an incident in which he, or Flambard, is said to have resorted to 'an expedient unprecedented in feudal practice',[3] an act which was 'not an enforcement, but a breach of feudal principles'.[4]

---

[1] Symeon of Durham, *Opera*, ed. T. Arnold (Rolls Series, London, 1882–85), I, 135.
[2] Davis, *Regesta*, p. 99, no. 388.   [3] Southern, 'Ranulf Flambard', p. 103.
[4] J. H. Round, *Feudal England* (London, 1895), p. 310.

This was the notorious exaction of a relief from the tenants of the bishopric of Worcester in 1095.[1] The exaction has been regarded as a deliberate attempt on the part of Flambard to compensate the royal treasury for the fact that the relief exacted from the heir of a lay fief on his entry into his estate could not be exacted from an incoming bishop.[2] The relief was therefore extorted from the undertenants direct.

The wording of the writ ordering the relief deserves careful attention. Rufus announces to the Worcester tenants:

Sciatis quia, mortuo episcopo, honor in manum meam rediit. Nunc volo, ut de terris vestris tale relevamen mihi detis sicut per barones meos disposui.

'Nunc' is significant; it implies a close connection between the coming of the *honor* into the king's hand and the exaction of the relief. Round points out that the writ must have been issued 'very shortly after the death of Wulfstan', that is at the beginning of the vacancy.

This gives particular weight to an alternative explanation of the relief, which Round mentions in a footnote, although he seems to reject it. 'It has been urged to me', he writes, 'that relief *mutatio domini* was a recognized practice but I cannot find proof of it in English feudalism.' This alternative interpretation is, however, accepted by Maitland[3] and Professor Stenton has observed that although the exaction of a relief by a new lord was not customary in English feudal practice,[4] he had found occasional traces of payments to a new lord by way of recognition of his lordship, in the twelfth century.[5] A particularly clear example of payment from tenants to a new lord in the twelfth century is provided by the act of Abbot Samson at Bury St. Edmunds in 1182, as described by Jocelin of Brakelond. The newly appointed abbot, says Jocelin, on receiving

---

[1] *Ibid.*, p. 309.

[2] 'But Ranulf must have argued that bishops and abbots who took reliefs from their tenants ought, in like manner, to pay reliefs to the crown. This they obviously would not do . . . And so he adopted . . . the unwarrantable device of extorting the relief from the under-tenants direct' (Round, *loc. cit.*, p. 310).

[3] F. Pollock and F. W. Maitland, *The History of English Law* (2nd edition, Cambridge 1911), I, 317–18.

[4] F. M. Stenton, *The First Century of English Feudalism* (Oxford, 1932), p. 160.

[5] *Ibid.*, pp. 161–2.

C

homage from his knights demanded from them an aid, and
they promised him twenty shillings each.[1] As a corollary to
this the abbot levied an aid and recognition on the lesser
tenants, *per maneria*, and it is specifically stated that this levy
was made 'secundum consuetudinem regni'.[2] The customary
nature of such levies both on knights and lesser tenants is
further strengthened by a more brief but otherwise strikingly
similar entry in the chronicle of Hugh Candidus. Hugh is des-
cribing the accession of the restless and ambitious Henry del
Angeli to the abbacy of Peterborough in 1128; he writes:

Cum venisset autem sicut diximus prefatus abbas ad monasterium
mansit ibi pene uno anno, et accepit homagium et pecuniam de militibus et de tota abbacia et nichil boni ibi fecit, . . .[3]

The statement is admittedly less explicit than that of Jocelin,
but the coupling of the act of taking homage with that of taking
money from the knights and from the whole abbacy in the first
year of entry upon the fief strongly suggests that the money
thus taken was by way of aid and recognition, as at Bury over
half a century later. It seems a warrantable inference that such
payments were not unfamiliar in abbeys in the twelfth century.
It is *possible*, presumably, that they were already known in the
last decade of the eleventh century, and may in that case have
served as a model for Rufus's exaction of a 'relief' on the occasion of the vacancy at Worcester. As a payment made in recognition of the king's temporarily immediate lordship over the
bishopric the Worcester relief seems more intelligible. The
honor had come into the king's hand; the king was lord of the
honor; 'Nunc volo ut relevamen mihi detis.'

Rufus in fact, even with Flambard close at hand to suggest,
can be made responsible for too much. As long as he commands
attention as a monster of iniquity he has too much power to

---

[1] *The Chronicle of Jocelin of Brakelond*, ed. H. E. Butler (London, 1949), p. 27.

[2] *Ibid.*, p. 31. It is interesting to reflect that Henry III levied an aid at the rate of
four marks on the knight's fee on the tenants of the bishopric of Durham on the
occasion of the vacancy of 1226, which they were said to have paid 'willingly'
(below, pp. 133–4). For further discussion of such payments *sede vacante* in the thirteenth century see below, pp. 121–42. The amounts paid by the Worcester tenants to
William Rufus as a relief were in some cases very high. They varied between £30
and £1 (Round, *loc. cit.*, p. 309).

[3] *The Chronicle of Hugh Candidus*, ed. W. T. Mellows (Oxford, 1949), p. 101.

obscure the development of English institutions in the late eleventh century. His measures were oppressive, but neither he nor Flambard invented regalian right. It is true that he failed to observe a traditional division of ecclesiastical property at Canterbury, but it is not true that he kept the monks of all vacant churches on an arbitrarily fixed, meagre ration during a vacancy. Finally there was no need to commit breaches of feudal principles, as it is alleged that he did at Worcester, when it was sufficient to press all available feudal precedents into the great task of making money.

CHAPTER II

The Development of the Right
in the Twelfth Century

HENRY I

Henry I's charter of liberties conveniently sums up the evil practices of the late king and draws in outline a picture of the better time coming in the reign of his successor.[1] This, at least, was what it was intended to convey, for the charter was, in part, a piece of political propaganda; it sharpened and heightened the contrast between the evil ways of Rufus and the moderation and legality which it was promised should characterize the new reign.

In the first clause of the charter the king made a promise concerning one of the most notorious oppressions of Rufus's reign, the treatment of vacant bishoprics and abbeys. There is little agreement as to exactly what the clause means, although there is complete agreement that it was the customary practice of Henry I some years afterwards to enjoy the issues of episcopal and abbatial vacancies.[2] This fact is more important than the promise of the charter. However, since the king's declared policy is a useful starting-point for investigating his actual

---

[1] Stubbs, *Select Charters*, pp. 116–19.

[2] Knowles, *Monastic Order*, p. 613, and F. Makower, *The Constitutional History and Constitution of the Church of England* (London, 1895), p. 314, n. 2.

The contemporary evidence leaves no room for doubt. The assembly of clergy in 1136 mention, among other charges against Henry I, '. . . terras ecclesiarum, pastoribus defunctis, in proprios usus redigere . . .', *Gesta Stephani Regis Anglorum*, ed. R. Howlett, in *Chronicles of the Reigns of Stephen, Henry II and Richard I*, III (Rolls Series, London, 1886), p. 17. See also *Chron. Abingdon*, II, 158–9 (1115–19); Hugh Candidus, p. 99 (1125 and above all the evidence of the Pipe Roll of 1130) (*Pipe R. 31 Henry I*), where there are references to the issues of vacancies of the bishoprics of Durham, pp. 130–3; Hereford, p. 140; Coventry, p. 140; and York, p. 31; and of the abbeys of Glastonbury, p. 68; Evesham, p. 109; and Chertsey, p. 140.

practice, the vexed problems of Henry I's promise to the church must be examined. The clause runs

> . . . sanctam Dei ecclesiam imprimis liberam facio, ita quod nec vendam nec ad firmam ponam, nec mortuo archiepiscopo sive episcopo sive abbate aliquid accipiam de dominio ecclesiae vel de hominibus ejus donec successor in eam ingrediatur.[1]

One fact is clear. Henry did not renounce the *custody* of vacant sees and abbeys, the right of the crown to superintend the administration of a widowed church. That right was renounced later by Stephen, but such a step is neither anticipated nor, I think, in any way implied in Henry's charter. The king does, however, make two distinct promises. The first is that he will not sell nor put to farm the church of God. Is this promise concerned with vacancy procedure or not?[2] There is evidence which tempts one to think that the problems of vacancies may have been in the mind of those who framed this statement. At Canterbury in the vacancy between Lanfranc and Anselm it was the practice of selling the custody of the vacancy to the highest bidder which had given rise to grave abuses.[3] Moreover, the *Anglo-Saxon Chronicle* under the year 1100 sums up Rufus's oppression:

> God's churches he depressed, and all the bishoprics and abbacies, whose heads died in his days, he either sold for money, or held in his own hand, and let for rent; . . .[4]

This coupling of the abuses of simony and the farming of vacancies reads almost like an echo of the wording of Henry's charter. On the other hand there are two reasons for thinking that Henry's first promise, 'quod nec vendam nec ad firmam ponam', cannot refer to vacancies alone. In the first place it precedes and is in no way grammatically governed by the phrase 'nec mortuo archiepiscopo sive episcopo sive abbate', and further it seems to read naturally as a more exact elucidation of the very general statement that the holy church of God should be free. This promise may well have been primarily a renunciation

---

[1] *Select Charters*, p. 177.
[2] Mr. McKechnie for instance accepts the view that the promise does relate to vacancies, *Magna Carta* (2nd edition), pp. 97–8.
[3] See above, p. 7.
[4] *The Anglo-Saxon Chronicle*, ed. B. Thorpe (London, 1861), pp. 203–4.

of simony, such as Stephen made in his charter before his promises concerning vacancies.[1] But this does not mean that the
promise might not have referred to vacancies as well. The
statement may intentionally have been worded to be understood in a general rather than in any very exact sense and it is
perhaps most convincingly interpreted as something devised
to look like a renunciation of all selling or letting to farm in
connection with the church, either *sede plena* or *sede vacante*.

Henry's second promise, that he will not take anything from
the demesne of the church or from its men until the successor
enters upon it, specifically relates to procedure on the part of the
king after a prelate's death. Beyond this point the statement
bristles with difficulties. It is perhaps most often taken to mean
that Henry hereby yielded the claim which Rufus had made to
appropriate the revenues of vacant churches to his own uses.[2]
If this interpretation is correct then Henry was guilty of obvious
perfidy. It is sometimes implied that the king may have kept his
promise to renounce vacancy issues at first but that he lapsed
later on. It is said that Henry was found taking the revenues of
vacancies 'some years later',[3] or that he 'afterwards resorted
to the practices of his brother Rufus'.[4] A statement made by
Hugh Candidus seems to undermine these modifying clauses.
Shortly before the end of the reign of William II, Thurold the
abbot of Peterborough died, and Hugh records what happened
during the vacancy:

> Willelmus Rufus habuit vacacionem abbacie per duos annos et
> Henricus rex per unum annum et amplius.[5]

No distinction is here drawn between the act of William Rufus
and that of Henry I. William Rufus did not merely hold the

[1] *Select Charters*, pp. 143–4. See also Stubbs, *Lectures on Early English History*
(London, 1906), pp. 109–10.
[2] Stubbs seems to imply this in *Select Charters*, p. 116, and it is the interpretation
accepted by Professor Knowles, *Monastic Order*, p. 613. In *Lectures on Early Eng. Hist.*,
p. 109, however, Stubbs sees it as a twofold renunciation, 'of the right of seizing the
property of the church and demanding extraordinary services from its vassals during the vacancy'. Round states firmly that this is a renunciation of revenues, not
of reliefs, but he does not give his reasons (*Feudal England*, pp. 310–11). Makower
considers this a possible interpretation, but suggests as an alternative that Henry
may be promising that he will not reduce the capital value of the see, rather than
that he will renounce the interim fruits (*loc. cit.*, p. 314).
[3] Knowles, *loc. cit.*, p. 613.   [4] Round, *loc. cit.*, p. 310.   [5] Hugh Candidus, p. 170.

abbey during the vacancy, he 'had the vacancy of the abbey', that is, he enjoyed the issues of the vacancy for two years, 'et Henricus rex per unum annum et amplius'. As far as the evidence goes there was no break in the exercise of regalian right in England though Rufus died and Henry I became king. This continuity of practice is, of course, far from proving that Henry had not made a promise to abstain from the practice of appropriating the revenues of vacant churches and abbeys; what is rather surprising perhaps is that no chronicler seems to mention that he immediately broke his promise.

There is another possible interpretation of the king's statement that on the prelate's death he would take nothing from the demesne of the church nor from its men. The phrase 'aliquid accipiam' occurs again in the third clause of the same charter,[1] where King Henry promises not to insist on any payment when one of his barons seeks licence to marry a daughter. Here he is clearly speaking of a single payment, which he promises not to receive or obtain, 'accipere'. The identical wording in clause (i) suggests, in the absence of any evidence to the contrary, that a similar single payment (as distinguished from the regular issues of a vacant see) may be referred to here as well.[2] The likelihood of this explanation is increased by the fact that there was a payment which is known to have been taken by Rufus on the death of a bishop and which might well have been referred to in this way, the relief exacted from the military tenants of the bishopric of Worcester in 1095.[3] That was a single payment taken 'mortuo episcopo' and 'de hominibus ecclesiae'.[4]

But Henry also promises to take nothing 'de dominio ecclesiae'. This is more difficult to explain. It is true that there is no direct evidence that Rufus charged the inhabitants of the

---

[1] *Select Charters*, p. 118.

[2] The argument that 'aliquid accipiam' refers to the receipt of a single payment in clause (1) of Henry's charter, as it undoubtedly does in clause (3), is perhaps strengthened by contrast with the wording of clause (12) of the Constitutions of Clarendon (*Select Charters*, p. 166), in which Henry II formally asserts his claim to appropriate the revenue of a vacant see. He does not use 'accipere', but the much more forceful 'percipere' (to lay hold on, take possession of): '. . . et inde [Rex] percipiet omnes redditus et exitus.'

[3] See above, pp. 16–18.

[4] Mr. McKechnie interprets this part of the clause as a promise not to take reliefs (*loc. cit.*, p. 98).

demesne of a vacant bishopric with any levy which might be considered parallel to the relief paid by the freeholders of the bishopric of Worcester in 1095. On the other hand it would be rash to argue from silence that he did not. Certainly, whatever happened in England, one of the first acts of the early Capetian kings in a vacancy in any French bishopric over which they were able to exercise regalian right was to levy a *taille* on the vacant see.[1] Moreover, in later English practice aids and tallages were levied on the demesne of vacant sees.[2] Clearly this evidence is not conclusive, but it is suggestive. It does not seem unlikely that Rufus may sometimes have levied an oppressive payment of some kind, whether he called it a tallage, gift or recognition, or whether he gave it a name at all, on the demesne of a vacant see or abbey.[3]

To sum up, the evidence relating to the first clause of Henry I's charter establishes one fact and suggests one working hypothesis. It is certain that Henry I continued to exercise a claim to the issues of vacant sees and abbeys; it seems a likely hypothesis that he never renounced it.

Contemporary chronicles provide comparatively little evidence with regard to the treatment of vacancies in Henry I's reign, but the total evidence is becoming gradually richer. In the *Liber Niger* of Peterborough[4] we have an extant example of one of those descriptions of the property of a vacant abbey to which there are frequent references in the chronicles of the Norman period.[5] More immediately relevant is the financial account rendered at the exchequer by Geoffrey Escolland for

---

[1] A. Luchaire, *Histoire des institutions monarchiques de la France sous les premiers capétiens, 987–1180* (2nd edition, Paris, 1891), ii, 60–1. It is also worth noting that when Abbot Samson of Bury St. Edmunds took an aid from his knights on entering his abbacy in 1182, he also levied an aid and recognition on his lesser tenants '*per maneria*' (see above, p. 18).

[2] For example in 1168 the keeper of the vacant see of Bath rendered account of £100 'de Assisa facta super Dominia Episcopatus ad maritandam Matildam filiam Regis' (*Pipe R., 14 Henry II, 1168*, p. 168). Similar levies were made on the demesnes of other sees in hand; for further examples see below, pp. 41–2.

[3] The St. Albans' chronicler accused him of taking money from the men of a vacant abbey 'causis cavillatoriis adinventis' (*Gesta Abbatum Mon. S. Albani*, i, 65).

[4] *Liber Niger.*

[5] See above, p. 6 and p. 7; also *Chron. Abingdon*, ii, 158, *Chronicon Monasterii de Bello*, ed. J. S. Brewer (Anglia Christiana Soc., London, 1846), p. 60 and Hugh Candidus, p. 99.

the issues of the vacant bishopric of Durham on the Pipe Roll of 1130.[1]

On the death of Ranulf Flambard, according to the chronicler Symeon, the bishopric of Durham was committed to the custody of two 'barons', John Amundevill and Geoffrey Escolland.[2] Escolland answers at the exchequer for the issues of the bishopric during the first two years of its vacancy,[3] and a subsidiary account is made for a small group of the episcopal manors by Ansketil of Worcester.[4] For convenience of analysis, Escolland's account may be divided into four sections. The first section is not strictly relevant to the vacancy; it concerns the remainder of the farm of the bishopric 'de tempore episcopi'. The keeper seems to have appropriated and to be here accounting for payments which strictly speaking relate to the period before Flambard's death.

The second section relates to the first year of the vacancy proper and Escolland accounts for the farm of the bishopric for this year. It seems that it was farmed at £428.18.0,[5] and a further sum of £110.5.5 was accounted for 'de cornagio animalium'. Not all this money, however, reached the treasury. Certain expenses are claimed by the keeper, and also some of the cornage money had not been paid at the time this account was made. Altogether £484.8.2 was paid *in thesauro*.

The third section of the account is closely parallel to the second section and is concerned with the issues for the second year of the vacancy. For this year, the farm stands at £428.18.1 and the cornage at the same figure as the previous year, that is, £110.5.5. However, on this occasion, by the time the account had been drawn up a total of £418.6.7 had reached the treasury.

---

[1] *Pipe R. 31 Henry I. 1130*, pp. 130-3.

[2] Symeon of Durham, I, 141. They were perhaps barons of exchequer. The bishoprics of Coventry and Hereford had been in the custody of the chancellor, Geoffrey Rufus, who was paid his expenses for forty-three days when he had not been at the exchequer 'cum aliis baronibus Regis' (*Pipe R. 31 Henry I, 1130*, p. 140).

[3] John Amundevill is mentioned in the course of the account as one of those on whose testimony Escolland is allowed expenses for restoring manors that were waste (*ibid.*, p. 130). He does not appear as an accountant.

[4] *Ibid.*, pp. 132-3. From a cancelled version of Ansketil's account (*ibid.*, p. 31), it seems that he was in charge of three manors.

[5] This figure is calculated from the addition of the money paid *in thesauro* and the expenses claimed. The figure of the farm is not given for either the first or the second year in the text of the account.

Again there are certain expenses, and it is from the expenditure items on the Pipe Roll accounts that much of the information about *sede vacante* administration comes. In the particular case of this early Durham vacancy, the record of expenses is short and unelaborate. They show that the alms payments customarily made by the bishop were being continued during the vacancy; houses on the manors were being repaired; three king's servants received livery while they were in the bishopric 'doing the king's necessary business'; and, finally, the archbishop of York received a corrody each year for coming to the bishopric and returning. We are not told what he did between coming and returning, but it seems possible that he may have been fulfilling some of the spiritual functions which would fall upon the bishop *sede plena*, in which case it is interesting that it should be the royal keepers who contribute to his expenses.

The fourth and final section of Escolland's account touches upon a difficult and controversial problem: royal taxation. There are three items accounted for. In the first place there is £58.6.8 by way of *donum* from the knights of the bishopric; secondly there is the sum of £46.5.4, an unspecified payment 'de Tainis et Dreinnis et Smalemannis inter Tinam et Teodam'; and thirdly a list of payments which would later be classed 'pleas and perquisites'. It is the first and second items which raise the difficulties.

The *donum* from the knights may have been levied not in 1130 but in 1129. This is suggested by the arrangement of items on a cancelled account for this Durham vacancy which precedes the final account on the Pipe Roll,[1] and which differs from it slightly in the arrangement of items, in some of the amounts paid *in thesauro* and, occasionally, in terminology. In the cancelled account the payment from the knights[2] appears immediately after the entries for the issues of the first year of the vacancy; and immediately after the entries for the issues of the second year, the *arrears* of this payment are accounted for.[3] A

[1] *Ibid.*, pp. 128–30. The cancelled account of Ansketil of Worcester for his share is on p. 31 (see above, p. 25, n. 4).

[2] In the cancelled account the payment is called an *auxilium*, not *donum*; but there is no doubt at all that it is the same payment.

[3] In the 'correct' account there is no division into original payment and arrears. The actual word arrears does not appear on the cancelled account, but as the

payment made by the knights of the bishopric in the first year of the vacancy does just rouse a memory of the Worcester relief,[1] but to identify the two would be quite unwarranted without much more substantial evidence. It may well be accidental that the knights of Durham probably paid their *donum* in the first year of the vacancy, and certainly it is never called a *relevamen*. At the same time, terminology is at best an uncertain guide in itself. Nor was this payment uniformly called a *donum*. In the 'cancelled' account it is called an *auxilium*. A rigid distinction between such terms in this early period may conceal rather than reveal the real nature of a particular levy.

On the Pipe Roll of 1130 there are records of *auxilia* levied on some of the towns; more spasmodic traces of an *auxilium comitatus*; and in three counties (Surrey, Essex and Devon) an *auxilium militum*.[2] The 'aid' or 'gift' from the knights of Durham may be closely connected with the latter, which Stubbs has suggested may represent arrears from a previous year 'in which there may have been some general impost of the sort'.[3] That description is masterly and perhaps close to the truth in its

debt in respect of the *auxilium* stands at £27.10.0 after the payments of the first year have been made and it is for £27.10.0 that Escolland accounts by way of *auxilium* at the end of the section relating to the second year there can, I think, be no doubt that the second entry of the *auxilium* concerns arrears only. The following tabulation of the sequence of items on the two accounts may clarify the argument:

CANCELLED ACCOUNT		FINAL ACCOUNT	
		Issues of bishopric *tempore episcopi*:	£82.18.6
Farm of bishopric (1st year):	£428.18.0	Farm of bishopric (1st year):	£428.18.0
Cornage (1st year):	£110.5.5	Cornage (1st year):	£110.5.5
Auxilium of knights (*In thesauro* £30.16.8; *Debet* £27.10.0)	£58.6.8		
Farm of bishopric (2nd year):	£428.18.1	Farm of bishopric (2nd year):	£428.18.1
Cornage (2nd year):	£110.5.5	Cornage (2nd year):	£110.5.5
Auxilium of knights:	£27.10.0	*Donum* of knights:	£58.6.8
Payment from thanes etc.	£46.5.4	Payment from thanes etc.	£46.5.4
Issues of bishopric *tempore episcopi*:	£82.6.8		
Pleas and perquisites.		Pleas and perquisites.	

[1] See above, pp. 16–18.
[2] Stubbs, *Constitutional History*, i, 412, n. 1.   [3] *Ibid.*

implication of comprehensiveness. If an *auxilium* or *donum* had been levied in 1129 which extended to the military tenants of sees in the king's hand it anticipated the levy of 1168 in its widespread incidence and thorough-going character.[1] The theory that a 'general impost' was extended to lands temporarily in the king's hand is supported by a reference to a debt to the crown of Walter Fitz Witson, a tenant of the *honor* of Pembroke which was in the king's hand in 1130. Walter it seems owed eight marks of the *donum* to the king.[2]

The knights of Durham, then, paid to the king a gift or aid. Whether it was paid as a recognition of the fact that the see had come into the king's hand, or whether because lands in the king's hand were being taxed incidentally to some more widespread 'impost', can perhaps not be determined.[3] But what did the thanes, drengs and smallmen pay? There are two references to them. Those between Tyne and Tees[4] paid £46.5.4. The drengs and smallmen on the separate group of manors of the bishopric of Durham accounted for by Ansketil of Worcester paid £12.13.4.[5] It might be suggested that these payments were simply yearly dues. But they only appear once in an account which covers two years,[6] and which, for the most part, is clearly divided into annual sections. Moreover, in the final account they are suggestively sandwiched between the *donum* of the knights and 'pleas and perquisites'. Professor Mitchell, meditating on the ultimate origin of royal tallage wrote: 'It is a great mistake to suppose that the baron's right of taxation was limited to his military tenants. The feudal aids were but one manifestation of a general authority exercised over all dependants.'[7] Perhaps it was not mere chance that the payment

---

[1] For the levy of 1168 see below, pp. 40–2.

[2] *Pipe R. 31 Henry I, 1130,* p. 136. This is cited by the late Professor S. K. Mitchell, *Taxation in Medieval England* (London etc., 1951), p. 270.

[3] On the whole the evidence for the taxation of vacant sees in Henry II's Pipe Rolls tends to strengthen the supposition of a general impost. See below, p. 43.

[4] And in Northamptonshire according to the 'cancelled' account.

[5] *Pipe R. 31 Henry I,* p. 133.

[6] Unlike the payment from the knights, there is no indication that the payment from the thanes, drengs and smallmen was paid in the first year of the vacancy. In both the cancelled and the final account it appears after the issues for the second year have been dealt with.

[7] *Op. cit.,* p. 267.

from the thanes, drengs and smallmen was accounted for immediately after the gift of the knights. Did the non-military tenants perhaps pay the king what would later be known as a tallage?

On the evidence of Henry I's Pipe Roll alone it is impossible to get much further than this. The knights of the vacant bishopric of Durham made a payment which could be called either an *auxilium* or a *donum* to the king, and the lesser tenants in some parts of the bishopric made an unspecified payment which may have been connected with that made by the knights. Whichever it was, there is an implied tribute to Henry I's initiative and efficiency in his financial administration. In short this vacancy was made to yield a good profit to the crown not only from its regular issues but also from 'imposts'. Thirty years earlier Henry had promised that he would not take anything, 'aliquid', from the demesne or from the men of a vacant bishopric. Perhaps it was the vagueness rather than the comprehensiveness of 'aliquid' which recommended the word to the king. In the years between 1128 and 1130, Henry had had some unusually heavy expenses, and a vacant see, especially a wealthy one, should not be allowed to slip too lightly from the royal grasp. The 'profligate' Rufus had taken £300 a year from the bishopric of Durham during the previous vacancy,[1] the Lion of Justice reaped a clear profit of over £1,200 from the regular issues of this vacancy in two years.[2]

STEPHEN

The reign of Stephen has been said to be the sole interruption in the practice of the royal claim to administer the temporalities of vacant sees in England.[3] The evidence for this statement is Stephen's charter of 1136, in which the king promises that he will commit vacant sees into the custody of clerks or good men of the bishopric until a successor has been appointed.[4] There

---

[1] Symeon of Durham, I, 135.

[2] See Appendix A, below. The sum actually paid *in thesauro* was £1238.1.5.

[3] Makower, *loc. cit.*, pp. 314–5.

[4] 'Dum vero sedes propriis pastoribus vacuae fuerint, ipsas et earum possessiones omnes in manu et custodia clericorum vel proborum hominum ejusdem ecclesiae committam, donec pastor canonice substituatur' (*Select Charters*, p. 144).

can be little doubt that Stephen is here promising more than a mere change in the type of custodian, that he is in fact renouncing the issues of vacancies.[1] Certainly the church seems to have interpreted the clause in this way. In 1139 Innocent II confirmed the liberty of the church of Lincoln as it had been granted by King Stephen,[2] and a letter from Eugenius III in 1149 forbids that the king or any other powerful person should presume to occupy the castles of the bishopric of Lincoln *sede vacante*.[3]

Was Stephen's promise kept? It is not easy to say. William of Malmesbury writing of Stephen's charter as a whole states, 'pene omnia . . . perperam mutavit',[4] and Henry of Huntingdon even more categorically remarks 'Haec principaliter Deo vovit, et alia, sed nihil horum tenuit.'[5] It may be that like the promise of canonical elections it was sometimes kept and sometimes broken. However that may be, the promise as it stands does not mean that the king had no part to play when a bishopric fell vacant. Stephen says that he will commit ('committam') the churches and their possessions to the custodians. The king could commit only what was already in his own hands. If he was renouncing his regalian right in the narrower sense as a source of revenue, he was not renouncing the right in its wider connotation as a source of authority. Thus, in 1141 when William, the treasurer of York, was elected as archbishop his first step apparently was to hasten to the king at Lincoln where Stephen 'electum . . . libenter suscepit, et in terris et possessionibus Eboracensibus confirmavit'.[6] In the light of this it is easier, perhaps, to see why Henry II was able to return to the practice of Henry I in regard to vacancies; if, indeed, there had been really any appreciable interruption of the custom in Stephen's reign, which is itself a matter of some doubt. At least there seems to have been no absolute

[1] See Stubbs, *Lectures on Early Eng. Hist.*, p. 183.

[2] *Lincoln Registrum Antiquissimum*, I, ed. C. W. Foster (Lincoln Record Soc., XXVII, Hereford, 1931), pp. 191–2.

[3] *Ibid.*, p. 194.

[4] *Historia Novella*, in *De Gestis Regum* etc., II, 542.

[5] Henry of Huntingdon, *Historia Anglorum*, ed. T. Arnold (Rolls Series, London, 1879), p. 258.

[6] John of Hexham, *Chronicle*, in Symeon of Durham, *Opera*, II, 307. The king later withheld the temporalities of this see from Henry Murdac for three years.

break in the continuity of the theory that the bishop's barony was received at the king's will.

Stephen's reign has been described as a time when the courage of the church was high.[1] The coming together of that high courage and the rule of a weak king threw a strain on every point at which the authority of the *regnum* and that of the *sacerdotum* were in uneasy contact. The gravest danger to the king's traditional rights in respect to vacancy issues lay in the fact that the church had a clear and articulate policy in the matter, a policy which was in direct conflict with the practice of Henry I. According to the ecclesiastical point of view the issues of a vacancy should be reserved to the church; their appropriation by the king was sacrilegious.[2] Regalian right therefore, became a useful bargaining instrument. Stephen had yielded it to gain a political advantage in his charter to the church. It is interesting to find Henry II's eldest son, the younger Henry, piously informing Pope Alexander III in 1173:

... Volumus vacantis ecclesiae bona in aliquos ejusdem ecclesiae necessarios usus converti, vel, si expedit, futuro ipsius pastori reservari. Nunquam enim, Deo miserante, sustinebimus res crucis ... in regios fastus seu luxus saeculares converti, sine quibus Reges esse non solent.[3]

The 'regios fastus' and 'luxus saeculares' are literary flourishes. Both church and crown were aware that the issue was less simple than this. The king had more serious expenses than personal luxury or display, and Anselm had shown a clearer perception of the importance of vacancy issues as revenue when he told Rufus that he was not given abbeys 'quo expeditiones et bella ... inde fiant'.[4] As the expenses of government and of war increased, the usefulness of episcopal vacancies to the crown became increasingly apparent. Yet Stephen had, at the very least, gone so far as to renounce this fruitful source of revenue in

[1] D. Knowles, *The Episcopal Colleagues of Archbishop Thomas Becket* (Cambridge, 1951), p. 8.
[2] Thomas Becket makes this point: '... respondit archipraesul ... res pauperum fisco minime applicandas ...', *Materials for the History of Thomas Becket*, ed. J. C. Robertson (Rolls Series, London, 1875–85), III, 283.
[3] *Recueil des historiens des gaules et de la France, XVI*, ed. M. J. J. Brial (Paris, 1814; general editor M. Bouquet), p. 646.
[4] Eadmer, *Hist. Novorum*, p. 50.

a general charter. It is true, as we have seen, that he had not renounced all control in a vacancy; he could still withhold or grant the temporalities to an incoming bishop. So all was not yet lost.

HENRY II

In the year that King Stephen died, the fate of regalian right in England hung in the balance. That balance was soon tipped in favour of the crown by his successor. There can be little doubt that Henry II exercised regalian right from the beginning of his reign. The absence of vacancy accounts on the Pipe Rolls before the death of Archbishop Theobald in 1161, and the reputation which the archbishop has for having exercised a beneficial influence over the ecclesiastical policy of Henry's early years,[1] might at first suggest that before Theobald's death the young king may have observed Stephen's promise to abstain from the issues of vacancies. Archbishop Theobald's will invites a different conclusion.[2] The will threatens with anathema all those who may harm the archbishopric during the coming vacancy. The king's officials are specifically mentioned; there seems no doubt that they will appear, and they are prohibited from interfering in any way with the lands set aside for the monks.[3] Further, there must be no alienation of the lands of the see and no damage done to the groves. This document is eloquent in its assumptions and omissions. It assumes royal custody of the see and it does not forbid it.

Moreover, although there are no vacancy accounts on the earliest Pipe Rolls of the reign, the explanation may be found in a letter written by John of Salisbury to Thomas Becket in 1161:[4]

Fama est apud nos quod trium vacantium episcopatuum redditus ad liberationem vestram vobis dominus rex concesserit.[5]

[1] R. Foreville, *L'Eglise et la royauté en Angleterre sous Henry II Plantagenet, 1154–89* (St. Dizier, 1943), pp. 96–7.

[2] A. Saltman, *Theobald, Archbishop of Canterbury* (London, 1956), pp. 255–7.

[3] '. . . interdicimus ne quis officialium domini Regis ad res que propriis monachorum Cant' ecclesie usibus dicate sunt temerariam manum presumat extendere . . .' (*ibid.*, p. 255).

[4] *Materials*, v, 14.

[5] Dr. A. L. Poole identifies the three bishoprics as Exeter, Worcester and Coventry (*Domesday to Magna Carta*, p. 172, n. 1).

The rumour was correct, for one of Becket's embarrassments in his controversy with the king was Henry II's demand that his ex-chancellor should render account for the issues of the vacant bishoprics, abbacies, baronies and honors which had been in his custody.[1] Thus the royal right of custody of ecclesiastical vacancies was almost certainly practised by Henry II from the beginning of his reign.

In clause (12) of the Constitutions of Clarendon the king defined his right with a precision that left nothing in doubt as to the general nature of the royal claim:

Cum vacaverit archiepiscopatus vel episcopatus, vel abbatia, vel prioratus de dominio regis, debet esse in manu ipsius, et inde percipiet omnes redditus et exitus sicut dominicos.[2]

The euphemistic word *custodia* is not mentioned in this passage.[3] Henry speaks plainly of *redditus* and *exitus*. The issues of a vacant see are to be taken *sicut dominicos*.[4] This unequivocal clarity, which is characteristic of the Constitutions of Clarendon, has been much criticized. Henry has been accused of committing a tactical blunder in putting the customs of his ancestors in writing. But the king himself thought otherwise. Sir Maurice Powicke has written in another but similar connection that, 'law in the long run must be met by law'.[5] Possibly Henry II grasped this truth. The clash between the king and Becket over the Constitutions of Clarendon was a clash between two sophisticated legal and administrative systems. Between these two systems, between church and state, there was a disputed territory. The canonists had for some time been engaged in defining their own claims to that territory; and to define a position was one step towards occupying it. The church was articulate in its demands, and Henry may well have been aware of the challenge which this presented to the state; law had to be met by law. The king committed himself to a definition, a very precise

---

[1] *Materials*, III, 299.

[2] *Select Charters*, p. 166.

[3] Contrast the relevant clauses in Stephen's charter of 1136 (*ibid.*, p. 144), and also in John's charter of 1214 (*ibid.*, p. 284).

[4] The term *dominicos* may mean the king's 'own' rather than the king's 'demesne', but the purport is the same in this case.

[5] F. M. Powicke, *Stephen Langton* (Oxford, 1928), p. 82.

D

definition of ancient customs. He forced the issue, and his en-
suing gains were considerable.

Becket's answer to clause (12) of the Constitutions of Clarendon savours of a slightly passive resistance:

> Sed ecclesiae semper clamandum, semper obviandum et quatenus
> potest resistandum; et si sustineatur quod corrigi non potest, tamen
> consentiendum nunquam.[1]

What concerned Henry was that the practice should remain
one 'which could not be corrected', and he was never obliged to
withdraw from the stand which he had taken on this point. It
is true that for a little political advantage the king was capable
of making fair promises of moderation in the exercise of his
right. In 1176 he assured the pope that in future he would not
keep sees vacant for more than a year; but he carefully left himself a loophole:

> Concedo etiam quod archiepiscopatus, episcopatus et abbatiae
> non teneantur in manu mea utra annum, nisi urgente necessitate et
> evidenti de causa quae propter hoc non fuerit inventa ut diutius
> teneantur.[2]

No doubt it was 'urgente necessitate' that the king was obliged
to keep the wealthy see of York vacant for the last eight years of
his reign with a regular intake of over £1,000 a year into the
exchequer.

William of Newburgh said of Henry II that although he was
somewhat immoderate in seeking money, a 'decent limit had
been observed by him with this exception, that he allowed
vacant bishoprics to remain void a long time in order that he
might receive the emoluments which thence accrued'.[3] In
estimating the truth of such an accusation, it is useful to remember that not all the sees were equally remunerative. Chichester
could be kept vacant for five or six years before it would yield as
much as the archbishopric of York did in one year. There was
greater incentive, therefore, for keeping vacant the more wealthy
sees. At this time the six most lucrative were Canterbury,

[1] Materials, III, 283–4.
[2] Ralph de Diceto, Opera Historica ed. W. Stubbs (Rolls Series London 1876), I, 410.
[3] William of Newburgh, Historia Rerum Anglicarum, ed. R. Howlett, in Chronicles
of the Reigns of Stephen, Henry II and Richard I, I and II (Rolls Series, London, 1884–5),
I, 280.

York, Winchester, Ely, Lincoln and Durham. Of these, the first three, on the evidence of the Pipe Rolls of Henry II, were each capable of rendering to the royal exchequer a net profit of approximately £1,000 during each year of vacancy.[1] The highest figures were a little under £1,500.[2] On the same basis, Ely and Lincoln can be valued at notional figures of £880[3] and £840 respectively.[4] Durham was worth nearly £600 in the reign of Henry I.[5] Of these six sees Canterbury is exceptional since it was the primatial see and many disadvantages ensued when it was not filled, not the least being the pilgrimage of other bishops to Rome for consecration. Durham was not vacant at all during Henry II's reign, and Winchester is only accounted for on two of the Pipe Rolls. York and Lincoln, however, were kept open for long periods and one can hardly doubt that this was done, in part at least, for the sake of the revenue. Ely fell vacant in 1169 and perforce remained vacant until 1174. There is an appreciable gap in net value between these six bishoprics and the rest, all of which come below the £500 line. Bath and Salisbury rendered about £425 and £400 respectively in a year; Exeter and London about £330 and £300; Hereford about £270, Chichester about £240 and Lichfield less than £200.[6]

There were several very long vacancies during the reign, but that in itself does not prove avarice on Henry's part. There are two distinct periods when the number of vacant sees in the king's hand was very large. The first is from 1166 to 1174, when

---

[1] See the tables in Appendix A below. It is interesting to compare these figures with those given by W. J. Corbett as rough estimates of the Domesday valuation of these sees. The evidence for York is too incomplete for a useful assessment, but he evaluates Canterbury at £1,750 and Winchester at 'over £1,000' (*The Cambridge Medieval History*, v (Cambridge, 1926), p. 509).

[2] Winchester in 1171–72 yielded a net income of £1,440.2.4½ (below, p. 229). The higher figures, at Canterbury 1167–68 (below, p. 214) and at York in 1182–83 (below, p. 231) cannot be considered as normal, in the first case because of the inclusion of an aid, and in the second instance because of the inclusion of some payments of arrears.

[3] Below, p. 219. Corbett's figure for Ely is £790 (*ibid.*, p. 509).

[4] Below, p. 223. Corbett's figure is £600 (*ibid.*, p. 511).

[5] Below, p. 217. The Domesday evidence for Durham, as for York, is too incomplete to be of use for comparison.

[6] Below, pp. 212–13 (Bath), 227 (Salisbury), 220 (Exeter), 225 (London), 221 (Hereford), 216 (Chichester), 222 (Lichfield). Corbett's figures (*ibid.*) are: Wells, £325; Salisbury, £600; Exeter, £360; London, £615; Hereford, £280; Chichester, £138; Chester, £85.

a steadily increasing number of vacancies appear year by year
on the Pipe Rolls. This is easily explained. While Becket was in
exile and during the vacancy following his death there was no
one to consecrate new bishops. Indeed the archbishop's prerogative of consecration was a powerful weapon in his struggle
with Henry II; it was that above all which made him indis-
pensable to the English church, and he relied on that right,
together with his right to consecrate the young prince as king,
to bring Henry to submission. Reginald, archdeacon of Salisbury, had suggested to Henry that the king should petition
the pope to allow another English bishop to perform the
consecrations.[1] Becket held his own, and the pope did not agree.

The second period when the vacancies were numerous,
although not as numerous as in the first, was from 1181 to 1189,
the last eight years of the reign. This was partly the result of a
natural fluctuation. The sees had almost all been filled in
1174, and a lull followed. From 1181 onwards there was a
renewed spate of episcopal deaths, and it seems clear that
Henry did not rush to fill these vacancies. The archbishopric of
York was vacant for the whole of this period. In 1186 the canons
of York proposed five candidates to Henry for the archbishopric: Hubert Walter, then dean of York; Haimon, the church's
precentor; Laurence, archdeacon of Bedford; Bernard, prior of
Newburgh and Master Roger Arundel.[2] They were a fair
selection. Laurence and Roger Arundel were two of the keepers
of the temporalities of the archbishopric,[3] but the king apparently found them very satisfactory as keepers, and preferred
them to continue to pay some £1,000 each year into the royal
treasury than to make one of them archbishop.

To sum up the evidence on this point, it seems very doubtful
whether Henry II would deliberately prolong episcopal vacancies without distinction in order to increase his income. His
anxiety to fill the bishoprics in 1172 shows that he regarded the
simultaneous vacancy of a large number of sees as an undesir-
able as well as an abnormal phenomenon. The king relied consider ably on the support of the bishops for counsel and in

---

[1] *Materials*, VII, 181.

[2] Benedict of Peterborough, *Gesta Regis Henrici Secundi* (Rolls Series, London,
1867), I, 352.

[3] *Pipe R. 32 Henry II, 1186*, p. 100.

administration. On the other hand, one or two wealthy sees in hand might be well worth any attendant inconveniences.

Henry II's financial policy in respect of vacancies is not to be found exclusively in the length of time they lasted nor even in the impressively large totals which conclude some of the accounts. It is a closer view of some of the individual items of receipt which reveals a more telling picture of Henry II's exchequer at work, that determined, self-confident and splendidly adaptable government department. There are two groups of these individual items which call for special comment. The first consists of items which may be classed as spiritualities, and the second will be referred to for convenience as 'taxation items'.

(1) The rule that the king's right in a vacancy extended only to the temporalities of a see, that is to the bishop's barony, was a commonplace in the thirteenth century, and there is an incident recorded by Ralph de Diceto which indicates that already in Henry II's reign the church opposed any tampering by the royal custodians with matters which it considered clearly lay outside the range of the temporalities. In 1187 Archbishop Baldwin wrote to the king's keepers of the vacant bishopric of London, ordering them not to overstep the bounds of their commission.[1] Their fault is the seizure of a sequestrated church, and they are ordered to give the custody of it to the archdeacon of Middlesex, in whose archdeaconry it lies.

On the other hand it is quite clear that the church had a long struggle in claiming bit by bit various sources of episcopal income as spiritualities, which should not be appropriated by the crown *sede vacante*. In Henry II's reign, to judge from Pipe Roll accounts, the struggle had only begun. Entries of Peter's Pence, for example, are found quite regularly on these accounts, and synodals frequently;[2] both of which items were later to be classed as spiritualities.[3] Again, in the diocese of York, towards the end of his reign, the king drew substantial sums from vacant

---

[1] Ralph de Diceto, II, 48.

[2] See for example the accounts for Hereford (*Pipe R. 13 Henry II, 1167*, p. 76); Carlisle (*Pipe R. 34 Henry II, 1188*, pp. 7–8); and York (*Pipe Rolls 28 Henry II, 1182*, p. 62; *29 Henry II, 1183*, p. 59; *30 Henry II, 1184*, p. 40; *31 Henry II, 1185*, p. 78).

[3] See *The Register of the Diocese of Worcester during the Vacancy of the See*, ed. J. W. Willis Bund (Worcs. Hist. Soc., Oxford, 1893–7), pp. xvi–xxi (General Introduction).

churches and prebends.[1] These seem to appear under various guises in the earlier York accounts, such as perquisites from the deaneries[2] or simply as perquisites.[3] Items which appear quite frequently are payments from archdeaconries. Sometimes they are quite small and they never rise above £167.18.8 in one year, which is the amount accounted for at Lincoln in 1182,[4] but there seems to be an interesting reluctance to pay them. At Lincoln they appear on successive accounts, but are frequently pardoned or *in respectu*,[5] and at Bath the charges are allowed to accumulate and for the most part are not paid.[6] These payments can probably be identified with the payments known as prestations, which the archdeacons of the diocese of Lincoln, at any rate, were later in the habit of making either annually or twice a year to the bishop *sede plena*.[7] In the two cases where comparison is possible between the sums mentioned on the Pipe Rolls of Henry II and the sums given in Bishop Dalderby's register there appears to be a remarkably close parallel.[8]

[1] On the Pipe Roll of 1187 the keepers account for £50.2.4 from vacant churches and £13.9.2 from vacant prebends (*Pipe R. 33 Henry II*, p. 98). Similar entries may be found in the accounts for Lichfield in 1184 (*Pipe R. 30 Henry II*, p. 24) and again in 1185 (*Pipe R. 31 Henry II*, p. 142); for Lincoln 1181–5 (e.g. *Pipe Rolls 27 Henry II*, p. 63 and *31 Henry II*, p. 125), and for Salisbury 1186–8 (*Pipe Rolls 32 Henry II*, p. 167, *33 Henry II*, p. 187, and *34 Henry II*, pp. 184–5).

[2] *Pipe R. 28 Henry II, 1182*, p. 62.

[3] *Pipe R. 29 Henry II, 1183*, p. 59.

[4] *Pipe R. 28 Henry II, 1182*, p. 59.

[5] See for example *Pipe R. 17 Henry II, 1171*, p. 111: 'remanent xxx li. super Robertum Archidiaconum qui fuerunt in respectu per Regem . . .' and 'In Quietantia Archidiaconatus Nicholai de Hunted.' ii m. 'Et Archidiaconatus Nicholai de Bedeford xx s.' (*ibid.*, p. 112).

[6] Thomas, archdeacon of Wells, owes £14 in 1171 (*ibid.*, p. 24) covering the payments due from him for two years, and he seems to be still increasing his debt at the rate of £7 a year in the next account (*Pipe R. 18 Henry II, 1172*, p. 128).

[7] The following example is taken from the Memoranda volume of the Register of John Dalderby, bishop of Lincoln 1300–26 (Archives of the Bishopric of Lincoln, Bishops' Registers no. III): 'Noverint universi quod nos J—Lincolniensis Episcopus recepimus de annua prestacione archidiaconatus Leyc' nobis debita . . . quindecim libras sterlingorum de termino Sancti Michelis anno domini mcccxvi' (f.385d). Prestations from the archdeaconry of Bedford are referred to on ff.308, 393d and 399; from the archdeaconry of Huntingdon, ff.308 and 399; from the archdeaconry of Buckingham, ff.379d and 393; from the archdeaconry of Stowe, ff.391d and 399; from the archdeaconry of Northampton, f.392d; and from the archdeaconry of Oxford, f.394.

[8] The prestation of the archdeacon of Northampton in Dalderby's time was £54.10.0 (see the entry for £27.5.0 for half the year; Dalderby Memorand. f.392d).

To sum up, there are few if any vacancy accounts of Henry II's reign which do not include some sort of revenue which was later to be classed as *spiritualia* and in some cases the revenue of this kind was considerable. On the Pipe Roll of 1188 there is an account for Carlisle which rouses even darker speculation. The entries are entirely confined to synodals, issues of churches, schools, pentecostal offerings, and pleas and perquisites.[1] The incidental reference to Carlisle in the *Registrum Roffense* is perhaps relevant:

Nihil enim tenet episcopatus Roffensis per baroniam de rege, set per puram elemosinam, quod non est dicendum de aliquo episcopatu Anglie, nec de archiepiscopatu, nisi duntaxat Karleolen.[2]

The case of Carlisle and the various entries of *spiritualia* on the other accounts cause one to wonder whether Henry II did not regard himself as taking over a bishopric rather than merely the temporalities of a bishopric. It is, however, worth noting that only £2.10.0 from the Carlisle vacancy account was actually paid into the treasury. The rest was spent on such commendable projects as work on the canons' dormitory. This may show Henry's discretion. In any case, the fact remains that the king held the bishopric of Carlisle, despite the 'spiritual' character of its revenues, *in manu sua*. That at least was deliberate, and it is interesting to remember Miss H. M. Chew's statement that it was Henry II who temporarily discredited the ecclesiastical policy which limited the application of the term barony to tenants-in-chief who held *per servicium militare*.[3] Henry II's government never jeopardized its rights by conceiving them too narrowly.

(2) The second group of items on the vacancy accounts of this reign which calls for further examination covers the entries

In 1172 one of the keepers of the vacant see of Lincoln is charged with £55 'de archidiaconatu de Norhanton' (*Pipe R. 18 Henry II*, p. 96).

The prestation paid to Dalderby by the archdeacon of Oxford annually was £20 (see the entry for £10 for half the year; Dalderby Memorand., f.394). On the Pipe Roll of 1170 there is the suggestive entry: 'In donis per breve Regis Magistro David' de Lund' x li. de dimidio anno in archidiaconatu de Oxenefordscir.' (*Pipe R. 16 Henry II*, p. 153).

[1] *Pipe R. 34 Henry II, 1188*, p. 7. The account covers a period of two years.
[2] *Registrum Roffense*, ed. J. Thorpe (London, 1769), p. 79.
[3] *The English Ecclesiastical Tenants-in-Chief and Knight Service* (Oxford, 1932), p. 187.

scutagium, auxilium, donum and *tallagium.* Scutage is the most easily dealt with. During a vacancy the king stood in the same relation to the tenants of the bishopric as did the bishop in his lifetime. When the king, therefore, levied a scutage on a bishopric during a vacancy he took payment not only on the 'recognized' fees, that is, the fees of the old *servicium debitum* but also on the 'unrecognized' fees.[1] This was logical since it is known that, at least by the end of Henry II's reign, the prelates themselves (despite lively protests from their own military tenants)[2] were in the habit of exacting scutage both on the recognized and on the unrecognized fees, while they paid to the king only on the recognized fees, and thus made a good profit each time the king levied a scutage. This was the profit which the king never succeeded in tapping except *sede vacante.*[3]

In the same way, when the king levied a feudal aid he was able to recoup himself more richly from the vacant sees than he was from those that were full. When Henry II levied a regular feudal aid for the marriage of his eldest daughter, Matilda, in 1168 he exacted from the sees that were vacant full payment on the unrecognized as well as on the recognized fees.[4]

---

[1] The fees on which the bishop recognized that he owed payment of scutage to the king were those of the old *servicium debitum,* which was the figure used for the assessment of scutage before the *Carte* of 1166. The 'unrecognised' fees consisted of the surplus of the fees of the Old Enfeoffment over the fees of the old *servicium debitum* (the fees of the Old Enfeoffment corresponded with the number of knights which the bishop had enfeoffed before the death of Henry I).

Thus 'recognised' fees=fees of the old *servicium debitum*; 'unrecognised fees' =fees of the Old Enfeoffment *minus* fees of the old *servicium debitum.* This has been worked out by Miss Chew (*op. cit.,* pp. 18–21).

[2] See Jocelin of Brakelond, p. 65 and appendix O, p. 152.

[3] Miss Chew says, 'There is no record of any payment upon fees "que non recognoscit" save when the fief was in the king's hand' (*op. cit.,* p. 22). Mr. E. Miller makes the same point in connection with the bishopric of Ely (*The Abbey and Bishopric of Ely* (Cambridge, 1951), p. 162).

[4] In the vacant see of Lincoln for example the keeper accounts for 60 marks from 60 fees which 'Robertus Episcopus recognovit se debere Regi' and for 42 marks 'de xlii militibus episcopatus quos episcopus non recognovit se debere Regi'. These 42 marks were duly paid *in thesauro* (*Pipe R. 15 Henry II, 1169,* p. 46).

Although in the case of Canterbury (also vacant) no distinction is made in the vacancy account between recognized and unrecognized fees, the keeper accounts on the basis of 84¾ fees (instead of the 60 fees of the old *servicium debitum*) (*Pipe R. 14 Henry II, 1168,* p. 154).

At Bath which was also vacant in 1168 it so happened that the old *servicium*

The king's exactions from vacant sees in connection with this aid of 1168, however, are particularly interesting in that they were not wholly 'feudal' in character. On the demesne lands of the vacant bishoprics, as on the royal demesnes proper, a levy was made on the *non*-military tenants as well as on the military tenants. That this levy was evidently considered as essentially the same exaction as the levy from the military tenants is made clear by the Pipe Roll account for the vacant see of Canterbury.[1] Under a heading 'De auxilio Matilde filie Regis', the keeper accounts to the exchequer for £56.10.0 'de militibus Archiepiscopatus'. The entry which immediately follows this one does not concern knights at all. It runs:

Homines de Norfleta reddunt compotum de xiij li. xs. de eodem auxilio.

Following this entry are the payments made by the other vills. It seems then that the aid paid by the men of Northfleet and by the other men of the demesnes of the archbishopric was the same aid, 'eodem auxilio' as that paid by the knights. Yet the aid from the men of the demesnes was levied vill by vill in the manner which came to be usual for royal tallages on a township. This is another warning, if such were needed, against attaching any rigid technical significance to such words as 'aid' or 'tallage' at this period. This same levy on the non-military tenants, for instance, is termed 'assisa' at Bath,[2] apparently to distinguish it from the *auxilium* levied on the knights. The exchequer was, no doubt, more concerned with the amount of the levy than with its name: and the amounts were heavy. The demesne of Canterbury was assessed for £222.16.8 as compared with the £56.10.0 levied from the knights of the see.[3] The Hereford demesne lands

---

debitum was a higher figure than the Old Enfeoffment and the aid was therefore accounted for on the basis of the old *servicium* (20 fees) (*ibid.*, p. 143; the entry is made in the name of the bishop).

In the vacant see of Hereford the situation is more complex (see H. M. Chew, *op. cit.*, p. 19.) The keeper accounts for 3½ marks 'de Militibus Episcopatus preter illos quos Episcopus dicit se debere Regi' (*Pipe R. 14 Henry II*, pp. 115–16). These 'extras' in this particular case are knights who have been enfeoffed since the death of Henry I (i.e. knights of the New Enfeoffment).

[1] *Ibid.*, p. 154.   [2] *Ibid.*, p. 168.
[3] *Ibid.*, pp. 154–6. The sums for the levy on the demesne are given separately, vill by vill.

were charged with £40,[1] those of Bath with £100[2] and those of Lincoln with £140.[3]

Two questions suggest themselves. Was this levy on the non-military tenants of the demesnes of vacant sees something essentially new? And, whether new or not, what was the significance of it? The first question is the more quickly dealt with. In the non-feudal aid which was levied in 1168 the exchequer cast its net very wide indeed, yet it is very difficult to pin down any single part of the exaction that was wholly unprecedented. As Professor Mitchell has said, 'There is no doubt of the expansion and of the desire of the government for it, and that such a general levy was unprecedented. But it was not wholly new.'[4] It was the scale of the levy that was unprecedented. As far as the scanty evidence goes for that part of the levy which concerned the demesnes of the vacant sees, it does nothing to disturb Professor Mitchell's judgement. It is true that there is no evidence of taxation of vacant bishoprics earlier in Henry II's reign; the levy of 1168 was undoubtedly a special effort. On the other hand, it would be inadvisable to state categorically that the levy on sees in hand was wholly new until a satisfactory alternative explanation has been found for the payment which the thanes, drengs and smallmen of the vacant bishopric of Durham paid to the crown in 1130.[5]

Secondly, the historical significance of the levy of 1168 depends not only on whether it was new but on whether it was repeated. A glance at the later history of taxation in Henry II's reign shows that the king did follow up the precedent of 1168 in extending non-feudal levies to the demesnes of sees and abbeys in hand on several other occasions. It will be convenient to call these levies tallages,[6] since that was the term increasingly applied to them in the later twelfth century, but they were by no means uniformly styled tallages as yet.[7] Tallages were levied

---

[1] *Pipe R. 15 Henry II, 1169*, p. 143.
[2] *Pipe R. 14 Henry II*, p. 168.
[3] *Pipe R. 15 Henry II*, p. 46.
[4] *Taxation in Medieval England*, p. 267.
[5] See above, p. 26.
[6] This convention is adopted by Professor Mitchell.
[7] In the levy of a tallage on the demesnes of the vacant see of Salisbury in 1187 the word *tallagium* is used in the heading, but the individual payments are listed

on royal demesnes in 1173 and in 1174, but it seems doubtful whether in these years there was a general taxation of the demesnes of vacant sees. The references to an aid in the vacancy accounts on the Rolls for these years are usually not sufficiently explicit to make it clear whether an aid from the knights or an aid from the demesnes is meant. In 1178 there comes the first mention of a tallage *eo nomine* in a vacancy when £71.6.8 is levied 'de tallagio terrarum abbatis de Burgo per plures comitatus'.[1] This may well have been a late collection of a levy made in connection with the tallage of the demesnes in 1177, for Peterborough was in hand in the previous year as well.[2] In 1187 the last tallage of the reign was taken, and the vacant sees of Salisbury and York both paid substantial sums *de tallagio*.[3] The burgesses of Malmesbury paid a *donum* because their abbey was vacant and the men of the manors an *auxilium*.[4] The demesnes of Glastonbury were tallaged 'quia honor est in manu regis'.[5] There seems, however, to be no record of payments from other vacant abbeys.[6]

As far as can be gleaned from the Pipe Rolls, Henry II's practice of tallaging vacant sees and abbeys was normally limited to those occasions on which he was tallaging the rest of the royal demesne.[7] This association of vacant sees in the taxation of the royal demesne is important. Professor R. S. Hoyt in tracing the development of tallage in Henry II's reign writes: 'These lands', that is vacant bishoprics and abbeys, 'could by no legal theory be considered to be royal demesne in the full sense of the phrase. But while in the king's hand they were subject to tallage, . . .'[8] Professor Hoyt sees in this an illustration of the

---

de dono (*Pipe R. 33 Henry II*, p. 188 and pp. 179–81). In the same year the men of the manors of Malmesbury paid an *auxilium* (*ibid.*, p. 182), whereas in 1188 the men of the town of Malmesbury owed £4.16.8 'de dono quia abbatia est in manu regis' (*Pipe R. 34 Henry II*, p. 139).

[1] *Pipe R. 24 Henry II, 1178*, p. 55.
[2] *Pipe R. 23 Henry II, 1177*, pp. 104–5.
[3] *Pipe R. 33 Henry II, 1187*, pp. 188 and 179–81 (Salisbury) and pp. 75–6 (York).
[4] See p. 42, n. 7.
[5] *Ibid.*, p. 179. See also *ibid.*, p. 163.
[6] Holme and Cirencester were also vacant (*ibid.*, p. 23 and pp. 26–7).
[7] The only exception seems to be a small *donum* of £6.18.6 paid at Abingdon in 1186 (*Pipe R. 32 Henry II*, p. 117).
[8] *The Royal Demesne in English Constitutional History 1066–1272* (New York, 1950), p. 121.

deliberate intensification and extension of its demesne rights on the part of the crown, especially in respect to matters of taxation. Certainly, as we have seen, Henry II did tend to treat ecclesiastical vacancies in the same way that he treated the royal demesne but it is, perhaps, wise not to stress too heavily either the illegality or the novelty of this practice. In the Constitutions of Clarendon Henry II had made clear his policy of taking the issues of a vacant bishopric or abbey 'sicut dominicos', and he claimed that it was customary.[1] The lands of sees in hand were not 'royal demesne in the full sense of the phrase'; Henry does not suggest it; he does not define their position at all. What he does define is his own policy. He will regard them in financial matters as his 'own'. He will take their fruits as he would take the fruits of his own demesne. In 1168 we find that he will also exact taxes from them 'sicut dominicos'. The inference does not seem legally unsound.

The skill of the government at the level of policy, however, is only half the explanation of its success. It was in the end efficient method which effectively brought the stream of silver *denarii* flowing from the vacant sees into the royal treasury. In the course of this reign there was a noticeable refinement in the methods of recording the accounts of the keepers of vacant sees and abbeys. For both receipts and expenses, the accounts become much more detailed. Even when a vacant see is farmed there are usually some items which the farm does not cover and which must be accounted for separately, and this list tends to grow. Between the beginning and the end of the reign, it would seem that the standards of the exchequer in relation to the accountant became markedly more exacting.

The reign of Henry II, then, saw not only the reassertion of regalian right but also a steady development and consolidation in the methods of exercising it.

RICHARD I

The reign of Richard I forms the last section in the consideration of the royal administration of vacant sees in the twelfth

[1] It would be difficult to prove this either way but the payment from the smallmen of Durham in 1130 may be a precedent; above, p. 26.

century. As an epilogue it is disappointingly indistinct, for the evidence about vacancies in this reign is fragmentary.

Between 1191 and 1193 there are no accounts of episcopal vacancies on the Pipe Rolls.[1] Some at least of the issues of these vacant sees may have gone to the commission for the ransoming of the king.[2] The only vacancy account of the reign which is of particular interest is that for Durham on the Roll of 1196.[3] It covers a period of only about one year,[4] and in this comparatively brief period a grand total of £4,581.10.0½ is accounted for by the keepers, apart from a scutage, and certain sums accounted for as a debt of the late bishop to the king. Of this large total, the assized rents, which formed the backbone of the receipts from vacant sees in Henry II's reign, comprise little more than a quarter of the whole.[5] Among the other items three deserve special notice. The first is the tallage which was assessed at £341.4.2, a higher sum than any tallage, gift or aid accounted for in the previous reign.[6] The other two items are payments of fines, among which are £611.16.8 under the heading of *fines clericorum* and £677.13.4 under the heading of *fines servientum H. Episcopi*. These two entries require more comment.

The *fines clericorum* is an obscure entry, but it seems just possible that it may be parallel to the *fines servientum*, and about this there is independent evidence. William of Newburgh, concluding a description of Bishop Hugh le Puiset's death at his manor of Howden in 1195, states that the king's ministers took charge of the bishopric and sought out all the hidden treasure of the late bishop.[7] He continues:

---

[1] *Pipe Rolls 3–5 Richard I (1191–3)*, inclusive. There were vacancies at Bath, Canterbury and Exeter during this period.

[2] Sir James Ramsay suggests this, *Revenues of the Kings of England*, I, 214.

[3] *Chancellor's R. 8 Richard I, 1196*, pp. 253–61.

[4] For the complexities of the dating see Appendix A.   [5] £1,259.7.11.

[6] The highest had been that levied at Canterbury in 1168: £222.16.8 (*Pipe R. 14 Henry II, 1168*, pp. 154–6).

[7] 'Illo autem mortuo et episcopatu illico per ministros regios in fiscum redacto, iidem omnia secreta ejus perscrutantes, quicquid repertum est regiis applicuere commodis' (William of Newburgh, I, 439–40).

See also Geoffrey of Coldingham in *Historiae Dunelmensis Scriptores Tres*, ed. J. Raine (Surtees Soc. IX, London, 1839), p. 16: 'De thesauris Episcopi diligentius inquirebant; et non solum familiares et Officiales Episcopi, sed eos etiam, qu nullius familiaritatis fuerant astricti, si aliquid abundantius videbantur habere, regii auctoritate imperii ad solvendum cogebant.'

Sed nec ministri et familiares ejus evasere quaestionem qui nimirum jussione regia tamquam subtractores bonorum ejus districtae
discussioni addicti, pro viribus quisque substantiae suae satisfacere
sunt compulsi.

The substance of some of the *servientes episcopi* seems to have
been considerable; at least three were charged with a fine of
£100 each.[1] The combined evidence of Newburgh's chronicle
and the exchequer Roll suggests two conclusions. First, the
servants of the late bishop seem to have been fining with the
king for money which had either been left to them in Hugh le
Puiset's will[2] or which they had appropriated at his death, perhaps a little of each. Secondly, the royal custodians of the
vacant see claimed the late bishop's personal property for the
crown, and therefore exacted these fines.

Was the personal treasure of a deceased bishop a lawful
royal perquisite? On at least one other occasion Richard I did
appropriate such personal treasure, on the death of Geoffrey
Ridel, bishop of Ely, in 1189:

. . . tria milia et cc marcae novo regi coronando collata sunt pro
anima episcopi . . . mimis et scurris dividendae.[3]

However, it would be hasty indeed to conclude from these two
instances that Richard I indulged in the indiscriminate plunder
which the so-called *jus spolii* is often taken to imply.[4] The circumstances of the two cases must be examined in the light of the
most specific statement that an English king had made on this
subject, the statement in the charter of Stephen. Stephen had
promised that the will of a bishop should normally be fully
and freely executed,[5] but if the prelate was suddenly and

[1] *Chancellor's R. 8 Richard I, 1196*, pp. 258–9.

[2] William of Newburgh states that he made a will (*loc. cit.*, p. 439).

[3] Gervase of Canterbury, *Opera Historica*, ed. W. Stubbs (Rolls Series, London,
1879–80), I, 457.

[4] Dr. A. L. Poole describes the *jus spolii* as 'the right to the personal belongings of a
deceased bishop' (*Domesday to Magna Carta*, p. 182). He later points out that
Stephen's charter meant that the bishop's goods 'could therefore no longer law-
fully be purloined by the king under colour of the so-called *jus spolii*' (*ibid.*, p. 190),
but notes that the king nevertheless seems to have appropriated such personal
property on various occasions. However, all but one of the instances which Dr.
Poole cites are mentioned in the explanation which is attempted below, and that
of the abbot of Cirencester might perhaps be similarly explained if we had more
evidence.   [5] *Select Charters*, p. 144.

unexpectedly seized by death the property should be distributed 'pro salute animae ejus'. This has a clear bearing on the case of Ridel. Geoffrey Ridel had died intestate and according to Stephen's promise his property should therefore have been distributed 'pro salute animae ejus'. Accordingly, the irony of Gervase's statement that Geoffrey Ridel's treasure was squandered on the king's coronation expenses 'pro anima episcopi', is fully apparent. Richard had not indeed acted within the spirit of Stephen's promise, but his seizure of the bishop's treasure on this occasion does not imply a claim to seize the personal property of all deceased prelates. The circumstances were special, and were legally recognized as such.

On the other hand, it will rightly be urged that Hugh le Puiset, bishop of Durham, had not died intestate. Newburgh expressly states that he had made a will.[1] Yet Richard claimed the bishop's goods and exacted heavy fines from those who had possession of them. Why was this? Stephen's promise, when examined carefully, leaves some loopholes. It applied to wills made 'ante mortem . . . rationabiliter'. As Hugh le Puiset made his will at Howden where he died, one may suppose that he only made it shortly before his death, and it might be argued that a will made in such circumstances was not made 'rationabiliter'. This was certainly a distinction made by Henry II. This king appropriated the accumulated wealth of Archbishop Roger of York in 1181, on the grounds that the archbishop had not made his will before the period of his last illness, and Henry noted with satisfaction that the late archbishop himself had once pronounced on the invalidity of a will made in these conditions.[2]

In the light of this digression into the exercise of the *jus spolii* the Durham account of 1196 has less sinister implications of a policy of spoliation than might at first be supposed. Yet the total accounted for is very high even when allowances have been

---

[1] See above, p. 46, n. 1.

[2] Benedict of Peterborough, 1, 283; 'Dicebat enim rex, quod praefatus archiepiscopus judicium fecerat, quod de jure non liceret alicui viro ecclesiastico divisam facere, nisi priusquam aegrotare inciperet.' There are a few other instances, but only a few, on the Pipe Rolls, of entries which may indicate an exercise of the *jus spolii*, although whether in the limited form suggested above or not, it is difficult to say. Thus £300 'de Pecunia Ricardi Wintoniensis Episcopi' was accounted for by the keepers of the vacant see of Winchester in 1189 (*Pipe R. 1 Richard I*, p. 5).

made for the fines imposed in connection with le Puiset's personal treasure, and there may be some justification, after all, for Newburgh's remark that the see was 'thoroughly despoiled'[1] in the course of this vacancy.

In the history of episcopal vacancies, Richard I's reign forms a rather obscure link between that of Henry II and that of John. There may, perhaps, have been some increase of pressure on the vacant sees as a result of the general financial strain, but the evidence is so fragmentary that the only warrant for this rather tentative conclusion is the account for Durham in 1196. The other accounts are too incomplete to be of much use, but as far as they go, there does not seem to be any sign of a particularly new or original treatment of vacancies. The issues still flow along the orthodox lines, straight from the bishopric to the treasury of the exchequer,[2] with the result that there is no information as to how they were subsequently spent. The practice of tallaging sees and abbeys in the king's hand when the royal demesne was tallaged appears to be continued on the same basis as in Henry II's time. Thus, in 1196 tallage is levied on Durham, and on York[3] which, although not technically vacant, was in the king's hand, and on the abbey of St. Mary's, York.[4] From the evidence which we have, there is no indication that ecclesiastical vacancies were tallaged on any occasion on which there was no general tallage of the royal demesne; but it should be stressed that the evidence is so incomplete that it is just possible that new developments were taking place of which there is no extant record.

The king's right to the custody of vacant sees emerges at the end of the twelfth century in a healthy and robust condition. It was not an abuse furtively resorted to, but a claim whose general nature had been clearly defined and which had been logically woven into the structure of that feudalization of the church which had come with the Norman Conquest and which had been fully articulated in the Constitutions of Clarendon. The reform promised in Stephen's reign had been quashed by the policy and consistent practice of Henry II and Richard I.

[1] William of Newburgh, i, 441.

[2] This statement is of course limited to the issues of sees whose vacancies are accounted for on the Pipe Rolls.

[3] *Chancellor's R. 8 Richard I*, pp. 255–6, and p. 189.　　　[4] *Ibid.*, p. 175.

CHAPTER III

The Development of the Right in the Reign of King John

THE haze of uncertainty which obscures the question of the administration of vacancies in the reign of Richard I is immediately dispersed with the accession of John. John's reign was a period of fiscal experiment and in his treatment of casual revenue he shows an originality and skill which is quite distinct from anything that has gone before.[1] Professor Cheney has described John's policy, especially during the interdict, as 'the financial devices of a ruthless fiscal expert, rather than the depredations of a king at war with the church'.[2] An examination of the king's treatment of vacancies over the whole of this reign in every way corroborates this conclusion.

The importance of the interdict from the point of view of general ecclesiastical and political history has perhaps created what is, in many ways, an artificial barrier between the earlier and later parts of the reign. The exaction of large sums from vacant bishoprics certainly does not begin with the beginning of the interdict in 1208 but with the beginning of the reign itself. If the see of Lincoln rendered £1,113.9.7 gross income in one year, 1211–12,[3] it had produced £1,838.6.9 (without Banbury) in one and a half years during the vacancy of 1206–9.[4] If the enormous sum of £1,154.1.8 was levied in tallage from the manors of the see of Durham in 1208–9,[5] the manors of Canterbury, a see of comparable resources, had already paid in 1206 the sum of £1,065.2.3 by way of a tallage.[6]

---

[1] See especially Mr. J. E. A. Jolliffe's paper, 'The Chamber and the Castle Treasures under King John', in *Studies in Medieval History Presented to Frederick Maurice Powicke* (Oxford, 1948), pp. 117–42.

[2] C. R. Cheney, 'King John and the Papal Interdict', *Bulletin of the John Rylands Library*, XXXI (1948), p. 306.

[3] *Pipe R. 14 John, 1212*, p. 2.   [4] *Pipe R. 9 John, 1207*, p. 13.

[5] *Pipe R. 13 John, 1211*, p. 35.   [6] *Pipe R. 8 John, 1206*, p. 54.

In fact wherever comparison is possible, at least as far as the official accounts are concerned, there is no sign of any sharp rise in exactions from episcopal vacancies during the period of the interdict.[1]

If, then, John's policy was generally speaking uniform, was it uniformly oppressive? Receipts from vacant bishoprics were generally higher in John's reign than they had been in that of his father or in that of his brother, and at first glance they produce an impression of considerably increased pressure.[2] But these figures on the Pipe Rolls invite very cautious handling. As they stand, the *summae* are not merely often unhelpful but sometimes they are positively misleading. The yearly total of gross income accounted for in Durham fluctuates from over £4,200 in 1208–9 to less than £2,600 in 1209–10.[3] At Canterbury over £5,000 gross income is accounted for in a year and three months on the Pipe Roll of 1206,[4] whereas during the interdict period (1211) an account for the archbishopric 'de dimidio anno' only reaches £1,105.17.5,[5] which at first suggests a much lower rate of income. In a smaller way Chichester produces a gross income of nearly £380 in 1210–11,[6] but in 1211–12 the sum was less than £212.[7] None of these cases would warrant the inference that there had been a change in the king's policy nor that there had been a change in the value of the bishoprics.

Yet the vacancy accounts are not completely unhelpful material. By John's reign the accounts of the keepers' receipts are sufficiently well itemized as to make it possible to break

[1] For further examples see Appendix A. Professor Cheney has suggested that in the case of the abbeys there was a marked increase of pressure during the interdict ('King John's Reaction to the Interdict on England', *Trans. Royal Hist. Soc. Fourth Series*, XXXI (1949), pp. 143–5), but the only clear example is that of Ramsey which has vacancy accounts both in the period before and during the interdict, and here the king had a special motive for oppression since he had quarrelled with the monks over the election of a new abbot (*Chronicon Abbatiae Rameseiensis*, ed. W. D. Macray (Rolls Series, London, 1886), p. 342).

[2] See Appendix A.

[3] *Pipe R. 13 John, 1211*, p. 35. The exact figures are £4,247.9.0½ (1208–9) and £2,572.14.2 (1209–10).

[4] £5,169.19.5 (*Pipe R. 8 John, 1206*, p. 54).

[5] *Pipe R. 13 John, 1211*, p. 244.

[6] £379.14.1 (*Pipe R. 14 John, 1212*, p. 9). This is the total of the account 'de anno praeterito'.   [7] £211.15.5½; *ibid.*

down the gross income into its component parts, and, by doing this, to understand which parts of the account may be used for purposes of comparison. Very large sales of corn and stock in an account covering the first year of a vacancy should be treated with caution, as possibly including some of the accumulated reserves of the late bishop.[1] Tallages have to be discounted in any calculation of purely regular income,[2] and a big difference may be made by the inclusion or exclusion of the money received from the sale of the corn harvest.[3] It is possible, if such pitfalls are borne in mind, to derive tentative figures as to the net income of the various bishoprics for the reigns of both Henry II and John, and then to compare the two sets of figures. From the calculations given in the tables in Appendix A it seems possible to say that on the whole the regular net income for most bishoprics appears at a higher figure on the rolls of John than on those of Henry II. May one go a step further and infer that John's policy towards vacancies was more extortionate than that of his father? I think that on the basis of these figures alone one cannot. In his investigation of the see of Ely, chiefly from the evidence of vacancy accounts, Mr. Miller has shown how the actual income figures rise consistently from the eleventh to the end of the thirteenth century, but, as he points out, the period covered was one both of economic expansion and also of rising prices.[4] The span from the beginning of the reign of Henry II to the end of John's reign lends itself perhaps more satisfactorily to comparison of the income totals than does the wider period covered by Mr. Miller, but, even so, caution is required. Towards the end of the twelfth century and in the early thirteenth century the practice of letting manors to farm

[1] Thus the very high total of £5,169.19.5 mentioned above, p. 50 n. 4 as coming from Canterbury in 1206 includes a sum of £1,019.8.1 for corn sold. It also includes 1,000 marks which the custodians of the see received 'de thesauro per manum Thesaurarii'. Whatever this mysterious payment may be it is distinctly suspect in the rôle of regular vacancy issues (*Pipe R. 8 John, 1206*, p. 54).

[2] It is a heavy tallage which in part explains the discrepancy between the totals accounted for in successive years at Durham, 1208–10.

[3] The variations in the Chichester accounts mentioned in the previous paragraph were in part due to this; in 1210–11 £159.10.2 was received 'de blado vendito', whereas only £17.14.5 was accounted for from this source in 1211–12 (*Pipe R. 14 John, 1212*, p. 9).

[4] Miller, *Abbey and Bishopric of Ely*, pp. 94–5.

for a fixed sum was being replaced by a more direct economic exploitation, and this change in general economic administration is reflected in the vacancy accounts on the Pipe Rolls of John when they are compared with those of the reign of Henry II, especially with the earlier ones of that reign. This change in methods would in itself tend to make for higher profits.

The figures of net income then, cannot be used with assurance to prove an oppressive policy towards vacancies on John's part. On the other hand, to think that John accepted passively the income which accrued to him from the vacant bishoprics without making any effort to make the returns as large as possible would be to do an injustice to the king's financial achievements and to underestimate his need of money.

The most casual glance at the vacancy accounts immediately suggests that there were some items in the income of a bishopric which were intrinsically much more capable of expansion *sede vacante* than others. Such very appreciable figures as £296.8.5 and £115.16.2 'de bosco vendito' are significant.[1] One might hew down the episcopal forests with greater impunity than one could take so noticeable a step as raising the figure of the assized rents. But the most promising item of all on Henry II's and Richard I's vacancy accounts from the point of view of potential expansion, was tallage.

John's reign was a turning-point in the general history of tallage. His general tallages were assessed heavily and during the first eight years of his reign he tallaged his demesne five times. Then comes a change of policy. Only two more general tallages were levied during the rest of the reign, that of 1210 and that of 1214; both were very heavy and covered a large number of counties. At the end of John's reign, tallage had in fact reverted to its position between 1168 and 1194; an occasional levy made to meet a special necessity, and in that form it could be levied very heavily.[2]

The tallage of vacant bishoprics had reached a turning-point

---

[1] On the account for Canterbury, 1205–6, *Pipe R. 8 John, 1206*, p. 54; and that for Winchester, 1204–5, *Pipe R. 7 John, 1205*, p. 12.

[2] This is a summary of the late Professor S. K. Mitchell's account of the tax in John's reign (*Studies in Taxation under John and Henry III* (London etc., 1914), pp. 287–8 and *Taxation in Medieval England*, pp. 17–83 and pp. 93–118, *passim*).

too, perhaps in part dependent on the development of tallage in general, although the path taken by the tallage of vacant sees was different from that taken by tallage of the royal demesne. Before John's reign vacant bishoprics had been tallaged, as far as one can see, incidentally to the tallage of the royal demesne; when there was no tallage of the demesne there was no tallage of the sees in hand. The development towards an annual tallage between 1194 and 1206 meant that it was possible for the crown to tallage nearly every vacant bishopric and abbey, if it so wished, because in almost every year in which a bishopric or abbey fell vacant, a tallage was being levied on the towns and on the royal demesne. A return to the practice of an occasional tallage, however, undermined this convenient possibility, and if a complete return to the methods of Henry II had been made by John, then some wealthy see such as Durham or Canterbury might well have slipped untallaged from the royal grasp.

This, John would not permit. The period of very frequent tallages no doubt made easier the evolution of a new principle, that every bishopric should be tallaged at least once during each vacancy, *whether the royal demesne was being tallaged or not*. Every vacant bishopric in John's reign was in fact tallaged at least once in each vacancy.[1] That this was not a mere accidental coincidence with general levies of tallage is indicated by the tallage of Exeter in 1210–11,[2] and of Durham in 1208–9.[3] These are particularly clear cases because in neither year was there a general tallage. It cannot be argued that these levies were really seignorial tallages, payments levied at will and often annually by a lord on his unfree tenants, and quite distinct from royal tallage which was a form of taxation.[4] In the case of Exeter on the roll of 1211 there are two consecutive entries, £139.18.4 'de tallagio maneriorum', and £32.11.8 'de auxilio maneriorum consueto'. It seems that a distinction is drawn between an accustomed aid and a presumably unaccustomed tallage. In the case of Durham, the other example, the vacancy account is rendered in four sections. The first section is for part

---

[1] See the tables in Appendix A. I have indicated which bishoprics were actually vacant and which were in the king's hand as a result of the interdict.

[2] *Pipe R. 13 John, 1211*, p. 272.

[3] *Ibid.*, p. 35.

[4] For this distinction see Hoyt, *op. cit.*, p. 108.

of a year only, but the other three are each for a year. In the first and third sections there is no indication at all of any payment in the nature of a tallage. But in the second section comprising the year 1208–9 there is a very heavy tallage of £1,154.1.8 accounted for; and in the fourth section covering the year 1210–11 there is a much smaller sum of £206.15.8 accounted for 'de tallagio'. Evidently one cannot explain the levy of £1,154.1.8 in 1208–9 in terms of an *auxilium consuetum*.

In the light of these considerations, it would seem that there can be little doubt that the tallages levied on vacancies by John were essentially a further extension of that royal tallage which Richard I and Henry II, and perhaps Henry I and Rufus, had levied on sees in hand on at least some of the occasions when they called on the royal demesne and the boroughs to provide them with special financial help. In this light, as the lineal descendant of *donum* and *auxilium*, the tallage of the royal demesne and of lands in hand is firmly designated by Professor Hoyt as taxation. 'Tallage was essentially royal (or public) rather than 'seignorial' as far as the question of origin is concerned.'[1] But the principles lying behind the various levies which the king made were anything but clear cut, anything but rigid. This was especially true when the government was treating custom a little roughly by working out new practices, or rather adapting and developing old practices until in effect they became new. It is now a commonplace that the urge for a distinction between tallage and aid in the thirteenth century came not from above but from below, not from the government but from those paying the taxes. In the same way there are some indications that the exchequer was not so anxious to distinguish firmly between the nature of seignorial tallage and royal tallage, as historians naturally tend to be. An interesting case in this connection comes from the bishopric of Exeter which was usually divided, for the purposes of vacancy accounts, into two parts, the manors in Cornwall and those outside Cornwall. In 1207 the manors of the bishopric outside Cornwall paid the king a tallage of £177.2.11½.[2] The manors within Cornwall paid an *auxilium*;

---

[1] *Ibid.*, p. 115.
[2] *Pipe R. 9 John, 1207*, p. 222. This figure is calculated from the individual sums levied from each manor.

the keeper rendered account for £34.9.7 from the Cornish manors, 'quod auxilium debetur per annum licet non in hac summa'.[1] How much of the aid paid by the Cornish manors can we designate royal 'taxation'? The question is clearly absurd. The principles on which John, or his exchequer, might have defended their policy, for it does seem to be a policy, of levying a tallage on a vacant bishopric at least once during the vacancy, unfortunately are not known. The question is of interest, for the practice of John's reign had the ultimate effect of making the king's right to tallage a vacant bishopric an integral part of that sum of rights which fell to the king when a vacancy of the see occurred. As a result, the tallage of vacant bishoprics gradually becomes something distinct from the tallage of the rest of the demesne. One might even say, with caution, that it perhaps loses some of that character of 'taxation' which the tallage of the demesne retained. It was no longer levied on an occasion of great necessity, but on every occasion that a vacancy occurred as an incidental part of the king's total rights of lordship over the vacant see. Indeed, it might perhaps be said that it became less 'public' and more, in the widest sense of the word, 'seignorial'.[2]

John, then, tallaged episcopal vacancies more frequently than either Henry II or Richard I as far as can be judged from the extant evidence. He also tallaged them more heavily. The largest recorded sum exacted in tallage from a vacant see before the reign of John was £341.4.2, levied on the bishopric of Durham in 1196.[3] On the first vacancy account of John's reign, that of the see of Lincoln on the roll of 1201, a tallage of over £520 was accounted for.[4] In 1205 the large sum of £1,217.19.4 was received from 'aids and perquisites and small sales' in the vacant see of Winchester.[5] This entry may well have covered a heavy tallage. In the following year the archbishopric of Canterbury was tallaged for £1,065.2.3.[6] The very heavy tallage of

[1] *Ibid.*
[2] For the development of the tallaging of vacant sees in the thirteenth century see below, pp. 121–42.
[3] *Chancellor's R. 8 Richard I, 1196*, pp. 255–6.
[4] £522.5.2 (*Pipe R. 3 John, 1201*, p. 193).
[5] *Pipe R. 7 John, 1205*, p. 12.
[6] *Pipe R. 8 John, 1206*, p. 54.

£1,154.1.8 levied at Durham in 1208–9 has already been mentioned.[1] It is a little curious that after this date, that is, roughly after the first year of the interdict, there is no record of any really high tallage in an episcopal vacancy for the rest of the reign.[2] Some of the sees in the king's hand during the interdict, but not vacant, are not recorded as being tallaged at all,[3] but the accounts do not always cover the full period during which the king had control of the see; however, it might be that the king sometimes drew a distinction between vacant sees and sees in hand but not vacant. Whatever the explanation of that downward trend in the recorded tallages towards the end of his reign, of the very high tallages of the period 1200–9, and of his more freqent levy of tallages on the vacant sees, John had undoubtedly heightened the importance of this element in vacancy revenue. It will later be seen how very important these developments were as precedents.[4] Henry III was to regard the practices of the reign of his father, as sufficiently old to be termed 'customary'.

Every account for the issues of a vacant see may be divided into two basic sections: receipts and expenditure. So far we have been concerned with the receipts on the accounts of John's reign, and of what they reveal of royal policy; but the items on the expenditure side hint at new developments too. In the vacancy accounts of the reigns of Henry II and Richard I, the expenditure was almost entirely confined to two types of payments; (a) those which the bishop himself would have made had he been alive, such as those connected with the agricultural administration of the bishopric and the accustomed payment of alms; and (b) the payments into the royal treasury. By far the greater part of the gross income accounted for normally found its way *in thesauro*.

In his discussion of the experiments in financial administration in the second part of John's reign Mr. Jolliffe has said that

---

[1] See above, p. 49.

[2] See Appendix A. The highest figure is that of the Durham tallage of 1210–11: £206.15.8 (*Pipe R. 13 John, 1211*, p. 36), and the next highest is that taken at Canterbury 1211–12: £184.2.5 (*Pipe R. 14 John, 1212*, p. 40).

[3] For example Salisbury 1210–11 (*Pipe R. 13 John, 1211*, pp. 244–5), Lincoln 1211–12 (*Pipe R. 14 John, 1212*, p. 2), and London (*ibid.*, pp. 9–10).

[4] See below, pp. 121–42, *passim*.

until the summer of 1207 the main supplies for the financing of the royal household were drawn in the orthodox way. The money went first to the treasury at Westminster, and was thence, by royal writ, delivered to the chamber when that was its real destination.[1] The vacancy accounts suggest that, in the case of this particular branch of casual revenue at any rate, the beginnings of a new emphasis on payments *in camera* instead of *in thesauro* may be traced to the earlier period of this reign. For example, on the Roll of 1202 in the Lincoln account of that year £487.18.11 was the sum paid *in thesauro*,[2] but £728.7.6 was paid to Geoffrey Fitz Peter, who then accounted for it (and for more) as having been paid by himself partly *in camera* and partly *ipsi Regi*.[3] Of course, it may be that Fitz Peter had in fact made these payments 'in the chamber' and 'to the king himself' before the money from the vacant see of Lincoln had reached him, in which case the payment to Fitz Peter from the issues of the vacancy was in the nature of the simple discharge of a royal debt. But even if this is so, the by-passing of the treasury still seems significant. Again, on the Winchester vacancy account of 1204–5 no money (except for one besant) was paid into the treasury.[4] Much was spent on the king's requirements for the Gascon campaign, and there was a payment of £266.13.4 *in camera*. At Canterbury, too, in 1205–6 there was no payment recorded *in thesauro*, but the very large sum of £2,000 was paid *ipsi Regi in camera*.[5] All this happened before the summer of 1207, and suggests that the king was experimenting with new methods early in his reign. In 1208 and 1209 the accounts of Lincoln and Exeter were actually rendered *in camera*.[6]

Mr. Jolliffe has shown from the evidence of the Misae Rolls how the issues of vacancies were involved in John's scheme of castle treasures, the hoarding of large quantities of wealth in provincial depôts in the charge of well-trusted castellans. These rolls show that £1,000, more than half of it from the issues of the bishoprics of Durham, Ely and Chester, went 'ad custodiendam' to Ralph Parmenter at Corfe;[7] £300 from Canterbury

---

[1] Jolliffe, *loc. cit.*, p. 120.
[2] *Pipe R. 4 John, 1202*, pp. 277–9, i.e. apart from fines for scutage.
[3] *Ibid.*   [4] *Pipe R. 7 John, 1205*, p. 12.
[5] *Pipe R. 8 John, 1206*, p. 54.   [6] *Pipe R. 11 John, 1209*, pp. 81 and 91.
[7] *Rot. de Liberate ac de Misis et Prestitis*, p. 110, in 1209.

and some fines were received by Reginald of Cornhill into Rochester.[1] So too were £110 from the bishopric of Exeter and the canons of Newburgh.[2] The Pipe Roll account for three and a half years, 1208–11, of the Durham vacancy, adds impressive corroboration of Mr. Jolliffe's thesis. Of the huge total of £16,787.14.10$\frac{1}{2}$[3] accounted for from Durham during this time, £5,946 are sent, 'Philippo Marc et Briano de Insula . . . ad ponendum in thesauro Regis apud Notingham', and £1,066.13.4 'Roberto de Braibroc, que misse fuerunt apud Bristo'.[4]

Sometimes, however, it seems to have been more convenient to by-pass not only the treasury at Westminster but also the chamber and the castle treasures and to pay sums direct to the payee. No doubt this was partly a question of whether the money was required immediately or not. Nor indeed was there anything startlingly new in this practice itself. From the time of the early twelfth-century records, sheriffs had been charged with the duty of making purchases for the king, payment for which would be allowed to them in their accounts at the exchequer. But when, as at Winchester in 1204–5, out of a grand total of £3,633.8.2 and one besant accounted for by the keepers,[5] only one besant is paid into the treasury, and only £466.13.4 is paid into the chamber, while considerable sums are claimed by the keepers for their payments, 'in liberationibus balistariorum et aliorum . . .', and 'Willelmo Ernald' et sociis suis galiotis' and 'pro expensis factis in cleiis et pontibus et aliis necessariis contra transfretationem Regis in Pictaviam', one is inclined to feel that the requirements of war colour these accounts to a particularly marked degree.[6] Similarly, at Canterbury, in 1205–6, 2,000 marks are spent in purchases made in the fairs of Winchester and sent to the king in Poitou,[7] while from Durham, 1208–11, large quantities of grain and pigs are sent for

---

[1] *Ibid.*, p. 145, in 1210.

[2] *Ibid.*, p. 115. Mr. Jolliffe gives this sum as £200, but I think this may be a slip for £110.

[3] *Pipe R. 13 John, 1211*, p. 38. Included in this sum are some arrears of a previous account and payments of fines and scutage. The gross income without these payments amounts to £13,575.5.5$\frac{1}{2}$; see p. 217, below.

[4] *Ibid.*

[5] *Pipe R. 7 John, 1205*, p. 12. Again, this figure includes payments of scutage. Without these the total gross income amounts to £3,189.8.2; see below, Appendix A.

[6] *Ibid.*   [7] *Pipe R. 8 John, 1206*, p. 54.

the king to Wales, Ireland and Scotland.[1] Vacancies were evidently freely used by John as direct sources of supply when he was waging war, and of all the sources of supply, over and above the regular income of the crown, vacant bishoprics with their large surpluses of food and their reserves of ready money were one of the most convenient.

In the light of John's skilful and original exploitation of ecclesiastical vacancies, his reserving of their custody to himself and his heirs in his charter to the church in 1214 cannot appear as either surprising or unimportant. That King John valued this right highly and had no intention of yielding it is suggested by the use that was made of it as a sanction for his good faith in February 1213. The pope orders John to promise that if the king breaks faith with the church 'tuque perpetuo custodiam vacancium ecclesiarum ammittes.'[2] John guaranteed his promise in this form in his own letter of May 1213.[3]

On the exercise of regalian right in England between 1066 and 1216, there could be no more apt comment than that made by Thomas Madox:

It may be observed, that albeit this part of the Crown Revenue was in itself purely casual: Yet as the Kings in the Five or Six Successions after the Conquest ordered matters, one may guess that they made it a Considerable Revenue. For the Bishopricks and Abbeys in England of Royal Patronage being Numerous, And the Kings using to keep some of them (especially the Rich and Well-endowd ones) Long Void, As they had generally Some or Other of them in their Hands, So the same amounted in the whole to a Fair Revenue.[4]

With the death of King John the five or six successions after the conquest had run their course. It now remains to be seen what happened to the right which had so far produced so 'fair', so 'considerable' a revenue. And it may be well to bear in mind that up to this point that revenue had been increasingly considerable.

[1] *Pipe R. 13 John, 1211*, pp. 38–40; for example 2,353 pigs were bought and sent to Ireland and to Wales, and 1,774 quarters 3 bushels of oats were dispatched 'ad opus Regis . . . in Ybernia'.

[2] *Selected Letters of Pope Innocent III concerning England (1198–1216)*, ed. C. R. Cheney and W. H. Semple (London, 1953), pp. 133–4.

[3] *Rot. Litt. Pat. 1201–16*, pp. 98–9.

[4] *The History and Antiquities of the Exchequer of the Kings of England, etc.* (1st edition, London, 1711), p. 209.

CHAPTER IV

The Machinery of Royal Administration of Vacant Bishoprics

IN 1214 King John granted a charter in which among other things he conceded freedom of episcopal election to all the cathedral churches of England.[1] He made several other important concessions and several equally important reservations. Among the latter was this:

salva nobis et haeredibus nostris custodia ecclesiarum et monasteriorum vacantium quae ad nos pertinent.

The clause is brief, but short texts may deserve, and often require, long glosses. In this case, there undoubtedly exists ample material for the gloss, so much material that it has only been possible to investigate systematically the evidence relating to the cathedral churches. Indeed the extent of the evidence may appear to exceed the interest or importance of the theme. However, when it is borne in mind that this was a matter which enjoyed the frequent personal attention of kings, archbishops and bishops and occupied a large proportion of the time and energy of hundreds of clerks in exchequer, chancery and wardrobe, giving rise to thousands of royal writs and over a hundred financial accounts in the course of a century, it may be accepted that such a matter is worth investigation.

If the investigation is to be primarily a gloss on the clause in King John's charter, certain limitations are implied. The charter is concerned with the *Ecclesia Anglicana*, that is the provinces of Canterbury and York. The king's regalian right extended beyond this, notably to Ireland,[2] but we are concerned

---

[1] Stubbs, *Select Charters*, p. 283.

[2] See for example a writ of 20 Feb. 1256, *Cal. Pat. R., 1247–58*, p. 463. Edward I attempted to exercise the right in Gascony but Gregory X informed him that his occupation of the temporalities of vacant sees within the province of Auxerre was

here only with the twenty-one sees in England and Wales.[1] Moreover, an investigation based on the charter of 1214 implies also a limit in time. By the reign of Edward III the system of papal provisions to bishoprics had become sufficiently well established to change the whole complexion of the problems of episcopal elections and of regalian right. Vacancies had become shorter, and, therefore, financially of less importance to the crown.[2] Admittedly the later period cannot be entirely left out of consideration because the changing relations between church and state in the fourteenth century sometimes throw the political and constitutional significance of the right into sudden relief. Nevertheless, broadly speaking, this survey must be confined to the period between the accession of Henry III and the death of Edward II, or very roughly the century succeeding the charter of 1214.

Within these appointed limits three questions may pertinently be asked of the evidence. (1) How was the king's right of custody over vacancies exercised? (2) What were the crown's material gains from the right? (3) Did the exercise of this royal right have any political and constitutional implications? The second and third of these questions will be considered in Chapters IV, V and VI. The first, the question of the machinery of royal administration of vacancies, will be dealt with now.

In the thirteenth and early fourteenth centuries there were seventeen dioceses in England, and over all but Rochester the king regularly exercised regalian right. Here the bishop held his temporalities of the archbishop of Canterbury in virtue of a charter of King John.[3] But there is reason to believe that even

---

justified neither 'de consuetudine vel de jure'. The pope's letter (22 Sep. 1274) is printed in *Foedera*, I, pars II, ed. T. Rymer (Record Commission, London, 1816), p. 515. In a letter of 25 July 1276 Edward I renounces his right to the custody of the temporalities of the see of Bordeaux during a vacancy (*Cal. Pat. R. 1272–81*, p. 155).

[1] Occasional reference is made in this and the following chapters to individual Welsh bishoprics, but their peculiar administrative problems form a subject on their own and this has not been dealt with here.

[2] In any case their relative financial importance was on the wane at this time for other reasons, such as the increasing emphasis on such potentially vast sources of royal revenue as customs duties and parliamentary taxation.

[3] *Anglia Sacra*, ed. H. Wharton (London, 1691), I, 386–7.

Rochester had not been allowed to slip entirely from the king's grasp.[1]

In the machinery of custody of a vacant see the most important single factor was the royal custodian himself. The keeper was the linch-pin between the central government and the vacant bishopric. *Vis-à-vis* the men of the bishopric he is the king's representative who controls day by day the economic administration and much of the judicial administration of the vacant see. *Vis-à-vis* the crown, the keeper is the recipient of royal orders, responsible to the king for all that he does within the bishopric and all that he reaps from it financially. It is in terms of royal keepers that the administration of vacancies must be studied.

When the king heard of a bishop's death he normally lost little time in appointing keepers to the vacant bishopric. On occasion, he seems to have been a little too precipitate. On 15 January 1302, Edward I ordered the escheator to take into the king's hand the temporalities of the see of Worcester void by the death of Godfrey, late bishop.[2] The entry on the Fine Roll was cancelled; Godfrey Giffard did not die until eleven days later.[3] On 10 December 1254, Henry III anticipated the death of Roger Weseham, bishop of Lichfield by nearly two years. The writ was cancelled 'because he is alive'.[4]

The evidence indicates that with some exceptions the commission of a vacant see to one or more royal custodians was

[1] There is no evidence that Henry III ever attempted to take seisin of Rochester in a vacancy, but in his concession of the custody to the archbishop of Canterbury in 1235 he does add the saving clause 'salvo jure nostro et omnium aliorum si qui in custodia predicti episcopatus jus sibi vendicent' (*Close R. 1234–37*, p. 55).
The first three Rochester vacancies of Edward I's reign seem to have passed without royal interference, but for the vacancy of 1291 there is an account on the Pipe Roll by the royal escheator, Malcolm de Harley, which is headed 'Episcopatus Roffensis' (Pipe R. 136 m.27d). This account is for three manors only, which the bishop of Rochester is here said to hold in chief of the king and the writ for the restitution of these manors to the new bishop, 11 Dec. 1291, explicitly states that the late bishop held them 'by reason of the bishopric' (*Cal. Close R., 1288–96*, p. 210). It may be that the king henceforth exercised regalian right over these manors when Rochester was vacant, for in an entry on the Fine Rolls of Edward III it is stated that these manors were taken into the king's hand during voidance of the bishopric in the times of Edward I and Edward II (*Cal. Fine R., 1347–56*, p. 354).
[2] *Cal. Fine R., 1272–1307*, p. 448.
[3] 26 January, *Handbook*, p. 174.
[4] *Cal. Pat. R., 1247–58*, p. 392.

made within a few days of the bishop's death, and that sometimes at least the sheriff or escheator took the see in hand for a short time before the 'permanent' commission was made.[1]

Keepers were usually appointed to each vacancy singly or in twos, and in the reigns of Edward I and Edward II there was usually only one commission of the vacant see, and the keepers then appointed remained in office until the end of th evacancy.[2] However, in some of the longer vacancies of Henry III's reign there were several changes of keepers during the single vacancy. At Durham, for instance, in the 1237-41 vacancy John Fitz Philip was keeper for a year and nine months;[3] Nicholas de Molis followed him for a further year and five months[4] and, finally, William le Brun and Henry de Neketon succeeded Nicholas and remained in office for the last eight months of this long interregnum.[5]

When the king committed the custody of a vacant see jointly to two keepers he did not necessarily intend that they should have identical duties and responsibilities. Sometimes the second of two keepers might be appointed for his special knowledge and for the value of his advice, although in some cases he was unable, because of other duties, to devote all his time to the affairs of the vacancy. In the Ely vacancy, 1302-3, Robert Hereward, sheriff of Norfolk and Suffolk and also steward of the late bishop, assisted in keeping the vacant bishopric. His intimate knowledge of the affairs of the see and of the locality

[1] At Canterbury in 1228 there was a preliminary commission of the archbishopric to the local sheriffs (Fine R. 27, m.4) and the bishopric of Norwich was in the hands of the local subescheator for over a month in 1288 before its final commission to William de Redham and Peter of Leicester (Pipe R. 133, m.20d).

[2] There were exceptions. At Ely in 1302-3 and at Winchester in 1323-4 one of the keepers was replaced part way through the vacancy but his colleague continued in office with the man newly appointed. For Ely see Pipe R. 150, m.34 and for Winchester Pipe R. 169, m.43.

[3] 19 Apr. 1237 to 2 Feb. 1239 (Pipe R. 84, m.2).

[4] 2 Feb. 1239 to 24 June 1240; *ibid.*

[5] 24 June 1240 to 10 Feb. 1241 (Pipe R. 84, m.6d). Other instances may be found. The see of Canterbury was committed to Ralph Trubblevill and Walter Kirkham 12 Sep. 1231 (Fine R. 30, m.2) and remained in their custody until its commission to Peter de Rivaux 30 June 1232 (*Pat. R. 1225-32*, p. 486). Norwich was committed to the care of Robert de Scotindon 20 Aug. 1236 (Fine R. 35, m.5) and was later committed to Jeremiah de Caxton instead 17 Mar. 1237 (*Cal. Pat. R., 1232-47*, p. 176).

would be well worth the twenty marks which the king paid for his assistance during these ten months.[1]

Again a second keeper might be appointed specifically to act as controller. At Winchester in 1261 Walter de Burgh the keeper is requested to admit to his company Adam Fitz Pain; to give Adam two horses, two grooms and a reasonable allowance for expenses, and to permit Adam to join him in hearing the accounts for the issues of the individual bailiwicks of the bishopric.[2] De Burgh's account at the exchequer is rendered 'per visum et testimonium Ade filii Pagani'.[3] Adam's function was that of controller, and controllers are also found *eo nomine* in the vacancies at Canterbury 1278–9[4] and at Ely 1286.[5]

These shades and gradations in the extent to which keepers might be personally involved in the day-to-day work of custody of vacant sees, raises this further question: did the custody of vacant bishoprics ever become a sinecure, a convenient method of pensioning faithful royal servants? The evidence clearly indicates that it did not. There might be a certain amount of absenteeism on the part of some of the keepers who might have been busy royal clerks with other commitments,[6] but, broadly

[1] Hereward's expenses are given in the account, 'et ideo minus quia per idem tempus fuit vicecomes Norff' et Suff' (Pipe R. 150, m.34 and 34d).

[2] Fine R. 58, m.3; 1 Oct. 1261.

[3] Pipe R. 106, m.21.

[4] *Cal. Close R., 1272–79*, pp. 460–1. The calendared version of the writ is worth quoting: 'To the barons of the exchequer. Although the king lately committed to Ralph de Sandewico and William de Saham the archbishopric of Canterbury, . . . to be kept during his pleasure, he does not wish that William shall be charged with the issues thereof or shall answer to the king for the same, but that he shall intend the custody aforesaid with the said Ralph and shall be controller of all the issues aforesaid, so that Ralph shall answer to the king for the issues by the view and testimony of William.' However, even the post of controller took up too much of Saham's time and he was replaced on 12 Oct. of the same year by William of Middleton (*Cal. Pat. R., 1272–81*, p. 279 and Pipe R. 124, m.23d).

[5] Pipe R. 144, m.34. The account for the Ely vacancy is said to be rendered 'per visum et testimonium Willelmi de Middelton Baronis Regis de Scaccario' and in this case the counter roll is preserved among the P.R.O. Ministers' Accounts (Bishops' Temporalities) 1132/9.

[6] In an inquiry into the conduct of the vacancy at Winchester, 1323–4 (K. R. Mem. R. 101, mm.113–128d), two of the keepers, admittedly badly in need of an alibi (see below, pp. 107–9), plead that they spent very little time in the bishopric. Robert of Wells was 'aliunde occupatus in negociis Regis' (m.127d) and he mentions his 'lieutenant' Robert de Ho. Richard Airmyn, another of the keepers, says that 'de dicta custodia in modico personaliter se intromisit eo quod fuit tunc temporis custos rotulorum cancellarie' (*ibid.*).

speaking, there seems reason to think that keepers of vacant sees were expected to spend a considerable proportion of their time on the spot and to devote a good deal of their attention to vacancy matters. Except where the see is in the hands of an escheator, it is very unusual for one keeper to be involved in the custody of more than one bishopric at a time.[1] The striking exception to this is the commission of several vacancies to a group of three clerks in 1254.[2] John Chishull, Robert de Manneby and William of Axmouth were made principal keepers of bishoprics and abbeys which were then vacant or which should fall vacant. The experiment was unusual and it had a special purpose. The king was, at the time, in desperate financial straits and he wished to divert all the money from vacancies to the payment of his debt of 5,000 marks to the citizens of Bordeaux. The concentration of responsibility for this in the hands of three principal or 'super' keepers was a temporary device of financial centralization. To sum up, it seems reasonable to suppose that in general the custodian of the vacant bishopric in the thirteenth and early fourteenth centuries was, like the sheriff, a hardworking servant of the king. And, as with the sheriff, any profit-making on the part of the keeper was illicit profit-making.

John Mansell, a competent and much-beneficed clerk of Henry III, took some share in the keeping of four separate vacancies at different times,[3] and in Edward I's reign, Nicholas Fermbaud was keeper of Ely 1290,[4] of Bath 1302,[5] and joint keeper of Winchester 1304–5.[6] Sometimes a keeper who had successfully managed the affairs of one vacancy was appointed to the custody of the next vacancy in the same see, especially when the vacancies followed in fairly swift succession; thus Walter de Burgh kept Winchester in 1261 and again in 1268.[7]

---

[1] Malcolm de Harley, escheator, for example, was keeper of Llandaff from 15 Apr. 1287 (L.T.R. Mem. R. 60, m.4) and at the same time of Chichester from 25 Oct. of that year (*Cal. Fine R., 1272–1307*, p. 241). His custodies of Salisbury and York in 1286 were not strictly contemporaneous although the two tasks followed hard one upon the other.

[2] *Cal. Pat. R., 1247–58*, p. 359.

[3] He was appointed keeper of Canterbury 5 Nov. 1240 (Fine R. 37, m.16); of Worcester 20 Aug. 1236 (Fine R. 35, m.5); of York 15 May 1258 (Fine R. 55, m 6) and of Durham 17 Aug. 1260 (Fine R. 57, m.4).

[4] Pipe R. 135, m.1.   [5] Pipe R. 150, m.32.
[6] Pipe R. 152B, m.20.   [7] Pipe R. 95, m.6d.

F

From this attempt to unfold the general pattern of the system of the appointing of royal custodians there already emerges some hint about the manner of men these keepers were. Very often they were king's clerks, sometimes they were men of experience in local administration. Robert Hereward, sheriff of the eastern counties, and keeper of Ely, was also the late bishop's steward[1] and he was not the only episcopal steward to appear later as a royal keeper. Lambert de Trikingham was appointed steward of Henry Newark, archbishop of York, in 1297.[2] In 1299 and again in 1304 he was appointed by the crown as one of the keepers in these two York vacancies.[3] Ralph of Sandwich, a seneschal of Archbishop Kilwardby[4] was one of the keepers of Canterbury in the vacancy of 1278–9 on Kilwardby's translation.[5]

It becomes increasingly clear that, as Mr. Edward Miller has observed from the evidence relating to Ely,

a common pool of administrative officials came into existence—men who gained the same sort of experience and grappled with the same sort of problems whether they served the king or the bishop.[6]

The careers of the men engaged in vacancy administration corroborate this at every point. Not merely might the steward of a bishop, an occasion, be promoted to a share in the custody of the particular see in which he had already been steward, but, on a much more general scale, men passed easily from the service of a private lord to the service of the king and *vice versa*. Elias de Derham, keeper of Salisbury 1228–9 was a man of influence in the sees of both Salisbury and Canterbury. He was a canon of

[1] Miller, *Abbey and Bishopric of Ely*, p. 268, where a summary of Hereward's career is given.

[2] The Register of Henry Newark in *The Registers of John le Romeyn 1286–96 Part II and of Henry Newark 1296–99*, ed. W. Brown (Surtees Soc. CXXVIII, London 1916), p. 250, 28 June 1297.

[3] Pipe R. 150, m.30 and 152B, m.16.

[4] See B.M. Additional MS. 29794, m.1. This document is an account roll for the see of Canterbury, manor by manor, which belongs to Kilwardby's pontificate and has been assigned by Miss D. Sutcliffe to the year 1273–4 ('The Financial Condition of the see of Canterbury 1279–1292', *Speculum*, x (1935), p. 61 n. 2). The relevant entry is: 'In expensis seneschallorum videlicet R. de Northwood R. de Sandwyc. et Ade de Illegh.' See also D. L. Douie, *Archbishop Pecham* (Oxford, 1952), p. 85.

[5] Pipe R. 124, m.23d.   [6] Miller, *op. cit.*, p. 269.

Salisbury and had been the steward of Archbishop Stephen Langton.[1] Another administrator, John de Estwood, acted as the king's subordinate keeper of the see of London in the vacancy of 1273-4.[2] In 1276 he was steward of the bishop of Ely.[3] John de Lythegreyns a former steward of the archbishop of York[4] was a royal custodian of this bishopric in 1296.[5] Men of such diversity of experience could on occasion be very useful. In 1278-9 there was a vacancy at Canterbury and it would seem that there had perhaps been some query about allowing the payment of £1.10.0 which the keepers claimed as alms customarily due from the revenues of the archbishopric to the master of the hospital of Sevenoaks and to certain friars. However, Roger de Northwood, a baron of the exchequer, testified to the payment; he was in a position to do so; he had formerly been seneschal of the aforesaid archbishopric.[6]

The picture, as a whole, is perhaps complex in its details, but fairly firm in its main lines. A vacant bishopric was normally committed to the custody of one or two professional administrators, experienced in the service of king or bishops or both, and responsible to the crown. Except in the case of a long vacancy they might be expected to continue in office until the temporalities were restored to the incoming bishop. While it lasted the affairs of the vacancy would occupy a good proportion of their time and attention. Yet, the system itself was one of which the church disapproved, and towards the end of this period, in Edward II's reign there are several instances of the commission of the care of a vacant see to the dean and chapter of the cathedral church. The chapter of Lincoln in 1316, and the chapters of Salisbury and London in 1317 made permanent arrangements with the crown that they might act as farmers of their respective sees during vacancies.[7] Exeter made a similar

---

[1] *Acta Stephani Langton, 1207-28*, ed. K. Major (Cant. and York Soc., Oxford, 1950), p. 66 n. and p. 180. He was also an executor of Langton's will (*Close R., 1227-31*, p. 110; 22 July, 1228).

[2] *Cal. Fine R., 1272-1307*, p. 11.   [3] Miller, *op. cit.*, p. 266.

[4] *The Register of John le Romeyn, 1286-96, Part I*, ed. W. Brown (Surtees Soc., CXXIII, London, 1913), p. 358.

[5] *Cal. Fine R., 1272-1307*, p. 371.

[6] '. . . sicut testificatum est per Rogerum de Northwode Baronem de Scaccario quondam senescallum archiepiscopatus predicti' (Pipe R. 124 m.23d).

[7] *Cal. Fine R., 1307-19*, p. 272 and pp. 348-9.

arrangement for a single vacancy in 1320.[1] In a statute of 1340, the king promised to give all chapters the opportunity of coming to an arrangement of this kind for the individual vacancy.[2] This was a sign of the waning importance of the custody of vacancies to the crown in the fourteenth century. In the thirteenth century this lay in the future. In the reigns of Henry III and Edward I and usually in Edward II's reign too, the death of a bishop still meant the speedy arrival of the royal keepers. It now remains to watch the keepers at work.

In a document connected with the Durham vacancy of 1226–8, it is stated that

On or about 15 September 1226, Master Stephen de Lucy came to the city of Durham accompanied by his clerk, Hugh Devon, and there the king's letters patent, committing the bishopric to Stephen de Lucy's custody, were read aloud.[3]

This is the exact statement of Hugh Devon himself who was there and heard the letters read, and it may have been that the royal custody of many vacancies began with a similar ceremony.[4]

A keeper on his first arrival had to take seisin of all the temporalities of the see, and he might have to make decisions as to exactly what these included. It was advisable to be circumspect. In 1260 John Mansell, the keeper of Durham, had taken into the king's hand the hospitals of Northallerton and Sherburn 'rege inconsulto et absque mandato regis speciali'. The keepers of the hospitals did not omit to mention this to the king, and

[1] *Ibid.*, *1319–1327*, pp. 38–9. Already in Henry III's reign there had been one instance of the farming of a vacancy to the dean and chapter, at Salisbury (*Cal. Pat. R.*, *1266–72*, pp. 543–4; 26 June 1271), but the experiment does not seem to have been repeated in Edward I's reign. However, as early as the reign of John the device of farming abbatial vacancies to a convent had been used: Peterborough (Pipe R. 59, m.5d) and St. Augustine's (*Pipe R. 14 John*, 1212, p. 15). There are numerous examples of similar arrangements between the crown and individual abbeys in the reigns of Henry III and Edward I.

[2] *Statutes of the Realm*, 1 (London, 1810), p. 294.

[3] This is an extract from an account of proceedings in the case of the Durham election in the vacancy of 1226–8, which was being heard in the court of the archbishop of York (MS. 5520 in the Durham Cathedral Archives, as transcribed in the appendix to an unpublished B.Litt. thesis by the late W. K. Evers in the Maitland Library, Oxford).

[4] In this case Stephen de Lucy was not the first keeper during this vacancy; he followed Luke the Chaplain.

Mansell received a royal writ reproving him for his action.[1] The keepers of Norwich in 1326 took the precaution of consulting the king before definitely taking into the king's hand the corn of the churches of Hoxne, Thornham, Terling and Langham, 'which belong to the bishopric'.[2] It was well that they did so, as the royal judgement was eventually given in favour of the claim of the bishop's executors over this corn.[3]

There was another respect in which some keepers had to be wary about the limits of their commission; in a conventual cathedral the niceties of the keeper's authority over the monastery could create friction. A simultaneous vacancy in the bishopric and the cathedral priory was a particularly delicate business. An inquisition into the status of the convent of St. Mary's, Carlisle, in 1329 found that, although the temporalities of the convent in its vacancy belonged by custom neither to king nor to bishop, the temporalities of the priory had in the late voidance of the see been taken into the king's hand.[4] In the see of Ely the problem was recurrent. In a vacancy of this bishopric in 1229, which coincided with a vacancy in the priory of that church, the king found by inquisition that neither king *sede vacante* nor bishop *sede plena* had been in the custom of enjoying the custody of the priory when it was void.[5] On that particular occasion the king restored the custody of the priory to the subprior and convent.[6] However, in 1298 on the death of the bishop of Ely, without even the pretext of a 'double' vacancy,[7] the royal keepers of the vacant bishopric also took seisin of the manors of the monks[8] and made an extent of them,[9]

---

[1] *Close R., 1259–61*, pp. 212–13.   [2] *Cal. Close R., 1323–27*, p. 471.
[3] The problems of appropriated churches are considered more fully later; see below, pp. 114–16.
[4] *Cal. Inq. Misc.*, 1307–49, p. 270.
[5] *Close R., 1227–31*, p. 167.   [6] *Ibid.*
[7] i.e. a vacancy in the priory as well as in the bishopric.
[8] The story is reconstructed by Dr. Rose Graham in 'The Administration of the Diocese of Ely during the Vacancies of the See, 1298–99 and 1302–03', *Trans. Royal Hist. Soc. Fourth Series*, XII (1929), pp. 49–54. The incident left its traces on the Pipe Roll account for this Ely vacancy of 1298–9 (Pipe R. 144, mm.29–31). For example: 'In expensis iiij clericorum capientium in manum Regis maneria prioratus eiusdem per xv dies' (m.29).
[9] See *ibid.*, m.30d. 'In vadiis duorum clericorum facientium extentas maneriorum predicti Prioratus et appreciantium bona et catalla in eisdem inventis et ad inquirendum de exitibus inde perceptis per priorem Eliensem. . . .'

and the monks eventually had to pay a fine of 1,000 marks for a
royal charter granting that the king should not in future have
custody of the priory during a vacancy of the see.[1] In the course
of this inquiry, it transpired that the royal custodians, in the
vacancies of the see of Ely in 1286 and in 1290, had in each
case taken formal seisin of the priory although subsequently the
prior had in fact been allowed to administer the property.[2]
The keepers in 1286 had obliged the chief administrative
officials of the priory to swear that they would be faithful to the
king, and even in the eventual settlement of 1299 the king did
not yield his right to collate to offices in the priory.[3] Another
hazardous moment for the rights of the convent, or of the secular chapter of a cathedral church *sede vacante* was the arrival
of the justices in eyre: if the convent or chapter had the right to
the amercements of their own tenants they would do well to
keep a watchful eye on the custodians of the bishopric. Thus,
in the vacancy of Bath, 1242–4, and of Ely, 1254, the keepers of
these bishoprics were ordered to allow the demand of the dean
and chapter of Wells in the one case,[4] and of the prior of Ely in
the other to have the amercements of their men.[5] In matters
such as these the keepers would, of course, normally act according to the custom and precedent, if this was known to them.[6]
But sometimes there had to be much searching of chancery or
exchequer records before precedents emerged. Nor did keepers

[1] *Cal. Fine R., 1272–1307*, p. 419.

[2] L.T.R. Mem. R. 70, m.19. In the case of the 1286 vacancy the jurors said 'idem
prioratus tempore illius vacacionis fuit in manu domini Regis per tres dies'. In
the case of the 1290 vacancy, the jurors said they knew that the keeper, Nicholas
Fermbaud, had taken seisin of the priory 'sed per quantum tempus predictus
Nicholaus continuavit seisinam nomine domini Regis in predicto prioratu dicunt
quod ignorant'.

[3] *Cal. Pat. R., 1292–1301*, pp. 457–8. The king held a similar right at Canterbury
and at Winchester and used it with effect. See below, pp. 198–9.

[4] *Close R., 1242–47*, p. 52.

[5] *Ibid., 1254–56*, p. 13.

[6] These were of course exceptions. In the case of the seizure of the priory of Ely
in 1298 it does seem possible that the king was deliberately trying out his claim,
and that the keepers were acting under the government's instructions. The last
vacancy, 1290, when the prior had been allowed custody of the priory, was well
within living memory, yet the keepers in 1298 were in no way tentative; the extents of the manors of the priory were taken to the exchequer ('cum dictis extentis
mittendis ad Scaccarium apud Ebor'; Pipe R. 144, m.30d). It seems likely that this
had been ordered by the government.

necessarily base their decisions exclusively on the precedents of
the individual bishopric in which they happened to be; they
were also influenced by what they believed to be usual in other
vacant sees. At Norwich in 1326 the keepers had detained
(though they had not appropriated) the corn of the four
churches of Hoxne, Thornham, Terling and Langham, 'because
they understood that the king received the issues of churches
annexed to bishoprics in certain other bishoprics during voidance'.[1] The uncertainty of this state of affairs left room for
change, and the church was pressing hard for change, in the
definition of the limits of *temporalia* at least.[2]

Even apart from the problems of taking seisin, the initial
stages of taking over the custody of a vacancy would necessarily
have been complicated. The death of the bishop meant, as we
have seen, a division of the episcopal property into temporalities
and spiritualities, each section being in quite distinct custody
during a vacancy.[3] It also meant a division between the temporalities of the bishopric on the one hand, and the personal
and devisable property of the bishop on the other. Over the
former the royal keepers had full control, but the latter was the
domain of the executors of the late bishop's will. The right of
bishops to make wills seems to have been long established in
England,[4] albeit as late as 1276 the clergy of St. Asaph were
complaining that the Welsh prince Llywelyn would not allow
bishops to make wills at all.[5] Nevertheless, although the cru-
dities of an unlimited *jus spolii* were a thing of the past in

[1] See above, p. 69, n. 2.

[2] The changing connotation of the term is discussed below, pp. 111–16.

[3] For a full discussion of the administration of the spiritualities of vacant sees
within the province of Canterbury see I. J. Churchill, *Canterbury Administration*
(London, 1933), I, 161–240.

[4] There are Anglo-Saxon precedents; see Mr. E. John on the implications of
Bishop Theodred's will; 'The Division of the Mensa in Early English Monasteries',
The Journal of Ecclesiastical History, VI, 150. On the likelihood that the *jus spolii* was
only exercised in a limited number of cases see above, pp. 46–7. See also the
account of the execution of the will of Archbishop Baldwin of Canterbury by Hubert
Walter (Ralph de Diceto, II, 88).

There seems to have been an interesting anomaly in this respect at Westminster,
where it would seem that the king did exercise a *jus spolii* over the property of the
abbots well into the thirteenth century; see *Cal. Pat. R., 1281–92*, pp. 222–3.

[5] *Councils and Ecclesiastical Documents relating to Great Britain and Ireland*, ed. A. W.
Haddan and W. Stubbs (Oxford, 1869), I, 512. By 1293 Edward I had extended the
English custom to the see of St Asaph (*Cal. Fine R., 1272–1307*, p. 319).

England, yet the practical details of executing a bishop's will were, in the thirteenth century, still a matter for experiment, for adjustment of claims in the light of equity and for the creation of useful precedents.

Prudent bishops took the precaution of foreseeing, and as far as they were able, forestalling some of the difficulties while they were still alive. In 1231 Hugh of Wells, bishop of Lincoln (1209–35), and his brother Jocelin, bishop of Bath (1206–42), were willing to pay substantially for an agreement with the crown which would benefit their successors as well as themselves. Hugh reserved to himself and his successors, bishops of Lincoln, all movable goods and all corn sown before the bishop's death and all fruits of orchards and vineyards from the time of his death to the following Michaelmas. The executors were to have full freedom to use the granaries and granges and the storehouses of the bishopric until the time when these might reasonably be required for the produce of the next year.[1]

It becomes apparent where the difficulties in the administration of a vacant bishopric were likely to arise. Harvests would not wait upon the death of bishops. The royal keeper might arrive to find the corn sown but not reaped. To whom did it belong? who was to pay for the labour of reaping? and where was the grain to be stored? Above all, where was the grain to come from for next year's sowing, if the executors made a clean

---

[1] Fine R. 30, m.3. The two entries are worth quoting:
'Hugo Lincolniensis Episcopus finem fecit cum domino Rege per quingentas marcas quod ipse et successores sui in perpetuum non obstante aliqua consuetudine quam Rex vel antecessores sui aliquo tempore usi fuerunt quacunque parte anni Idem episcopus vel aliquis successorum suorum decesserit habeat omnia bona sua mobilia et omnes fructus tam de bladis in terra sua seminatis ante mortem suam quam fructus virgulatorum vinearum eodem anno scilicet usque ad festum Sancti Michaelis proximum post mortem eorundem provenientes. Ita quod nec Rex nec aliquis heredum suorum nec aliquis ballivorum suorum inde in aliquo se nunquam intromittat vel ad ea manum extendat. Set liberum sit eidem episcopo et successoribus suis et executoribus eorum inde facere et disponere omnino pro voluntate sua absque impedimento ipsius Regis vel heredum suorum vel ballivorum suorum. Et quod executores eorum absque impedimento Regis . . . habeant aisiamenta curiarum grangiarum cortulariorum granariorum et aliarum domorum que eorundem episcoporum fuerunt ad reponenda et conservanda bona sua predicta in eis donec rationaliter debeant provisoribus fructuum anni sequentis per eosdem executores liberari. J. Bathoniensis Episcopus finem fecit per ccc marcas pro habenda consimili concessione sibi et successoribus suis.'

sweep of this year's harvest? And where were the keepers to find ploughs and ploughmen if the bishop disposed of these in his will? The cultivation of the land was essentially a continuous process, and unregulated testamentary rights on the part of the bishop might cause upheaval and damage.

In the execution of episcopal wills it is evident that the bishops considered the king obstructive. In a council in 1257 they begged that the king would not impede the carrying out of such wills nor extend his hands to the corn which the bishop had sown nor to other goods of deceased prelates.[1] In fact the evidence of the Patent Rolls suggests that the king did normally grant the executors free administration of the will quite quickly, but there was normally a reservation clause providing that the executors should first give security that they would pay the late bishop's debts to the crown. Considering how frequently debts were not paid in the Middle Ages, this might seem a pretty innocent proviso, but in this particular case the king was not slow to see the possibility of implementing his claim. If he wished to appropriate some of the stock or other property of the late bishop he could simply allow its cost to the executors in the account of their debts to the crown. This was perhaps the surest, although maybe sometimes a slightly rough and ready method of ensuring that the king's claims would be satisfied.[2]

The second part of the bishops' complaint in 1257, that the king did not always allow the executors to have the corn sown by the late bishop, has substance. At Canterbury in 1228 the executors fined for 300 marks for the corn sown by the late archbishop.[3] In the next vacancy, 1231, however, the king ordered the keepers to give the executors full seisin of the autumn corn of that year 'sine aliquo retinemento'.[4] But again in 1240 on the death of Edmund Rich the king ordered free administration of the late archbishop's will, with the express proviso

---

[1] *Concilia Magnae Britanniae*, ed. D. Wilkins (London, 1737), I, 724.

[2] For example see the writs concerning the property of Richard Marsh (*Close R., 1234–37*, p. 456); Thomas Blundeville (*ibid.*, p. 384) and Walter Kirkham (*ibid., 1259–61*, pp. 103–4).

[3] Fine R. 28, m.13; 11 Nov. 1228.

[4] *Close R., 1227–31*, p. 561. The king later bought at least some of the late archbishop's corn from the executors (*Pat. R., 1225–32*, p. 472).

'salvis regi bladis in terra seminatis'.[1] The explanation of these apparent variations in royal policy may perhaps lie in part in a statement made by the editors of two episcopal wills of the early fourteenth century: 'Where there was any part of the harvest remaining uncut at the time of the bishop's death the produce would be an escheat and the property of the Crown.'[2] In 1231 when the king had ordered the keepers to hand over the autumn corn to the executors the vacancy had not begun until 3 August, by which time the harvest may have been reaped, and might therefore be expected to go to the executors. On the other hand, this distinction between reaped and unreaped corn does not seem an infallible touchstone. The bishops, in their petition of 1257 had requested the king not to take the corn *sown* by the late bishop, presumably irrespective of whether or not it had been reaped; and it is interesting therefore to find that in the case of Salisbury, which fell vacant in January 1256 the executors of the late bishop seem to have successfully pressed their claim to the winter corn already sown in the lands of the bishopric, although this corn could obviously not have been reaped by the date of the bishop's death.[3] There are two other pieces of evidence which also seem to indicate some uncertainty of practice in this matter. Lichfield fell vacant in December 1238 and a certain Robert of Lonsdale was to have paid a fine of £100 for all the corn which the late bishop sowed in the bishopric before his death. Again the corn could not have been reaped by the bishop, but the fine was pardoned.[4] Similarly, at Bath in 1266, the king eventually conceded to Walter Giffard the corn which he had sown before his translation to York, but conceded

[1] *Close R.*, *1237–42*, p. 273. This limited concession was itself at least temporarily revoked (*ibid.*, *c.* 13 Feb. 1241). The king in this case paid for the goods (*bona*) which he retained (*ibid.*, pp. 387–8; and pp. 418–19), but this may not have included the corn.

[2] *Account of the Executors of Richard Bishop of London, 1303* (R. Gravesend) *and of the Executors of Thomas Bishop of Exeter, 1310* (Thomas Bitton), ed. W. H. Hale and H. T. Ellacombe (Camden Soc., New Series x, London, 1874), p. xii.

[3] A writ of 24 Sep. 1256 (Fine R. 53 m.3) leaves the claims of king and executors on the corn sown by the late bishop still in abeyance, 'prout mediante Justicia fuerit declaratum utrum dictum ybernagia ad Regem vel ad dictum defunctum debeant pertinere.' However a writ of 16 Oct. 1256 (*Close R. 1254–56*, p. 367), orders that the executors shall have free administration of the late bishop's property 'una cum bladis hiemalibus per ipsum defunctum seminatis . . . '.

[4] *Ibid.*, *1237–42*, p. 171 and Pipe R. 84, m.12d.

it *de dono*.[1] In short, there does not seem to have been a very clear ruling on this question. It would seem that uncut corn did not invariably escheat to the king, and individual cases may have been decided by arrangement between the crown and the executors.

Whatever the arrangements for the execution of the bishop's will, it was always essential that provision of some sort should be made for the continuation of the ordinary round of ploughing, sowing and reaping while the vacancy lasted. There were two solutions of this problem, not mutually exclusive solutions. One was the reservation by the king of sufficient corn and stock out of the late bishop's property for the custodian to keep the course of agriculture running. At Chichester in 1244, the king explains that although he promised the late bishop that he might make his will of the corn still growing as well as of that in the granges, 'it was not our intention that we should not have wheat for sowing the lands of the bishopric and for the sustenance of the servants and ploughs of the bishopric until the appearance of the new grain'.[2] In many Pipe Roll accounts for the issues of vacancies, the custodians claim for their outlay in buying corn for sowing and liveries,[3] and in some cases these may well represent payments made to the executors.

The second device for ensuring continuity in the cultivation of the manors of the bishoprics was in many ways the more satisfactory for it covered some of the problems occurring at the end of vacancies as well as those at their beginning. In several bishoprics in the course of the thirteenth century a permanent system of minimum endowment was established, an endowment of stock, corn and agricultural implements. Fixed quantities of these had to be left in the episcopal manors by the bishop

---

[1] Pipe R. 112, m.2d. The fact that Walter Giffard had suffered translation and not death may have made some difference, but it is clear that the 'gift' was not a foregone conclusion. Giffard eventually sold the corn to his successor at Bath for 600 marks (*The Register of Walter Giffard, 1266–79*, ed. W. Brown (Surtees Soc., CIX, London, 1904), p. 133; July 1267).

[2] *Close R. 1242–47*, pp. 161–2.

[3] For example £162.16.9 on the Winchester account, 1304–5 (Pipe R. 152B, m.20); £194.14.0 and £150.0.9½ on the Salisbury accounts for 1286–7 (Pipe R. 133, m.28d) and for 1291 (Pipe R. 137 m.26d) respectively; £42.17.3 and £216.14.6 on the London accounts for 1273 (Pipe R. 117, m.7d) and for 1303–4 (Pipe R. 149, m.37) respectively.

at his death; that is he could not dispose of them in his will; and the same quantities had to be left by the king when his keepers quitted the bishopric at the end of the vacancy. There are quite early examples of the notion that a bishop should leave on the manors of the bishopric the same amounts in stock and equipment as he himself found on his entry into the see.[1] During the thirteenth century this principle blossomed into clearly defined 'endowments'. The earliest example of a definite endowment seems to be at Chichester where, before his death in 1222 Ralph Wareham had made a charter fixing the amount of stock to be left in the bishopric on the death of a bishop for the use of his successor.[2] The charter seems to have been fully observed by the king.[3] At Winchester in 1238 Peter des Roches had, in his will, left a certain amount of stock for his successor in the see,[4] and a permanent endowment seems to be implied in an entry on the exchequer account for the Winchester vacancy of 1250–1.[5] A Close Roll entry of 1284, again relating to this see is similar but even more explicit. The keepers had to pay £64.9.4 to the incoming bishop, John de Pontissaria,

for the defect of one hundred and eleven oxen and eight hundred and twenty four lambs delivered to him for the defect of the sheep (*bidentum*) and lambs of the stock pertaining to the bishopric . . .[6]

After the Canterbury vacancy of 1270–2 the keeper was ordered to deliver to the archbishop-elect, the ploughs, oxen and harrowers

---

[1] See Bishop Theodred's will, D.Whitelock, *Anglo Saxon Wills* (Cambridge, 1930), p. 4, and for thirteenth-century examples, at Exeter, Fine R. 18, m.1 (23 Oct. 1223) and at London, *Close R. 1227–31*, p. 122 (7 Nov. 1228).

[2] See royal confirmation, *Cal. Charter R., 1226–57*, p. 34; 26 Apr. 1227.

[3] See for example *Close R., 1242–47*, p. 179. Compare similar writ, 1 May 1253 (*Cal. Pat. R., 1247–58*, p. 190).

[4] Fine R. 41, m.2; 10 Sep. 1244. The keeper was to restore to the new bishop the manors of the bishopric, 'simul cum Instauro quod P. quondam Winton Episcopus reliquit in eodem Episcopatu ad opus successoris sui et quod vos per manus executorum testamenti eiusdem Episcopi recepistis . . .'. In an entry on the Close Rolls, 17 June 1238, des Roches is described as having left this stock 'to the bishopric (*episcopatui*)'; *Close R., 1237–42*, p. 62.

[5] The keeper is allowed £24.14.3 'pro vij affris, ix bobus, ccxv matricibus ovibus, cxxxv multonibus et clxij hogastris emptis ad perficiendum numerum instauri dimissi in maneriis episcopatus post mortem W. quondam Winton' episcopi' (Pipe R. 95, m.6).

[6] *Cal. Close R., 1279–88*, p. 268.

(*herciatores*) which he had received 'as pertaining to the archbishopric from the executors of Boniface, the late archbishop',[1]
and at Ely in 1302–3 such an arrangement was described as 'an
ancient custom'.[2] Exeter,[3] and London[4] seem to have had
similar arrangements. There is, therefore, reason to believe that
by this time such a plan was fairly general. Certainly it was
widespread and eminently sensible.

Behind the variations in the treatment of one bishop's will
and that of another, behind the complaints of the bishops and
the signs of the king's determination to make the most of his
opportunities, there is nevertheless a strong sense of lawfulness
in this picture, and a strong sense of what is equitable, what is
reasonable and, above all, what is workable.

In this complex matter of carrying out the bishop's will and
at the same time making possible the continued cultivation of
the bishopric, the wider decisions were made by the king or by
his advisors. It was the keepers or their bailiffs who had to carry
out the decisions and who had to deal with the executors or
their representatives within the manors of the bishopric. No
doubt there was friction on occasion. The executors of Thomas
Bitton of Exeter state that they had to make payments to the
keepers for their help in the business of executing the will,[5]
while the executors of the will of Richard Gravesend of London
account for four quarters, five bushels of hay seised in the manor
of Fulham by the ministers of the escheator and kept against the
will of the executors.[6] At Clacton, the subescheator Henry of
Gloucester took off a cart-horse also 'contra voluntatem executorum'.[7] It is not in the least surprising that the keeper took
one cart-horse too many but it is a tribute to both executors and
keepers that they could not only work in close contact in the
complicated circumstances of the early weeks of the vacancy, but

[1] *Cal. Close R., 1272–79*, p. 5.

[2] Pipe R. 150, m.34 (in the account of 20 Mar. 1302 to 18 July 1302).

[3] *Accounts of the Executors of Gravesend and Bitton*, pp. 13–22.

[4] At London the executors were by custom reponsible for sowing some of the
lands of the bishopric *sede vacante* (*Cal. Close R., 1272–79*, p. 65).

[5] *Accounts of the Executors of Gravesend and Bitton*, p. 36. This may of course have
been a lawful payment for services rendered.

[6] *Ibid.*, p. 61.

[7] *Ibid.*, p. 84.

that they could on either side produce the minutely detailed
financial accounts that they did for that period.

Occasionally the executors and the keepers were in a position
which almost amounted to joint control of the bishopric
through the early weeks or even months of the vacancy. At
Canterbury in 1228 the *servientes*[1] in office in Archbishop
Langton's time were to continue in office until the corn of the
coming autumn, which had been granted to the executors, had
been harvested. The *servientes* were to take oaths to the royal
custodians for their lawful conduct, but the custodians were to
observe the wishes of the executors if the latter should wish to
change any of the *servientes*.[2] Similarly at Winchester in 1238
the *servientes* already officiating were to remain until the following Michaelmas to serve the king, but also to be 'helpful' in the
custody of the goods of the late bishop.[3]

The next aspect of a royal custodian's work was the machinery of the day-to-day administration of the vacant bishopric.
But perhaps this concern was only a nominal one, and the
machinery in fact ran itself? That question is far from easy to
answer. The vacancy accounts on the Pipe Rolls often give
glimpses of an impressive administrative hierarchy at work
within the bishopric. Reeves, bedels, smiths and ploughmen are
allowed quittances of rents,[4] foresters and park keepers are
allowed their expenses and wages;[5] there are *servientes* or *ballivi*
in charge of manors or groups of manors and receiving wages,
liveries and sometimes robes,[6] clerks go from manor to manor

---

[1] The term is of wide connotation. Here it means the manorial officials.
[2] *Close R., 1227–31*, pp. 110–11.   [3] *Ibid., 1237–42*, p. 62.
[4] '. . . in relaxatione redditus prepositorum bercariorum . . .' at Ely 1254 (Pipe
R. 101, m.4); '. . . in quietancia redditus prepositorum bedellorum fabrorum
carucariorum . . .' at Winchester, 1260–2 (Pipe R. 106, m.21); '. . . in acquietancia
redditus prepositorum messorum bedellorum wodewardorum et carucariorum . . .'
at Salisbury, 1297 (Pipe R. 143, m.25d).
[5] '. . . in stipendiis et sustentacione . . . xv parcariorum et forestariorum . . .'
at York, 1255–6 (Pipe R. 101, m.4d). See also the account for Durham, 1237–9
(Pipe R. 84, m.2, *passim*).
[6] '. . . in liberacione et stipendiis xxvij ballivorum custodiencium maneria
quorum quilibet capit in die ij d . . . et liberacione iij clericorum quorum quilibet
capit in die j d. j ob. et stipendiis vij subservientium . . . et pro panno et ferruris ad
robas predictorum ballivorum et iij clericorum . . .' at Winchester 1260–2 (Pipe R.,
106, m.21); '. . . in vadiis et stipendiis quinque servientium custodiencium maneria
dicti episcopatus quorum quilibet cepit per septimanam ij s . . .' at Salisbury, 1297
(Pipe R. 143, m.25d).

hearing accounts,[1] and receivers sit at episcopal exchequers.[2] Other accounts are so condensed and simplified that there is no mention at all of any of these officials.[3] The detailed accounts from the larger bishoprics indicate this much: that the complex administrative hierarchy which was employed by the bishop to administer his estates *sede plena* is also detectable *sede vacante*, helping the keepers to administer the episcopal estates for the king. What the Pipe Roll accounts so rarely answer is the interesting question of what changes, if any, the royal keepers did make. Did they invariably accept the machinery just as they found it working or did they sometimes make changes either in the administrative personnel, or even in the general pattern of administration itself?

It is safest to assume continuity unless there is clear evidence against it. Certainly there is evidence in some cases of marked continuity both of machinery and of personnel. Two instances may serve as illustrations of this. On the Pipe Roll account for the vacancy at York in 1299, there happens to be a reference by name to four of the six bailiffs who, *sede vacante*, were in charge of the six bailiwicks into which the manors of the archbishopric were grouped.[4] Each of the four bailiffs named in this vacancy account (if the identification of Roger de Wycheton with Roger de Wyneton is correct) is found keeping a bailiwick in the time of the late archbishop, Henry Newark, and in each case it is the same bailiwick which is being kept by the same man. Moreover, three of the bailiffs mentioned *sede vacante* continue for some time as bailiffs under the next archbishop Thomas Corbridge, after the vacancy has ended. The following table may clarify this:

---

[1] '... in vadiis duorum clericorum ... audientium compotos prepositorum et ministrorum eorundem maneriorum ...' at Ely, 1298 (Pipe R. 144, m.30d).

[2] 'Et eisdem W. de Sancto Claro et W. de Hamelton pro expensis et stipendiis constabularii castri de Wolveseye qui fuit receptor et thesaurarius thesauri Regis ibidem ...' at Winchester, 1280–2 (Pipe R. 128, m.28).
'... Pro stipendiis et expensis unius receptoris commorantis ad scaccarium Elyensem capienti [*sic*] per diem vj d ...' at Ely, 1290 (Pipe R. 135, m.1).

[3] For example the London account, 1228–9 (Pipe R. 72, m.10d).

[4] 'Item in thesauro per Johannem de Pinkersham ballivum de Suwell. Rogerum Goldston ballivum de Chirchedon. Rogerum de Wyneton [*sic*] ballivum Beverl' et Patricium de Brafferton ballivum de Rypon xliiij li. x s.' (Pipe R. 150, m.31).

Bailiwicks	Bailiffs in office before 16 Aug. 1299 (i.e. *sede plena*)	Bailiffs in office *sede vacante*[6] 16 Aug. 1299 to 30 Apr. 1300	Bailiffs in office after 30 Apr. 1300
Beverley	Roger de Wycheton[1]	Roger de Wyneton (i.e. Wycheton?)	
Southwell	John Pinkersham[2]	John Pinkersham	John Pinkersham[7]
Ripon	Patrick de Brafferton[3]	Patrick de Brafferton	Patrick de Brafferton[8]
Hexham	Roger de Wycheton[4]		
Churchdown	Roger Goldston[5]	Roger Goldston	Roger Goldston[9]
Sherburn			

The second example of apparent continuity *sede vacante* comes from the short Winchester vacancy of 20 January 1268–2 May 1268. According to the vacancy account on the exchequer Pipe Roll wages are paid to twenty-one *capitales servientes* and to certain *subservientes*.[10] Among the so-called Winchester Pipe Rolls, the collection of manorial accounts compiled by the bishop's ministers *sede plena*, there is one roll which covers the financial year which includes the last months of the pontificate of John Gervais and the first months of that of Nicholas of Ely and also the period of this vacancy; that is, the roll begins at Michaelmas 1267 and ends at Michaelmas 1268.[11] For the complete financial year the account is rendered in the case of each manor by a reeve and a *serviens*, and the payments which went to the king during the vacancy are included with the rest.[12]

[1] Appointed 30 Sep. 1298 (*Reg. H. Newark*, p. 261).

[2] Appointed to receive seisin of bailiwick on behalf of the archbishop, 22 June 1297 (*ibid.*, p. 249).

[3] Reference as for Pinkersham in n. 2.

[4] Appointed 7 Dec. 1297 (*ibid.*, p. 254).

[5] Appointed 24 Aug. 1297 (*ibid.*, p. 252).   [6] See above, p. 79, n. 4.

[7] Reference to Pinkersham as bailiff; 15 June 1300 (*The Register of Thomas Corbbridge, etc., 1300–4* (Surtees Soc. CXXXVII, CXLI, Durham etc., 1925–8), II, 33).

[8] Reference to Brafferton as bailiff; 2 Nov. 1300; *ibid.*, II, 41.

[9] Appointed 15 May 1300 (*ibid.*, II, 32).   [10] Chancellor's R. 61, m.6d.

[11] (P.R.O.) Eccles. 2/159298. The inclusion of the vacancy period on these episcopal 'Pipe Rolls' is quite exceptional in the thirteenth century, although it is significant that after Edward III's statute of 1340, which allowed chapters the opportunity of farming their vacancies (see above p. 68), the vacancy periods are regularly represented by specially compiled rolls within this series; see Sir W. H. Beveridge, 'The Winchester Rolls and their Dating', *Econ. History Review*, II (1929–30), p. 106.

[12] The account for the assized rents for instance is in every case for all four terms (Christmas, Easter, St. John the Baptist and Michaelmas) and the payments of 'recognitions' to the king are included too. There is no doubt of the completeness of the account.

From this account it would seem that the administrative officials who had been appointed before the death of Bishop John Gervais remained in office throughout the financial year which included the short vacancy period.

It is not often that one is able to check matters so closely as this, but there are several other cases where a similarity in the payments made to *servientes* or bailiffs in successive vacancy accounts suggests a similar continuity at least in the pattern of administration, even though the question of continuity of personnel *sede plena* and *sede vacante* usually remains unproven. For example, the Durham accounts on the Pipe Rolls for the vacancies of 1226–8,[1] 1237–41,[2] 1274,[3] and 1283[4] show a steady repetition of payments made to a small number of *servientes*, each of whom, like the *ballivi* of the York account had control over traditional groupings of manors.[5] It seems likely that so regular a repetition implies a fairly faithful reflection of arrangements *sede plena*. At Ely in 1256–8 wages of 6d. a day are paid to eighteen *servientes*,[6] and in 1290 wages of 4d. a day are paid to twenty bailiffs,[7] arrangements which again suggest a certain amount of continuity in the general pattern. It may be mentioned, in this connection, that no fixed significance can be attached to the terms *ballivi* and *servientes*. The two terms seem to be used almost interchangeably at the exchequer. At Winchester in the 1238–44 vacancy twenty-four *servientes* keeping the manors of the bishopric received 2d. a day each. There are no bailiffs on this account. On the other hand in the vacancy of 1260–2 twenty-seven bailiffs (*ballivi*) received this same wage of 2d. a day and there are no *servientes*.[8] However, in the 1268 vacancy the *servientes* have reappeared; twenty-one *capitales*

---

[1] Pipe R. 73, m.1.

[2] Pipe R. 84, m.2.

[3] Pipe R. 118, m.18d.

[4] Pipe R. 127. m.2d.

[5] These groupings were sometimes called 'shires' in the see of Durham. The roll of the 1237–41 vacancy mentions Stocktonshire, Middlehamshire, Aucklandshire, Howdenshire, Allertonshire (Pipe R. 84, m.2).

[6] 'Pro stipendiis et sustentacione xviij servientium custodientium maneria . . . qui omnes capiunt in die vj d . . .' (Pipe R. 101, m.4d).

[7] 'Pro stipendiis et expensis xx ballivorum custodiencium maneria dicti episcopatus videlicet cuilibet eorum iiijd. per diem . . .' (Pipe R. 135, m.1).

[8] Pipe R. 106, m.21. There are also seven *subservientes* (see the passage quoted in n. 6, p. 78, above).

G

servientes receive 2d. a day.[1] Evidently whether they go by the name of *ballivi* or *servientes*, these men who get 2d. a day are essentially men of the same standing and of comparable duties.

When the vacancy accounts on the Pipe Rolls do show differences in the administrative pattern between one vacancy and another, it is often impossible to know for certain whether this indicates some flexibility in the treatment of the administration of the see *sede vacante* on the part of the royal keepers, or whether in fact the changes have really taken place *sede plena* and the keepers are, in each case, merely taking over the administrative machine of the last bishop. For example, at Salisbury in 1256 the exchequer allowed payment at the rate of 2d. a day to fifteen *servientes* keeping the fifteen manors of the bishopric.[2] In the Salisbury vacancy of 1291, on the other hand, there are only five *servientes* keeping the fifteen manors, but they receive 6d. a day each.[3] But unfortunately it is impossible to say whether this apparent move towards centralization in the *sede vacante* administration of Salisbury was merely a reflection of a change in episcopal administration *sede plena* or not.[4]

However, there is some evidence which does seem to suggest that the royal keepers did not invariably preserve the machinery just as it had been *sede plena*. The most interesting example of this is provided by the see of Canterbury. In the Canterbury vacancy of 1240–5, although there is no Pipe Roll account there is fortunately a writ entered on the Liberate Rolls[5] ordering the payment of wages to various administrative officials

---

[1] Chancellor's R. 61, m.6d. Wages are also paid 'quorundam subservientium'.

[2] Pipe R. 100, m.19: '. . . in liberacione xv servientium custodientium xv maneria episcopatus quorum quilibet habuit ij d. in die . . .' It is interesting to notice that this is exactly the wage of the *servientes* at Winchester, already mentioned, and there were *servientes* receiving 2d. a day at Canterbury in the vacancies of 1270–2 and 1278–9. See below, p. 83 n. 2. and n. 3. It was perhaps a fairly standard rate of payment for men who were in charge of single manors.

[3] Pipe R. 137, m.26d. 'Et in liberacione quinque servientium custodiencium xv maneria dicti episcopatus quorum quilibet cepit in die vjd. . . .' It will be noticed that the *total* rate of payment was exactly the same as in the earlier vacancy of the see.

[4] The intervening vacancy accounts for Salisbury on the Pipe Rolls are unhelpful. The account for the vacancy of 1262–3 (Chancellor's R. 61, m.6d) only records payment to one *serviens* at Sonning; the account for 1271 (Pipe R. 116, m.2d) does not mention any payments to *servientes* as a separate item of account. The accounts for 1284–5 (Pipe R. 133, m.29) and for 1286–7 (Pipe R. 133, m.28d) again make no mention of such payments.

[5] *Cal. Liberate R., 1240–45*, p. 131 and pp. 239–40.

within the see. Several of these are obviously men of the standing of the six bailiffs of the archbishopric of York. Twelve are actually called *ballivi* and they receive high payment, usually 6d a day.[1] However, in the next vacancy at Canterbury, 1270–2, there is no mention in the Pipe Roll account of the wages of bailiffs, but twenty-seven *servientes* keeping twenty-seven manors are paid 2d. a day each.[2] These are clearly much smaller men than the bailiffs of 1244. Similarly in the next vacancy in this see, 1278–9, there are again no highly paid bailiffs but only *servientes* obviously keeping single manors or perhaps in some cases two manors, and paid at the rate of 2d. a day.[3] The two vacancies, those of 1270–2 and 1278–9 in which the low paid *servientes* seem to have replaced the smaller group of higher paid officials who appear as bailiffs in the 1240–5 vacancy, fall on either side of the pontificate of Robert Kilwardby. It so happens that one of Kilwardby's own manorial account rolls for the archbishopric is still extant.[4] It is similar in form to the Winchester Pipe Rolls and it belongs to the financial year 1273–4.[5] On this roll, with the exceptions of the manors of Saltwood, Shirley and Hethe the organization is entirely in terms of groups of manors (bailiwicks) and of nine highly paid bailiffs and not in terms of *servientes* each looking after one manor.[6] The appearance in two successive vacancies of *servientes*

[1] This is the wage of the York bailiffs too and of the small group of highly paid officials at Salisbury in 1291.

[2] Pipe R. 119, m.21d. One other *serviens* is paid for a portion of the vacancy until the manor which he supervises is given into the custody of the queen. There is mention among the *expensae* of certain *parvi ballivi*, who are classed with the reeves, and bedels. But if these were men worthy of 6d. a day they would not be described as *parvi* and they should receive wages along with the *servientes* in the section of the account which comes immediately after the *summa* of the ordinary expenditure on cultivation.

[3] Pipe R. 124, m.23d. 'Et in expensis et stipendiis xxv serviencium custodientium omnia maneria . . . Archiepiscopatus . . . quorum quilibet cepit in die ij d.' There are in all 34 manors in the archbishopric mentioned on the most complete list, B.M. Additional MS. 29794.

[4] B.M. Additional MS. 29794.   [5] See above, p. 66, n. 4.

[6] The number of 9 compares interestingly with that of 12 bailiffs in the 1240–5 vacancy. See above. In addition to the 9 bailiffs there were three people who go by the title *servientes*; Stephen de Ledenne at Shirley (*ibid.*, m.5); William de Hunderchive at Hethe (*ibid.*, m.5d) and Robert Roffin at Saltwood (*ibid.*, m.6d). One of the bailiffs, Richard Attenoke received as wages in the course of the account £14.1.4½ (*ibid.*, mm. 1 and 2, *passim*). Richard kept five manors (the Surrey and Middlesex group); some of the other bailiffs only kept two manors.

receiving 2d. a day, who seem to be quite foreign to the *sede plena* administration of the intervening pontificate, together with the absence of payments to men of higher status on either of the vacancy accounts, does seem significant. At the same time, it is recognized that usually it is dangerous to infer anything from the absence of certain payments, especially wage payments, on a vacancy account on the Pipe Rolls. The keeper may sometimes be left with a deficit in the main account, and out of that deficit the wages of administrative officials may eventually be claimed. However, in this particular case, this argument has no weight. The 1278–9 account is balanced[1] and that of 1270–2 leaves the keepers not with a deficit but with a surplus.[2] So far the tentative inference would seem to be that in these two vacancies the keepers were imposing on the archbishopric a system of administration that was unfamiliar to the see *sede plena*. Such a conclusion, however, is complicated by the fact that in the vacancy of 1278–9, the see was in the custody of two of the late archbishop's servants; his steward Ralph of Sandwich and William of Middleton, another official.[3] On the other hand, this does not absolutely preclude the possibility of these men making administrative changes when the see had become vacant. Ralph of Sandwich was a royal servant as well as an archiepiscopal one; he had kept the vacant see of London for the king, 1273–4,[4] and was about that time a royal steward.[5] William of Middleton was to be appointed as a keeper to the see of Ely in 1286 and was at that time a baron of exchequer.[6] Already in 1278 he was a king's clerk.[7] It may well be that these keepers looked to other traditions as well as to those of the late archbishop.[8]

The two vacancies at Canterbury, for lack of other clear evidence, provide the only example of what may possibly have

[1] Pipe R. 124, m.23d.

[2] Pipe R. 119, m.20, where the account is carried forward from m.21d. Richard de Clifford's 'surplus' is £3.12.4.

[3] Douie, *Archbishop Pecham*, p. 85.

[4] *Cal. Fine R., 1272–1307*, p. 11.

[5] *Ibid.*, p. 64; 23 Jan. 1276, and 5 Feb.

[6] See p. 64, n. 5, above.

[7] *Cal. Pat. R., 1272–81*, p. 279.

[8] It is of course possible that Kilwardby himself had made a change in the pattern of administration *sede plena*, at some time later than 1273–4.

been a thorough-going reorganization *sede vacante*. But minor regroupings or changes of pattern *sede vacante* were perhaps not unusual. At York the six highly paid bailiffs of the 1299 vacancy[1] can be traced back as far as the first York vacancy of Henry III's reign (1255–6). They appear here as *servientes*, but they are clearly the same officials; they receive 6d. a day and they have two horses each.[2] They reappear in the 1265 vacancy[3] and again in 1279.[4] In addition to these six, there are in each case several lesser men with only one horse and a lower wage; and both the number of these lesser officials and their wage level seem to vary a little from account to account. In the 1255–6 vacancy there are six of them each receiving 4d. a day,[5] in 1265 there are only three, each receiving 3d. a day,[6] and in 1279 there are three at 4d. a day.[7] This evidence seems to point to slight alterations; they may, of course, be reflections of alterations which took place in each case *sede plena*, but this seems doubtful in view of the fact that both in 1265 and in 1279 the expenditure on the wages in the vacancy account is justified by an appeal to what is called 'a similar payment' in the Pipe Roll account for the vacancy immediately preceding.[8]

The impression that at least some of the subordinate officials were regarded as being the keepers' special assistants rather than members of the permanent staff of the episcopal administration is perhaps strengthened by an entry in the Pipe Roll account for

---

[1] See above, pp. 79–80.

[2] Pipe R. 101, m.4d. '. . . vj servientibus custodientibus maneria archiepiscopatus qui fuerunt ad duos equos quorum quilibet cepit in die vj d. pro expensis suis . . .'

[3] Pipe R. 110, m.13. There are in fact only five mentioned on this account: 'Et v servientibus custodientibus maneria . . . quorum quilibet habuit duos equos et cepit in die vj d. pro expensis suis . . .' but Churchdown is not accounted for, being in the custody of another keeper.

[4] 'Chancellor's R. 74, m.7. 'Et vj servientibus custodientibus maneria de Extildeham Ripon Schireburn Berverlac. et Swell et Chirchedon qui fuerunt ad ij equos quorum quilibet cepit in die vj d. . . .'

[5] Pipe R. 101, m.4d. 'Et vj aliis servientibus qui fuerunt ad unum equum quorum quilibet cepit in die iiij d. pro expensis suis . . . '

[6] Pipe R. 110, m.13.

[7] Chancellor's R. 74, m.7.

[8] In the 1279 account for instance these payments are made, 'sicut continetur in compoto magistri Johannis de Clarel de eodem archiepiscopatu in Rotulo xLj Regis Henrici in Rotulo compotorum et in compoto magistri Willelmi de Clifford de eodem in Rotulo L ejusdem Regis ubi facta est consimilis allocatio pro servientibus predictis' (*ibid.*).

the Salisbury vacancy of 1246–7. Admittedly the vacancy was
an exceptionally short one, and so it should not be regarded as
necessarily typical. In the account for this vacancy no payments
were made to servants keeping the manors, but £14.5.0 is
allowed 'eidem Anketill' (i.e. the keeper) 'ad expensas suas et
clericorum et servientium suorum'.[1] The clerks and *servientes*
were in some sense Anketill's clerks and *servientes*. It would be
interesting to know what this implied. Did keepers sometimes
take with them their own côterie of assistants? On the Ely
accounts for the vacancies of 1290 and 1298 there are references
to officials who seem to be in special dependence on the keepers.[2]
Moreover, the evidence for the two Durham vacancies 1226–8
and 1237–41 makes it clear that some at least of the administrative staff of a vacancy might be either dependents of the
keepers themselves or else royal appointments. We have already
seen that in 1226, Hugh Devon, Stephen de Lucy's clerk had
accompanied the new keeper to Durham. He stayed with de
Lucy in Durham castle and he was one of the men appointed
by the king to assist the keeper assessing an aid.[3] In fact de
Lucy seems to have been helped by a little group of royal
servants including Hugh Bolbeck who acts as an itinerant
justice,[4] William de Blockley, who is also resident in Durham
castle[5] and William Thornour who appears to be a trusted servant of the king.[6] In the next Durham vacancy in 1237 the king
sent Roger le Engleis to help the keeper to view and price the
stock on the episcopal manors.[7] When this has been done the

[1] Pipe R. 92, m.16.
[2] Pipe R. 135, m.1. (in the account of Nicholas Fermbaud): 'Eidem Nicholao
pro expensis suis et ij clericorum suorum . . .'
[3] '. . . in expensis . . . magistri S.' (Stephen de Lucy) 'et W. de Thornour. W
de Blockele et H. Devoniensis auxilium assidencium per maneria episcopatus x li.'
(Pipe R. 73, m.1).
[4] *Close R., 1227–31*, p. 34.
[5] Pipe R. 73, m.1.
[6] Stephen de Lucy was ordered to assess a tallage of the bishopric with the advice
of (*per consilium*) Thornour and Blockley (Fine R. 25, m.12). Indeed Thornour was
sent to Durham specially to help in this matter (see the Pipe Roll entry: '. . . in
expensis W. de Thornour venientis a London usque Dunelm ad assidendum auxilium et revertentis usque London v m.' (Pipe R. 73, m.1). On 6 Aug. 1226 Thornour
had been made a joint keeper of the lands of the bishopric in Yorkshire with
Stephen de Lucy (*Pat. R., 1225–32*, p. 57).
[7] *Close R. 1234–37*, p. 441.

keeper is to put Roger in some bailiwick in his custody until the king orders otherwise.[1] William de Blockley who had proved his usefulness in the previous vacancy is appointed by the same royal writ as receiver at the Durham exchequer,[2] and a little later William of London is sent by the king to reside at the Durham exchequer.[3] From this evidence it appears that at least the group of central officials who helped to administer a bishopric *sede vacante* was sometimes an importation into the see.[4]

This picture that we have attempted to piece together of the administrative personnel of a vacant bishopric is not a distinct one. If it were it would probably be untrue. Tentative as our inferences must be, they produce a picture in which the key-note is diversity, and that seems an authentic note in any study of medieval administration. The keepers seem sometimes to have taken over the machinery of episcopal administration practically intact and to have made no alterations, no new appointments even; but they do not seem to have considered themselves bound to do this. Their precedents ran from vacancy to vacancy rather than from pontificate to vacancy, and when a comparatively small number of senior officials was involved it was an easy matter to experiment in some rearrangements in the grouping of manors or the status of the men in charge of the manors. Even when the administrative pattern remained fairly constant there may have been changes of the people who worked it, some bailiffs dismissed and others appointed, and above all

---

[1] *Ibid.*, p. 449. [2] *Ibid.* [3] *Ibid.*, p. 457.

[4] Such a conclusion is strengthened by this complaint of the clergy in 1309 against the keepers of vacant sees, who introduce 'foreign' bailiffs: 'Ballivos insuper foraneos libertates ecclesiarum ipsarum sine sufficienti waranto ingredi ac summoniciones et districciones injustas in eisdem facere permittunt' (*Registrum Roberti Winchelsey, 1294–1313*, ed. R. Graham (Cant. and York Soc., Oxford, 1917–42), p. 1018).

There is a reference to changes of subordinate officials on the part of new keepers at Durham in a late twelfth-century vacancy, in the chronicle of Geoffrey of Coldingham: 'Possessiones interea Episcopi et oppida ballivi Regis occupabant; qui primo Hugoni Bardolf, deinde Archidiacono Herefordensi, novissime Ricardo Briwere et Gilberto filio Raynfridi Episcopatum commisit. Qui cum sibi vicissim succederent, et singulis fere mensibus novos in custodiis praepositos instituerant; illi, commodis suis ardentius insistentes ex alterna mutatione provincialibus mala innovabant' (*Hist. Dunelm. Script. Tres.*, p. 16). *Praepositus* may mean reeve, but it seems more likely that it is here used in its less technical sense of 'a person in authority.'

it does seem likely that the little group of central officials, the key men, as it were, who surrounded the keeper may frequently have included outsiders.

The clerks, auditors and receivers at the centre and the bailiffs or *servientes* in the scattered manors formed the keeper's administrative staff. His relations with them were similar to the relations of the bishop's steward with his staff *sede plena* and they relieved him of most of the routine work of running the bishopric. What remained to the keeper in the sphere of routine administration differed from place to place. The hearing of the bailiff's accounts was in some cases a keeper's duty,[1] and an entry in a Salisbury vacancy account of 1262–3 suggests that the holding of courts may sometimes have been another personal duty. A clerk is paid expenses for going round the manors to hold courts in the absence of the keeper.[2] However, at least by the time of Edward I's reign, it seems to have been usual for the holding of courts to be done by bailiffs or clerks, and the hearing of accounts by clerks too.[3] At Ely where stewards held the manorial courts, the keepers had the heavier responsibility of defending the liberties of the bishopric when the king held an eyre.[4] It would seem on the whole that when keepers did involve themselves in routine administration it was mainly at the level of justice, and a good proportion even of this could be delegated.

This does not mean that the purely economic aspect of vacancy affairs was hardly a matter for the keeper's attention

---

[1] See above, p. 64.

[2] 'In expensis cuiusdam clerici euntis per maneria ad tenendas curias in absentia dicti J.' (i.e. John Bell, the keeper; Chancellor's R. 61, m.6d).

[3] At York 1304–6 there were bailiffs holding courts (Pipe R. 152B, m.16).

On the account for the Bath vacancy of 1302 there is the entry 'In vadiis ballivorum custodiencium maneria episcopatus et tenencium curias' (Pipe R. 150, m.32).

At Winchester in 1304 four clerks go about, hearing accounts and holding courts (Pipe R. 152B, m.20); and at Ely in 1298 where the courts are held by stewards, two clerks are occupied in hearing accounts (Pipe R. 144, m.30d).

[4] '. . . eisdem Willelmo et Johanni custodibus dicti episcopatus pro misis et expensis suis factis pro libertatibus dicti episcopatus sic vacantis prosequendis et defendendis in eodem itinere xxvj li. xiij s. iiij d.' (Pipe R. 144, m.30d).

Compare a payment to the keepers of Canterbury, 1278–9: 'pro expensis suis factis in itinere Kancie pro libertatibus Archiepiscopatus predicti calumpniandis et defendendis xl li.' (Pipe R. 124, m.23d).

at all. It was the routine aspect of the administration that was largely delegated by the keepers, but it was they themselves who decided matters of policy, or executed specific royal orders. Many decisions they would make themselves, and always they had to bear in mind that at short notice the vacancy might end and their account be demanded. The vacancy had to be run on short-term lines. In the see of Ely in two successive vacancies in the early fourteenth century, the keepers seem to have been haunted by the idea of a bishop about to arrive. Master Richard of Abingdon and Robert Hereward in 1302, account for £125.19.3¾ received for hay sold before it had been reaped, 'pro eo quod timebant celerem adventum episcopi',[1] and, a little later in the account, two clerks receive wages of one shilling a day each for going round the manors of the bishopric making sales of wood and hay 'celeriter', and levying debts due to the king 'cum festinatione'. This sense of urgency seems to have pursued the custodians of Ely in the next vacancy, in 1310, for they too sold the hay before reaping 'pro eo quod timebatur de adventu episcopi'.[2] Perhaps it was felt that this little explanatory phrase was a mark of special efficiency worth copying.

The keeper's freedom of decision only ranged over matters where the king had not already given distinct instructions. The keeper had to be continually responsive to royal commands. Sometimes the king summoned the keeper to him for personal consultation, especially at the beginnings and at the ends of vacancies. At Ely in 1228, the custodians Thomas Ingoldsthorp and Matthew Christien were to keep the late bishop's property safe and let nothing be moved 'until they have come to the king and spoken with him'.[3] Ralph Trubblevill, a keeper of Canterbury in 1231, was summoned to personal interview with the king at the beginning of the vacancy,[4] and Stephen de Lucy came to the king after he had restored the episcopal manors to the new bishop of Durham in 1228.[5]

Long vacancies in wealthy sees might necessitate interviews between king and keeper in the middle of the vacancy too. In

[1] Pipe R. 150, m.34.
[2] Pipe R. 155B, m.6.
[3] '. . . donec ad dominum Regem venerunt et cum eo locuti fuerunt' (Fine R. 28, m. 11; 22 Dec. 1228).
[4] *Close R., 1227–31*, pp. 600–1.   [5] Pipe R. 73, m.1.

1240 the king addressed a writ to the custodians of the vacant
see of Winchester,[1] demanding money. The content of the writ
was not indeed unusual, but the tone was particularly personal
and although both keepers are addressed in the opening clause
of the writ Paul Peyvre is later singled out:

> Tu etiam prefate Paule, facias ccc marcas venire ad Turrim, sicut
> vobis viva voce nuper injunximus, . . .

The destination of the issues of this vacancy had clearly been a
matter which king and keeper had actually talked about.
Another keeper of a Winchester vacancy, the reluctant Nicholas
de Haudlo,[2] was forbidden by the king from carrying out an
earlier royal mandate: 'donec cum rege habuerit colloquium'.[3]

The extant evidence, however, naturally consists almost
exclusively of written mandates from king to keepers and of
these there was a constant stream during most vacancies. One
group of these may be separated from the rest, the class of writs
which are to be found mainly on the Liberate and Close Rolls,
demands by the king for money, or for issues in kind from the
vacant see.[4] The tone of these orders is often urgent, and in
the tense months of 1260 and 1261 it becomes almost shrill.
Repeated demands for money[5] culminate in an order of 27
October 1261 that the issues of the bishopric of Winchester
shall be delivered into the wardrobe 'de die in diem'.[6]

It was not money only that the king wanted. The chancery

---

[1] Close R., 1237–42, p. 224.

[2] Aymer de Valence was bishop-elect of Winchester but in 1258 the barons decided to regard the see as vacant (Aymer was not consecrated until 16 May 1260),
and they appointed a 'baronial' custodian of the bishopric, Nicholas de Haudlo
(Cal. Pat. R., 1258–66, p. 7; 24 Dec. 1258) but it is said that Nicholas took the
office 'much against his will' (ibid., 25 Dec.).

[3] Close R., 1259–61, p. 214.

[4] For typical examples of demands for money see Cal. Lib. R., 1240–45, p. 210
(12 Jan. 1244), where the keepers of the see of Winchester are ordered to send
all the money that they can get of the issues of the bishopric after the king without delay to Kent, whither he is going. See also mandates to the keepers of Hereford (Close R., 1237–42, p. 220; c. 23 June 1240); and to the keeper of Lichfield
(Close R., 1242–47, p. 376; 10 Dec. 1245).

[5] Note the phrases 'Quia rex denariis ad presens plurimum indiget . . .' (Close
R., 1261–64, p. 5; 18 Nov. 1261, to the keepers of Winchester); and 'Quia rex
plurimum indiget pecunia . . .' (Close R., 1259–61, p. 288; 29 Oct. 1260, to Thomas
de Penros who seems to have been assisting in the custody of Durham).

[6] Close R., 1261–64, p. 1.

rolls show orders for hundreds of eggs, eels, bream, does and pigs for the royal household, and the keepers had to arrange for the necessary fishing, hunting, salting, packing in barrels and carriage to Windsor, Westminster, Gloucester; wherever the king might be.[1] The keepers of Canterbury in November 1243 were ordered to take 300 rabbits in the warrens of the archbishopric, to buy twelve boars, and to search out all swans, cranes, peacocks and fowl of every kind that they can find in their bailiwick for the king and send the whole to Westminster by Saturday, the morrow of St. Edmund, at the latest.[2] The keepers seem to have been encouraged in thoroughness rather than in moderation.[3]

Apart from writs demanding money or issues in kind, the keepers received many other orders, some of which certainly seem to have demanded personal attention. In 1262, the king decided to sell the corn of Winchester to the incoming bishop, John Gervais, and he ordered an inquisition by good and lawful men to price the corn before sale.[4] The keeper, Walter de Burgh, is told to go to Farnham this coming Tuesday and to arrive there *summo mane* to meet the two other royal servants who have been sent to help to organize the making of the assessment. There is only one excuse which the king would be willing to accept for Walter's absence at Farnham, and that is, if this mission would hinder the king's business or (heaven forbid!) slow down the payment of money from the bishopric to the king.[5]

The assessing of an aid or tallage was another matter worthy of a keeper's personal attention. The two keepers of Lincoln in 1235 were directed to assess a tallage 'super singulas terras et

---

[1] In the bishopric of London in 1242 the keepers were ordered to fish in the episcopal fishpond 'contra Pascha' and to send the fish to the king in London (*Close R., 1237–42*, p. 412); and at Ely in 1256, 300 luce, 200 bream and 5,000 eels were to be taken and sent to London (*ibid., 1256–59*, p. 110).

[2] *Cal. Lib. R., 1240–457*, p. 19.

[3] For the question of the king's depreciation of the value of bishoprics during vacancies see below, pp. 142–6.

[4] *Close R., 1261–64*, p. 87.

[5] At Canterbury in the 1270–2 vacancy there is a hint that the king made the decision to sell the harvest without previous discussion with the keeper. The grain was sold 'per Regem et consilium suum et absque consilio eiusdem magistri Ricardi' [Richard de Clifford, the keeper] ut dicit' (Pipe R. 119, m.21d).

singula maneria episcopatus'. The sheriffs were to assist them and it seems clear that at least one of the keepers was expected to be present in person at the assessment of each manor.[1] Certainly, Stephen de Lucy seems to have dealt personally with the levy of an aid at Durham in 1226.[2] And one certainly could not leave to underlings the entertainment of royal guests. When Master Rostand, the papal chaplain was to be lodged in one of the manors of the vacant archbishopric of York, the keeper John Clarel had to touch up the manor in readiness, and to meet the guest personally and entertain him honourably.[3]

Occasionally keepers were called upon to enforce royal decisions in issues which might be broadly classed 'political'. When the chapter of St. Peter's, York, seemed reluctant to admit John Mansell to the vacant treasurership of their church, on royal nomination, the king wrote to them ordering the immediate induction of Mansell by his proxy; and as a final line of persuasion he added that he had also sent letters to the keeper John Clarel, that

. . . si vos post recepcionem presencium infra trium dierum spacium predictum mandatum nostrum exequi neglexeritis ipse extunc illud amoto cujuslibet difficultatis obstaculo exequatur.[4]

In particular keepers of the temporalities might be useful in the more important business of the election to the bishopric. Royal influence over episcopal election in the thirteenth century was not primarily a matter of sending letters of solicitation to the

[1] Fine R. 34, m.11; 20 Feb. 1235. The enrolment suffered a good deal of correction: 'Et mandatum est eisdem (vel eorum alteri) (Radulfoᶜ) quod (in propria personaᶜ) accedant (vel alter eorumⁱ) ad omnia et singula maneria (de predictoᶜ) episcopatus (predictiⁱ) [c=cancelled; i=interlined.] The keepers were Ralph de Warvill and John de Burgh.

[2] For a fuller discussion of this particular levy, based on the Durham MS. 5520 see below, pp. 129–30. Stephen de Lucy is here frequently mentioned by name in connection with the aid. '. . . homines de Hovedenscir rogati essent a magistro Stephano de Lucy ex parte domini regis ut conferrent ei auxilium,' and again 'convenit inter ipsos' (i.e. the men of the bishopric), 'et magistrum Stephanum quod auxilium darent domino regi.' Similarly at Norwich in 1236–7 the aid is said to be assessed by the keeper, Robert de Scotindon: 'Idem reddit compotum de xxxj li. viijs. et iiijd. de auxilio (Regisⁱ) assiso per predictum Robertum in predictis maneriis . . .' (Pipe R. 81, m.13.)

[3] *Close R.*, *1254–56*, p. 129. The keeper of Durham in 1260 was ordered to entertain the king and queen of Scotland (*Close R.*, *1259–61*, p. 211).

[4] *Ibid.*, *1254–56*, pp. 387–8; *c.* 9 Jan. 1256.

canons or monks, or even of the king appearing in person in cathedral chapters to deliver speeches: fundamentally by far the most important single weapon in the king's armoury was his regalian right. The king had seisin of the bishopric; his keepers were there in person with royal authority to support their every act. If the chapter perversely elected a bishop unwelcome to the king, the elect could be shut out of his bishopric. The keeper of Chichester in 1245 was ordered, day and night to guard over the gates of the city of Chichester,

quod nec Magister Ricardus de Wicio qui se gerit episcopum Cycestr' aut aliquis suorum, civitatem illam ingrediatur.[1]

At Winchester in 1244, the keepers were ordered to use boycotting tactics if William Raleigh attempted to act as bishop. They are

neither to lodge him nor permit him to be lodged by any lay person, nor any of his clerks, nor any of those who bear themselves as his officials; and to prohibit all lay persons of their bailiwicks from making contracts or having commerce with these, and they are to take and keep until further order all persons doing so.[2]

It is true that at both Chichester and Winchester the candidates whom the king opposed in this way were accepted by him eventually, but not before he had caused them inconvenience and hardship. Perhaps even more effective than temporarily shutting out the bishop-elect, were two other devices dependent upon regalian right: the deliberate impoverishment of the bishopric[3] and, where the cathedral was conventual, the harrying of the monks. In this same Winchester vacancy, 1238-1244, the prior of St. Swithins in 1241 turned out many of the monks who had supported the election of William Raleigh, and to assist him the prior called in certain satellites regis.[4] In the

---

[1] Close R., 1242-47, p. 352; 21 Apr. 1245. A few days later, and quite possibly for the same purpose, the keeper was ordered to place one serviens, mounted, and eight on foot to guard the vill of Chichester (ibid., p. 306; 28 Apr. 1245).

[2] Cal. Pat. R., 1232-47, p. 439. Compare Matthew Paris, Chronica Majora, ed. H. R. Luard (Rolls Series, London 1872-83), iv, 265.

[3] This will be considered below, pp. 142-6. It may be mentioned here that Matthew Paris accuses Henry III of doing this in the Winchester vacancy of 1238-44 and in the Ely vacancy of 1256-8, in each case to vent his anger against a chapter which had made an election contrary to his wishes (Chron. Majora, iv, 264 and v, 589).   [4] Ibid., iv, 159-60.

see of Lichfield in 1241 the priory of Coventry underwent great loss and hardships in a disputed election,

> Adversantibus itaque tam rege cum suis satellitibus quam quibusdam canonicis Lichefeldensibus.[1]

It does not seem unlikely that these *satellites regis* at Winchester and Coventry might have been subordinates of the keepers; certainly the presence of the keepers would strengthen their position. Moreover, at Durham in 1226 Thomas de Bendenges, who was keeper of Durham castle, prevented the bishop-elect, who was prior of Durham, from re-entering his own priory. When the prior demanded admission, Bendenges replied that he had other orders from the king.[2] Pressure of this kind was a possibility which monks bent on freedom of election had always to bear in mind, and it may well have been a strong deterrent from electing other than royal candidates. Matthew Paris writes that the monks of Coventry in 1238 elected William Raleigh to the see:

> . . . timentes ne si alium quam regi specialem accepissent rex in faciem contradicens eos more solito inquietasset.[3]

The occasions on which the king actually interfered in an election do not necessarily indicate the extent of royal influence.

The whole duty of the keeper of a vacant bishopric was to carry out the will of his royal master; to administer the bishopric efficiently and to exploit it advantageously to the crown. However he might delegate the more routine duties, he was himself ultimately responsible to the king for both the economic and the judicial administration of the see. Apart from this he had to respond promptly to every royal command; demands for money or issues in kind, orders to assess a tallage, to hold an inquisition or to sell the corn harvest; to turn the monks out of their convent or to entertain the king's guests. Every order had to be obeyed quickly, effectively and with discretion. It was no task for the incompetent.

---

[1] *Ibid.*, IV, 172.

[2] Durham MS. 5520: 'Thomas de Bendenges et servientes sui qui tunc custodivit castrum non permiserunt ipsum electum vel suos intrare set clausis portis eisdem restiterunt dicentes quod aliud mandatum habuerunt a rege.'

[3] *Chron. Majora*, III, 531. In this election, unlike that at Winchester, Raleigh was the king's nominee. Raleigh declined the see of Lichfield in favour of that of Norwich.

From the point of view of clergy and chroniclers the tale was
one of spoliation and oppression. It was naturally the cases of
the abuse of regalian right that normally drew the attention
of these critics; where there was no abuse they did not comment.
This is worth remembering; for the keepers did in reality come
to defend, to protect, to maintain order as well as to exploit, on
the crown's behalf.[1] The northern chronicler, Robert Gray-
stanes gives a vivid account of a disturbance in the streets of
Durham in 1283 when, in defiance of the chapter of Durham,
the archbishop of York attempted to enforce his right of visita-
tion *sede vacante*.[2] The situation became dangerous; some of the
wilder element in the town came near enough to lop off the
ears of the archbishop's palfrey:

et ipsum (i.e. the archbishop), [adds Graystanes], si Wycardus de
Charrons et Petrus de Thorsbi non impedissent, ut creditur occi-
dissent.

Guichard de Charron was the royal custodian of the temporalities;[3] when the sharpness of ecclesiastical controversy threatened the peace of the realm it was the much abused *satellites*
of the king who rescued the archbishop of York from the wrath-
ful citizens of Durham.

After months or sometimes years, the vacancy would end, and
the bishopric would be transferred to a new set of administrators, the ministers of the bishop-elect. The Register of John

---

[1] An incident in a vacancy at Hyde Abbey in 1282 shows that a vacancy was
regarded as an opportunity to seize coveted rights: Commission of oyer and terminer 'on complaint by the abbot of Hyde that whereas by reason of the liberty of
the hundred of Micheldever . . . held by his predecessors from time immemorial,
attachments for all trespasses committed within the said hundred belong to the
abbey of Hyde, Walter de Valle, mayor of Winchester, Walter de Caperugg' and
Richard Gabriel, bailiffs, and Richard Stocbrigg', citizens of the said town, with
a great multitude, during the voidance of the said abbey, entered the enclosures
(*septa*) of the said abbey within the precincts of the said hundred, seized the attachments for certain trespasses there, and took and imprisoned certain men of the
said abbey and certain ministers of the keeper of the said abbey' (*Cal. Pat. R.,
1281–92*, pp. 47–8).

Similarly the keepers of York in 1263 were ordered to inquire who it was 'while
the archbishopric was void and in the king's hands, felled trees in certain woods
belonging to the archbishopric in the county of Nottingham and made waste and
sale thereof without the king's licence' (*ibid., 1258–66*, p. 481).

[2] *Hist. Dunelm. Script. Tres.*, p. 65.

[3] Pipe R. 127, m.2d.

de Pontissaria, bishop of Winchester, 1282–1304, shows the machinery of this transference at work. The writ of restitution of the temporalities by the king[1] has, of course, hundreds of counterparts on the Patent Rolls. There are, however, other documents less commonly found. Among them are the writ of the keepers to the bailiffs, in this case dated eight days after the writ of restitution, ordering them to pay the issues of their bailiwicks henceforth to the bishop,[2] the bishop's appointment of an attorney to receive the temporalities in his name,[3] and the letters relating to the sale of corn and stock of the vacancy to the new bishop. Over this there was trouble. The king, on this occasion at least, seems to have allowed the custodians almost complete freedom in negotiating with Pontissaria over the price that he should pay for the corn which the king had sown, and the stock which the king had bought.[4] Pontissaria complained that he had found the keepers 'difficult',[5] and the king's chancellor Robert Burnell, who had been the king's candidate for the vacant see of Winchester in this election, wrote to the keepers urging them to be reasonable and not extortionate.[6]

It was usual for the incoming bishop to make an agreement with the king or keepers for some of the corn and stock which remained to the king at the end of the vacancy. Sometimes this was carefully and exactly priced, as in this Winchester vacancy of 1280–2, where Pontissaria eventually paid £2853.2.4 for the wheat and hay;[7] as at Canterbury in 1295 where Archbishop

[1] *Regisistrum Johannis de Pontissaria, 1282–1304*, ed. C. Deedes (Cant. and York Soc., London, 1915–24), II, 385; 11 Aug. 1282.

[2] *Ibid.*, p. 386; 19 Aug. 1282.

[3] *Ibid.*, p. 385; date not specified.

[4] *Ibid.*, p. 384. It is true that the king orders that an assessment shall be made, but one feels that much is left to the discretion of the custodians: 'Mandamus vobis quod omnia blada et fructus ad Episcopatum Wyntoniensem pertinentes qui sunt in manu vestra et in Custodia vestra una cum affris et alio instauro nostro quod est de emptione nostra ibidem, facta inde legali appreciacione, venerabili patri J nunc Wyntoniensi Episcopo vendatis pro justo precio et prout ad opus nostrum videbitis expedire.'

[5] *Ibid.*, p. 392. The reference is in the letter of Robert Burnell to the keepers, 12 Nov.

[6] *Ibid.*

[7] This is the figure given on the Pipe Roll account 'de toto blado et feno ejusdem episcopatus proveniente de anno x eidem episcopo in grosso vendito' (Pipe R. 128, m.28). In Pontissaria's Register the price is given as '4,280 marks except 4 shillings' (i.e. £2,853.2.8) (*Reg. J. Pontissaria*, II, 398; 18 Jan. 1283).

Winchelsey paid £1471.1.10½ for grain sold to him *in grosso*[1] and as at York in 1300 when the grain sown but not reaped was sold to Thomas Corbridge for £574.9.3.[2] But it seems to have been equally common for the incoming bishop simply to fine with the king for the grain.[3] It is difficult to say whether in any specific instance, the king drove an unfair bargain, but the evidence suggests that he was not wildly extortionate. John Mansell, keeper of Durham in 1261, was ordered to let the bishop-elect have the crops of the bishopric 'for as much as any other would give for them'.[4] And in the same see in 1283 the stock bought by the king from the executors of the late bishop was to be sold to Anthony Bek, the incoming prelate for exactly the same price as had been paid to the executors, saving to the king his 'expenses for wainage and the collection of any fruits there'.[5] No doubt the king would drive a harder bargain in some cases than in others, according to his feelings towards the bishop-elect and to his own immediate need of money, but considering the strength of his position[6] his policy does not in general seem to have been unduly harsh.

The date of the restitution of the temporalities to the new bishop marked the end of the vacancy[7]—but not the end of the

[1] Pipe R. 141, m.28d.

[2] The price was said to have been arranged 'coram Thesaurario et Baronibus de Scaccario' (Pipe R. 150, m.31d).

[3] For example at Bath in 1244: 'Rex concessit R. Bathoniensi Electo per finem cccc li. omnia blada seminata in terris maneriorum Episcopatus Bathoniensis . . .' (Fine R. 41, m.4; 17 July 1244). At Norwich in the same year Walter Suffield fined for £100 'pro habendis bladis seminatis in terris maneriorum eiusdem Episcopatus . . .' (*ibid.*; 19 July 1244). At Lincoln in 1279 the keeper accounted for 40 marks 'receptis de predicto Magistro Olivero Episcopo' [i.e. Oliver Sutton] 'pro quibusdam terris per eundem custodem seminatis arura eorundem et fimis eidem episcopo venditis' (Pipe R. 125, m.3d). And John Salmon at Norwich fined with the king for 1,000 marks in 1299 'pro omnibus bladis in terris episcopatus Norwic' tempore vacacionis seminatis ' (Pipe R. 145, m.12).

[4] *Cal. Pat. R., 1258–66*, p. 139.

[5] *Cal. Fine R., 1272–1307*, p. 189.

[6] The bishop-elect might be in an unhappy state until he had been able to secure some arrangement of this kind with the crown. Walter Stapeldon, newly elected to Exeter, wrote plaintively on 20 Mar. 1308 '. . . sum ad presens quasi in puris et nudis, et Maneria Episcopatus, de instauro nuda, de bladis Regiis, tempore vacacionis excultis sunt vestita' (*The Register of Walter de Stapeldon, 1307–26*, ed. F. C. Hingeston Randolph (London, 1892), p. 8).

[7] That is from the secular point of view. From the ecclesiastical point of view of course the date of consecration was the dividing line.

keeper's responsibilities. The day which would finally release the custodian was the day on which his account before the barons of the exchequer was concluded. Meanwhile there might be much still to be done within the bishopric. Nicholas Fermbaud, keeper of Ely, yielded the temporalities to the new bishop, William of Louth, on 30 May 1290, but Nicholas and his clerk were paid their expenses for five weeks which they spent in the autumn of that year going round the various manors of the bishopric viewing the corn which had been sown during the vacancy and which William of Louth was to buy.[1] In the next Ely vacancy although the temporalities were restored in October 1299, as late as March of the following year there were still men

custodientium blada in grangiis et in terris crescentibus [sic] staurum fenum et alia bona existencia in omnibus maneriis pertinentibus ad Episcopatum predictum preter ballivam Insule[2]

on the king's behalf. Ely was not exceptional. At Canterbury, in 1278–9, £22 was allowed to the custodians in the expenses of *servientes*, reeves and *contratalliatores* and others who remained to see to the continued harvesting of the crops and the collection of money due to the king 'post vacacionem predictam'.[3] At Winchester in 1282 the keepers released the temporalities on 11 August, but their expenses are paid until the following Christmas,[4] and over £4,800 of the issues of Winchester in this vacancy were taken to the royal wardrobe or elsewhere after the temporalities had been restored.[5]

From the keeper's point of view the effectual end of his task was the rendering of his account at the exchequer. But since twenty-two of the sixty-seven vacancies of Henry III's reign produced no account on the Pipe Rolls[6] the very assumption

---

[1] Pipe R. 135, m.1.   [2] Pipe R. 144, m.31.
[3] Pipe R. 124, m.23d.   [4] Pipe R. 128, m.28.
[5] The exact figure based on the carriage expenses recorded on the Pipe Roll account as specifically belonging to the eleventh or in some cases the twelfth year of this reign (i.e. 20 Nov. 1282 to 19 Nov. 1284) is £4,866.13.4 (*ibid.*). However, this figure is probably too low an estimate, for the enrolled wardrobe account, for the eleventh and twelth years show a payment of £6,516.13.4 received from the bishopric of Winchester *sede vacante* (Pipe R. 130, m.5) and, provided that the wardrobe accounts were up to date, this figure should be reliable.
[6] These figures exclude the Welsh sees and Rochester.

that the keeper normally accounted at the exchequer seems to require investigation. In the first eleven years of the reign, that is up to and including the exchequer year ending Michaelmas 1227, there is only one vacancy account on the Pipe Rolls proper,[1] and two on the collection of membranes known as the Foreign Roll of Henry III.[2] The exact relation of the Foreign Roll to the early Pipe Rolls of the reign is not easy to determine, but it would not, I think, be safe to assume that we still have all the vacancy accounts that were in fact rendered at the exchequer in the period before 1227.[3] From the twelfth year to the end of the reign there is a fairly regular incidence of vacancy accounts on the Pipe Rolls and if we base our figures on this second, more surely documented period, the proportion of vacancies which had Pipe Roll accounts to the 'silent'

[1] The account for the vacant bishopric of Norwich, 13 Dec. 1218 to 17 Mar. 1219, on the Roll of 1219 (Pipe R. 63, m.4d). The account is not mentioned in the *P.R.O. Lists and Indexes* XI, 133.

[2] The accounts for Exeter and Ely on Foreign R. 1, m.3d.

[3] This 'Foreign Roll of Henry III' is described in the introduction to *P.R.O. Lists and Indexes*, XI as consisting apparently of the detached foreign membranes of the first five years of that reign. However, it would seem from the internal evidence of the six membranes which constitute this roll that in fact it extends over a considerably longer period. Membrane 6 is headed 'Rotulus Quadragesime assesse et concesse Regi anno regni suo sextodecimo'. The wardrobe account on membrane 4 (printed in an Appendix by T. F. Tout in *Chapters in the Administrative History of Medieval England* (Manchester 1920–33), I, 233–8) covers part of year 11 (1226–7) as well as the whole of the ninth and tenth and a part of the eighth year.

In the case of the Exeter account referred to above there is an interesting cross reference: 'Et debet W. [William Brewer, the keeper] xx marcas de quibus W. Exoniensis episcopus debet eum adquietare sicut recognovit et respondet in magno Rotulo in Devon in compoto ipsius Episcopi tallagii maneriorum episcopatus.' This reference is in fact to the Pipe Roll of the ninth year (Pipe R. 69, m.3d) where the bishop of Exeter does account for the tallage and 'de xx marcis de remanenti firme maneriorum prescriptorum sicut continetur in Rotulo compotorum.' It will be noticed that neither of these two complementary cross references specifies the regnal year of the roll to which it is referring (contrast a reference in the Exeter account on the Foreign Roll to an account 'in Devon in rotulo viij')—presumably because it would be assumed that it was the same year, i.e. the ninth year of the reign. It would seeem therefore that membrane 3 of this Foreign Roll is in fact the *rotulus compotorum* of 9 Henry III. Further, the reference on the *rotulus compotorum* to the Pipe Roll of that same year as the 'Great Roll' ('in magno Rotulo in Devon' rather than simply 'in Devon') perhaps implies that the *rotulus compotorum* was more fully separate from the Pipe Roll proper than was customary later in the reign, in which case the dearth of vacancy accounts for this early part of the reign might possibly be the result of a loss of certain loose membranes of *rotuli compotorum*.

vacancies becomes forty-two to thirteen. In at least six of these thirteen 'silent' vacancies, moreover, it would seem that the king had originally intended that the keepers should make an account at the exchequer, for this is actually specified in their commission,[1] and there are in several cases special reasons why the account was not in the end rendered there.[2] This leaves us with seven vacancies where there was neither an account on the Pipe Rolls nor a commission which anticipated that such an account would be made. In two of these seven cases, the exchequer demanded an account, but the king remitted it,[3] in one other the issues of the vacancy were in fact paid into the exchequer but were assigned for a special purpose,[4] and in a fourth the issues were paid to the bishop-elect.[5] We are left with three.

---

[1] For example the commission of Chichester to Adam de Aston: 'Rex commisit Ade de Aston Episcopatum Cicestrensem vacantem cum omnibus pertinentibus suis custodiendum quamdiu Regi placuerit. Ita quod de exitibus eiusdem respondeat ad scaccarium Regis . . .' (Fine R. 50, m.12; 4 Apr. 1253). See also the commission of Canterbury to Bertram de Crioil and John Mansell (Fine R. 37, m.16, 5 Nov. 1240); the commission of Carlisle to Robert de Dacre (*Cal. Pat. R.*, *1247–58*, p. 366; 24 Mar. 1254; and Fine R. 51, m.9); and of the same see to Walter de Rudham and Martin de Chamflur (*Cal. Pat. R.*, *1247–58*, p. 503; 14 Oct. 1256); the commission of York to John Mansell (Fine R. 55, m.6; 15 May 1258) and of Durham to the same (*Cal. Pat. R.*, *1258–66*, p. 90; 17 Aug. 1260 and Fine R. 57, m.4). The specification of accounting at the exchequer was by no means an invariable clause in the original commission, even in cases where an account was rendered there.

[2] For example the death of one of the accountants. In the case of the issues of the Canterbury vacancy of 1240–5 the king acquitted the heirs and executors of Bertram de Crioil from accounting and as Mansell could not account without his colleague, he is acquitted too (*Cal. Pat. R.*, *1247–58*, p. 480; 12 June 1256. See also K.R. Mem. R. 30, m.15 and K.R. Mem. R. 31, m.4). John Mansell's executors were later acquitted in respect of the accounts he should have rendered for York and Durham because Mansell's property did not suffice for the acquittance of the said debts (*Cal. Pat. R.*, *1258–66*, p. 506; 16 Nov. 1265; and p. 508; 24 Nov. 1265 Compare also K.R. Mem. R. 40, m.14d).

[3] The exchequer had ordered Henry Wingham to make his account for Bath 1247–8 (L.T.R. Mem. R. 21, m.6) but the king remitted the account (*Cal. Pat. R.*, *1247–58*, p. 188; 18 April 1253). The two keepers of Norwich, 1244, were similarly ordered to account (L.T.R. Mem. R. 18, m.3d) but subsequently acquitted, (*ibid.*, m.3d and m.4) for a consideration of two palfreys in one case and one in the other.

[4] The treasurer Philip Lovel was ordered to pay the issues of Exeter in the vacancy of 1257–8 to William of Gloucester to buy gold for the king (*Close R.*, *1256–59*, pp. 208–9; 4 Apr. 1258).

[5] The issues of London in the 1259 vacancy were paid to Henry Wingham 'by counsel of the nobles of the council' (*Cal. Pat. R.*, *1258–66*, p. 33; 25 July 1259).

In the case of one of these, Hereford, 1239–40, we are very much in the dark.[1] In the case of Lichfield in 1256 Robert Walerand was ordered to answer 'to the king' for the issues.[2] As for the other, Norwich in 1266, we have a writ of commission which was altogether exceptional. The issues were assigned to the king's son Edmund (not in itself an unusual arrangement) but the exchequer is expressly ordered not to intermeddle.[3]

In the light of these explanations, it seems permissible to say that it was *normal* for the keeper to account for the issues of a vacant see at the exchequer. In Edward I's reign the number of vacancies for which there do not appear to be Pipe Roll accounts dwindled to four out of a total of forty-one vacancies and in three out of the four cases the keeper was the king's escheator. It may, therefore, well be that the issues were in fact accounted for at the exchequer but are embedded in the massive accounts which the escheators rendered there.[4]

The rendering of the account might be a lengthy business involving the keeper or his clerks in a stay of some weeks at the exchequer.[5] The keeper had to appear with tallies, writs authorizing his 'extraordinary' expenditure and finally rolls of particulars giving details of the receipts and routine expenditure

[1] A 'controller' seems to have been appointed to help in the custody of the see and was to have 'unum rotulum de exitibus ejusdem episcopatus et de expensis necessariis' (*Close R., 1237–42*, p. 218; 3 Aug. 1240). The financial aspect of the vacancy was evidently to be properly documented. It may just conceivably be significant that the name of the chief custodian was William de Camera (*ibid.*).

[2] 'Rex commisit Roberto Wallerand Episcopatum Cestrensem vacantem . . . custodiendum quamdiu Regi placuerit ad respondendum Regi de exitibus eiusdem episcopatus' (Fine R. 54, m.14. 29 Oct. 1256).

[3] *Cal. Pat. R., 1258–66*, p. 528. This may be compared with the command to Nicholas Fermbaud, keeper of Bath, 1302, to answer for the issues before Amadeus of Savoy to whom the king had committed the issues (*Cal. Close R., 1302–07*, pp. 9–10). But in the latter case there was an account enrolled on the Pipe Roll, covering the whole vacancy (Pipe R. 150, m.32), and the account is carried forward to Pipe R. 151, m.7d.

[4] As for instance in the case of the vacancies at Norwich in 1299 and London 1303–4 which are both accounted for among Walter of Gloucester's accounts as escheator (Pipe R. 149, m.29d and m.37 respectively). The latter is not mentioned in *P.R.O. Lists and Indexes*, XI, 133.

[5] The keeper of Ely in 1290, Nicholas Fermbaud and his clerk claimed the expenses 'quas fecerunt per v. septimanas Lond' compoto suo de exitibus eiusdem episcopatus reddendo iiij li. xvjs.iijd.' (Pipe R. 135, m.1). After the next Ely vacancy two of the keepers' clerks spent over three weeks at the exchequer for the business of rendering the account (Pipe R. 144, m.31).

manor by manor.[1] These rolls of particulars were based on the accounts by which the bailiffs and reeves of the individual manors had accounted before the keeper himself. This, at least, seems to be what the barons of the exchequer expected from the keepers of the Winchester vacancy of 1323–4,[2] and there are many examples of this type of account among the class of Ministers' Accounts in the Lord Treasurer's Remembrancer's records. Sometimes these accounts are actually in the name of the local accounting officers, the bailiffs and reeves,[3] but more often they are in the keeper's name, though presumably still based on the accounts of the local officials.[4]

It would be easy, however, to oversimplify the elaborate procedure of compilation that lies behind the succinct enrolments on the Pipe Rolls. Among the Winchester group of records in the 'Ministers' Accounts' there are many documents which seem to lie one stage further back even than the rolls of particulars as we have defined them so far. There is a list of allowances made to reeves and other officials,[5] a stock account for divers manors of the see,[6] a grain account from Nicholas de Haudlo's keepership, 1258–60,[7] and particulars of provender

[1] K.R. Mem. R. 40, m.13d: Richard de Compton, the keeper of Worcester is to appear at the exchequer 'cum rotulis brevibus talliis et omnibus aliis in compotum suum tangentibus'.

[2] The passage relates to the accounts made by the reeves of the manors '. . . per quos rotulos prepositorum de particulis etc. ipsi custodes compotos suos fecisse debuerunt . . .' (K.R. Mem. R. 101, m.127d).

[3] E.g. the roll of particulars for a part of the Winchester vacancy of 1280–2 (Min. Acc. 1142/1).

[4] E.g. the roll of Henry de Bray, keeper of Ely 1286, sewn together with William of Middelton's counter-roll (Min. Acc. 1132/9); a part of the roll of Nicholas Fermbaud and Robert de Harwedon for Winchester, 1304–5 (Min. Acc. 1142/15); the account of Humphrey de Walden for Worcester, 1302 (Min. Acc. 1143/18—this is printed in The Red Book of Worcester, ed. M. Hollings (Worcs. Hist. Soc., London, 1934–9) Appendix II, pp. 498–547).

Even more interesting is Richard de Clifford's roll of particulars for one year of the Canterbury vacancy of 1270–2. The various items have signs placed against them so that they will be easily grouped together into such categories as 'wages' or 'stock bought' for the purposes of the final compressed Pipe Roll account. Each item among the receipts is separately cancelled by a horizontal line and in the few cases where it is not cancelled there is a marginal note 'nondum in Rotulo' (Min. Acc. 1128/1).

[5] Min. Acc, 1143/7.

[6] Min. Acc. 1143/4.

[7] Min. Acc. 1143/2. Documents of this type would naturally be produced in the ordinary course of administration within the vacant bishopric. It is not surprising to find them locally (e.g. an estimate of grain prices made in a Lincoln vacancy of

for stock in the 1319–20 vacancy.[1] When the barons of the exchequer demanded rolls of particulars therefore, it may well have been that they expected much more than the comparatively compact lists of receipts and expenditure manor by manor.

Then there is a third type of roll among the bundles of Ministers' Accounts, distinct from both the manorial accounts and from the miscellaneous lists that we have just mentioned. It seems to lie between the manorial accounts and the final enrolment. These documents may easily be mistaken for what we have called manorial accounts, because they are for the most part drawn up manor by manor[2] although some of them are much more condensed.[3] Their distinguishing feature is their constant reference to rolls of particulars. In fact, they are the final draft from which the Pipe Roll account itself is compiled, very often word for word. Yet these, too, in the contemporary terminology of the exchequer, go under that comprehensive classification *rotuli de particulis*.[4] In short any document which lies behind the final enrolment may be called a roll of particulars but on analysis they represent several distinct stages in the process of accounting. It seems clear that the entry concerning the vacant see that is eventually made on the Pipe Roll is only the part of the iceberg that appears above the water; it is dependent upon an impressive base of stratified layers of accounts.

The exchequer standards were undoubtedly exacting. When Bernard of Savoy, the keeper of Chichester, 1244–6, failed to produce a roll of particulars, the omission was noted in the

the late thirteenth or early fourteenth century; Lincoln Cathedral, Dean and Chapter Archives Bj/5/17/5), but it is interesting to find them also at the exchequer.

[1] Min. Acc. 1143/12.

[2] For example the account for Ely 1298–9 (Min. Acc. 1132/10). This is partly arranged bailiwick by bailiwick (for the first 'year' of the account) and, then in more detail, manor by manor. See also the Worcester account for 1302 (*Red Book of Worcester*, pp. 498–547) and the Norwich account for 1326 (Min. Acc. 1141/1).

[3] E.g. the Worcester account for the vacancy of 1317 (Min. Acc. 1143/19) and the Winchester accounts for 1304 (Min. Acc. 1143/3) and for 1323–4 (Min. Acc. 1143/8 and 1143/9).

[4] There is a contemporary endorsement on the final draft of the Winchester account of 1304 (see n. 3, above): 'Rotuli de particulis compoti Nicholai Fermbaud et Roberti de Harewedon custodum Episcopatus Wintoniensis de exitibus eiusdem Episcopatus . . .'

Memoranda Roll.[1] Sometimes extents as well as accounts were demanded from keepers,[2] and watchful exchequer officials seem to have kept earlier vacancy accounts close at hand as a check on the ones that they were auditing. Again Bernard of Savoy was found wanting:

> Idem Bernardus non respondit super compotum suum de firma ecclesie de Eplinton de qua responsum fuit tempore Regis Johannis de xvi li.[3]

When John Fitz Philip and Nicholas de Molis, keepers of the see of Durham, only accounted for £5 a year for the wards of Norham, it was duly noted that the keeper in the last vacancy had answered for £6 a year from this source.[4]

The accounts which appear on the Pipe Rolls and among the rolls of particulars are essentially the keepers' *official* statements of their receipts and expenditure during a vacancy. Were they, on the whole, true statements? Certainly there are complaints, both general and specific, against the fraudulency of keepers. In Archbishop Winchelsey's Register, at the head of a list of *antiqua gravamina* of the clergy there is a paragraph on vacancies which includes one interesting accusation against the keepers; that the royal custodians sometimes did not pay to the king a third part of that which they levied by the racking of the tenants and destruction of the woods, parks and fish-ponds.[5] The figure of one-third has perhaps a literary flavour, but nevertheless this is or should have been responsible criticism. This, however, is general accusation. Where specific complaints

---

[1] L.T.R. Mem. R. 19, m.3d. 'Idem Bernardus non protulit Rotulum de particulis episcopatus super compotum suum unde debet respondere.'

[2] In the Ely vacancy of 1298–9 wages were allowed to two keepers' clerks who made extents of the manors of the bishopric: 'in vadiis ij clericorum predictorum custodum facientium extentas maneriorum Episcopatus (Pipe R. 144, m.29). In 1244 the barons of exchequer demanded from Ralph Dayrell, keeper of the vacant see of London, an impressively long list of 'particulars', some of which related only to this particular vacancy, e.g. 'omnes particulas placitorum et amerciamentorum per se', but some of which seem to be the basis of extents, e.g. 'quantum quilibet liber homo reddit in qualibet villa et quantum quilibet villanus per annum de redditu in denariis' (L.T.R. Mem. R. 15, m.5).

[3] L.T.R. Mem. R. 19, m.3d.

[4] 'Memorandum quod J. filius Philippi Willelmus de London pro eodem et Nicholas de Molis non respondunt nisi de c s. de Wardis de Norham per annum et magister Stephanus de Lucy responderat de vj li. per annum de eadem [*sic*]' (L.T.R. Mem. R. 13, m.9d).   [5] *Reg. R. Winchelsey*, p. 1018.

are preserved, usually in chronicles, it is often not possible to distinguish between what was due to abuse by the keepers themselves and what was due to deliberate oppression by the king. If the king gave practically a free hand to the keepers to waste the bishopric, as Matthew Paris states that Henry III did at Ely, 1256-8,[1] then the keepers themselves cannot be held solely responsible, and at the moment our concern is strictly with abuse, and particularly with peculation on the part of the keepers themselves. For the same reason one cannot attach too much weight to Matthew Paris's onslaught against the keepers of the see of Winchester, 1238-44, or their subordinates, because the king happened on that occasion to be angry with the convent of that see and the responsibility for extortion may again rest largely with him.[2]

More promising evidence, although it is rarely forthcoming, is a royal order either for abuse to stop or for an inquiry to be made into suspected abuses. On 11 July 1243 Henry III wrote from Bordeaux to the regents in England stating that he had heard unsatisfactory reports of the conduct of Ralph Dayrell, keeper of the vacancies of Evesham abbey and of the bishopric of London.[3] The regents were directed to look into the matter and to remove Dayrell immediately if these reports were well founded. In the troubled period of 1258-61 there are two other inquiries into the conduct of royal keepers; one is for the Ely vacancy of 1256-8[4] and the other for the keepership of Winchester, 1258-60, by Nicholas de Haudlo.[5] But the date of

---

[1] *Chron. Majora*, v, 589.

[2] The passage may be quoted, however, because it does purport to be general as well: 'Rex autem, persistens in ira sua, ad maneria sua arctam posuit custodiam per suos satellites; qui, ut de more solent, limites praecepti tirannici saeviendo transgredientes, episcopatui subjectos satis inhumane tractantes propriis emolumentis avidius intendebant'; *ibid.*, iv, p. 264.

[3] *Close R., 1242-47*, p. 33.

[4] 'Commission to William le Bretun, to make inquisition touching a complaint by H. bishop of Ely, that immense trespasses and damages have been done in his bishopric by the king's guardians of the same and their ministers while the bishopric was in the king's hands, . . .' (*Cal. Pat. R., 1258-66*, p. 48; 4 Nov. 1258). It is interesting to notice that William Breton was himself keeper of the bishopric in the previous vacancy, of 1254.

[5] Appointment of John de la Lynde and Gerard de la Grue 'to enquire by jurors of the bishopric of Winchester how the bishopric was kept after it came to the king's hands after the recess of A. sometime bishop of Winchester, the king's brother, from England, and how Nicholas de Haudlo and his bailiffs treated the

these two writs suggests a warning. The inquest at Ely was a part of the general programme of inquiries into crimes committed by the king's ministers which was a part of the baronial plan of reform; Nicholas de Haudlo was a 'baronial' keeper and the king for that reason alone, may have been more determined to suspect him of ill-treatment of the inhabitants of the bishopric of Winchester. Again, in 1302, Edward I ordered Humphrey de Walden, keeper of Worcester, to desist from causing waste and destruction in the lands of the see.[1]

For two vacancies, we still have the detailed returns to such inquiries into mismanagement. The complaints against Richard de Clifford's behaviour in the see of Canterbury in 1270-2 are to be found on page after page of the Hundred Rolls,[2] the returns to Edward I's commission of inquiry into the misdeeds of his officials made immediately after his return from the Holy Land. Miss Sutcliffe has described Clifford's administration as 'wicked mismanagement and tyranny'.[3] Certainly Clifford and his bailiffs seem to have exacted fines for everything they could think of, and in some cases to have cheated the inhabitants.[4] They made waste in the woods[5] and charged the men of the see for expenses which were never incurred.[6] It is likely there

men of the bishopric, how much they received of the issues of the bishopric and what they did with it. . . .' (*Cal. Pat. R.*, *1258–66*, p. 185; 8 June 1261).

[1] *Reg. Worcs. Sede Vacante*, p. 3, 10 Apr. 1302. There does not seem to be an enrolment on Patent or Close Rolls. Also coming from this period is an accusation of oppressive keepership on the part of the custodian of Wenlock Abbey, Geoffrey of Northampton. He had to pay a fine of 70 marks to the prior and convent 'pro dampnis que fecit predictis priori et conventui in predicta vacacione' (*Close R.*, *1259–61*, pp. 476–7. *c.* 23 May 1261).

[2] *Rotuli Hundredorum*, I, 200–36, *passim* and II, part I, 211.

[3] 'Financial Conditions of the See of Canterbury', p. 64.

[4] 'Idem Ricardus cepit de Willelmo de Edeste preposito de Cerryng c s. quos in compoto suo allocare noluit (*Rotuli Hundredorum*, I, 213). 'Item dicunt quod magister Ricardus de Clifford . . . cepit de Elia le Prude et sociis suis de summonitione scaccarii x marcas per manus magistri Hugonis de Thornham permittens [*rectius* promittens?] quod ad scaccarium eos aquietaret et non fecit nec unquam unde habuerunt allocanciam ad grave dampnum eorum' (*ibid.*, p. 204b).

'Item dicunt quod magister Ricardus de Clifford . . . cepit de hundredo de Westgate xl s. ita quod eos sustineret eo modo quo ballivi archiepiscopi eos tenuerunt et occasione illius finis fecit injuste levare de eodem hundredo iiij marcas' (*ibid.*, p. 205b).   [5] *Ibid.*, p. 208b.

[6] 'Item dicunt magister R. de Clifford . . . cepit de villata de Gillingeham . . . x li. ad terras seminandas in dicta villa . . . et illas x li. asportavit et terras non seminavit' (*ibid.*, p. 222).

was substance in these complaints, but, of course, the tenants of a bishopric when given an opportunity to present grievances would not understate their case. There are frequent complaints about the 'recognitions' paid to the keepers[1] but it is not clear whether it is the amount that is objected to or the principle; if it was the latter the keepers were not responsible and there is no means of judging whether the amounts themselves were unreasonable.[2]

The evidence for the Winchester vacancy of 1323–4 is in some ways the most informative of all. It relates exclusively to the question whether the keepers cheated the exchequer. In April 1323 Edward II appointed Robert of Wells and Richard Airmyn as keepers of the vacant see of Winchester. Over five months later Robert of Wells was relieved of his responsibilities and for a further nine months his colleague Richard Airmyn shared the keepership with William de Pillande. The vacancy ended in June 1324, and the accounts were rendered at the exchequer and enrolled on the Pipe Roll.[3] But the king was told that these three keepers had concealed some of their receipts and had claimed undue expenses. An inquisition was ordered and twelve sworn men from each of the Winchester manors were given two sets of rolls to compare. The first set were said by the jurors to be true copies of the rolls by which the reeves had made their account before the royal keepers; in other words, the reeves' manorial accounts had been made in duplicate, one set handed to the keepers and the other set kept by the reeves. With these true copies of the reeves' rolls the jurors were asked to compare the rolls of receipts and expenses manor by manor by which the keepers had in their turn accounted at the exchequer. It soon became obvious that the rolls presented at the exchequer were not the twins of the true copies which had been kept in the manors. The jurors found grave discrepancies. The keepers had received £3 from butter and

---

[1] 'Magister Ricardus . . . cepit de villatis de Reculre et Westhalimot de recognitionibus ad opus domini Regis x li.'; *ibid.*, p. 204b.; and '. . . idem Ricardus cepit x li. de tenentibus hundredi de Tenham injuste nomine tallagii in primo adventu suo' (*ibid.*, p. 211b).

[2] That is the individual amounts. On the total sum levied in tallage or recognitions from the archbishopric on this occasion see below, p. 124, n. 6.

[3] Pipe R. 169, m.43.

cheese on the manor of Cheriton and had accounted for only
£1.16.0 from this source.[1] They had levied £35.7.2 in fines at
Downton but they only mentioned £14.14.0 in their accounts.[2]
They had claimed 2/4d. in expenses for the wage of a harrower
at Bitterne—and there was no harrower at Bitterne.[3] The lists
continue, membrane after membrane. In the final calculation
Robert of Wells, Richard Airmyn and William de Pillande
among them had defrauded the exchequer of £905.17.4¾,[4]
that was very roughly about one seventh of the net total of
receipts during the whole vacancy.[5]

The exchequer pressed the keepers for explanation. The
keepers denied that the 'true copies' of the reeves' rolls were
true copies at all. But, perhaps significantly, they were unable
or unwilling to produce the rolls by which the reeves had
originally accounted to the keepers.[6] They foisted the responsibility on to each other, or to the treasurer at Wolvesey, or on to
William de Pillande's clerk, who was said by Pillande to have
the reeves' original rolls for the second part of the vacancy in a
chest at Winchester, but neither clerk nor chest was ever found.

The case ends in the next reign in almost, but perhaps not
quite, complete anticlimax. Robert of Wells did not live to see
the end, but Airmyn and Pillande procured writs of acquittance from the new king. The writs are interesting. They imply
that the keepers were victims of an intrigue, for the inquisition
is said to have been made:

ad procuracionem Hugonis le Despenser Junioris et Magistri
Roberti de Baldok suggerencium.

---

[1] K.R. Mem. R. 101, m.117.   [2] Ibid., m.126.   [3] Ibid., m.120d.

[4] Ibid., m. 127. It is interesting that the apparent misappropriation of revenue
seems to have been maintained at a very steady rate throughout the vacancy despite
the partial change in keepership. £352.2.10¾ was lost to the crown in the first five
and a half months (13 Apr. 1323 to 30 Sep. 1323) and £553.14.6 in the nine
months following (to 28 June 1324).

[5] The net totals (without deduction of keepers' expenses) as given on the Pipe
Roll accounts are £2,339.15.3½ and £4,309.11.2½ for the first and second periods
of the vacancy respectively, making a grand total of £6,649.6.6.

[6] There are among the Ministers' Accounts, bundles 1141 and 1142, various
sets of rolls from individual Winchester manors. Many are fragmentary but a
complete set (e.g. 1141/11, for the manor of Bentley) has three membranes: (1)
a record of the inquisition of 1326 for that particular manor, as is to be found on the
Memoranda Roll; (2) the reeves' 'true copy' of the account for the first part of the
vacancy and (3) the 'true copy' for the second half of the vacancy.

Maybe, but it is difficult to believe that there had not been some peculation somewhere. The details seem to be too circumstantial to be complete invention, although there may have been some exaggeration. But whether £905.17.4¾ found its way to the purses of the keepers or to those of their subordinates, or perhaps both, it seems impossible to say for certain. But the exchequer never saw it, and the incident seems to confirm what *a priori* one would suspect, that not all the profits of a vacant see always reached the royal treasury. The custody of vacancies, like other aspects of medieval government, had its occasional big scandals and, no doubt, its more continual petty malpractices.

The administration of vacant sees is simply one aspect of medieval central government at work in the provinces. The evidence lies mainly in the stream of royal writs that flowed out of the chancery and the stream of financial accounts that flowed into the exchequer. The recipient of the writs and the accountant at the exchequer was the royal keeper. The keeper was the pivot of every vacancy. He dealt with bailiffs and reeves, with the late bishop's executors and with the stewards of the bishop-elect; with the exchequer and even with the king himself. He was responsible ultimately for the auditing of the manorial accounts, for the administration of justice and for the economic exploitation of the bishopric. He was the executor of royal policy within the vacant see. In the course of such work the various royal custodians were creating precedents for each other and were advising and informing and thus influencing the policy of the central government. They were more than cogs in one part of an impressive administrative machine; the machine was still in the making in the thirteenth century and the royal keepers were in part its creators.

CHAPTER V

The Emoluments of Episcopal Vacancies: (I) Revenue

W HEN the king took in hand a bishop's barony he seems sometimes to have made a distinction between two kinds of wealth which pertained to it. In the first place there was the ordinary revenue of the bishopric in rents, profits of agriculture and of justice and the capital wealth from which some of this revenue was derived; and in the second place there were the occasional emoluments derived from the bishop's rights of advowson, from the issues of escheats and wardships and the profits of reliefs, marriages and other 'feudal' perquisites.[1] The distinction was of practical importance because this second section of a prelate's revenue was very often reserved to the king when he relinquished the 'ordinary' revenue of a vacant bishopric or abbacy to be farmed by the chapter or when he sold it to the chapter for a fine.[2] For convenience these occasional emolu-

[1] Such for example was the profit which the bishop normally made when the king levied a scutage or feudal aid and the bishop recouped himself by exacting the payment from *all* his enfeoffed knights. See above, pp. 39–40.

[2] In 1229 the convent of Bury St. Edmunds fined with the king for the custody of the abbey during a single vacancy for 300 marks 'salvis domino Regi donationibus ecclesiarum ad eandem Abbatiam spectantium si quas infra illum terminum vacare contigerit. Salvis Regi interim Wardis escaetis et aliis que ad Abbatem eiusdem loci pertinent . . .' (Fine R. 28, m.6).

There are many examples. Compare for instance the fines made by the convent of St. Albans (Fine R. 34, m.11; 28 Feb. 1235), that made by Ramsey (*Cal. Pat. R., 1266–72*, p. 196; 20 Feb. 1268) and by St. Benet's Holme (*ibid.*, p. 253; 26 Aug. 1268), in each case, saving to the king 'wards, reliefs and advowsons of churches'; and that made by Shaftesbury (*Cal. Fine R., 1272–1307*, p. 110; 7 May 1279) saving to the king 'advowsons of churches, wards and escheats and the keeping of the abbey in other voidances'.

In the case of the arrangement for the farming of the temporalities of the see of Exeter by the chapter in 1320 there is a more fully specific reservation: 'saving to the king knights' fees, advowsons of churches, wards, reliefs and escheats if any fall in by reason of that voidance' (*Cal. Fine R., 1319–27*, pp. 38–9). The reservations in the similar arrangements for the sees of Salisbury and London in 1317 only mention advowsons and escheats (*Cal. Fine R., 1307–19*, p. 348 and p. 349); and in that for Lincoln in 1316 only escheats are mentioned (*ibid.*, pp. 272–3).

ments will be treated separately in the following chapter. The present chapter will be concerned only with the first section of the bishop's wealth, the ordinary revenue and the capital which lay at the back of it. Normally, it was this which came under the direct exploitation of the royal custodians. Escheats and wardships, on the other hand, were often granted out for personal exploitation.[1]

There is a simple preliminary question to be asked. Of what did this ordinary revenue from vacant sees consist? There were certain items in this source of royal revenue which came under bitter criticism from the church, either because of the method of their exaction or, in some cases, the very fact of their exaction. To watch the solution of these disputes at the level of practical administration may at least underline some of the peculiar characteristics of Angevin financial administration, its consistency of purpose in extracting money from every possible source and the intellectual subtlety of its devices in attaining its purpose.

The ordinary revenue from vacancies was, of course, temporal revenue. Perhaps the crown in the thirteenth century would never have denied, if challenged, that the royal claim extended only to the temporalities of a vacant see, although the word *temporalia* was not commonly used in this connection until the second half of the century.[2] On the other hand, the government conceived a wide interpretation of the term temporalities and

---

[1] See below, pp. 170–1.

[2] Mr. W. E. Lunt points out that the word *temporalia* was not much used before 1250 in the writs for the restitution of the temporalities of a bishopric to the new bishop (*Valuation of Norwich* (Oxford, 1926), p. 74). More detailed phrases were used instead. Thus the keepers of Worcester in 1218 were ordered to give seisin to the bishop-elect 'de omnibus terris, redditibus, tenementis, et rebus ad dictum episcopatum pertinentibus' (*Pat. R., 1216–25*, p. 169). Mr. Lunt gives many other examples (*loc. cit.*). The term *temporalia* was used increasingly after 1250 and by 1260 had almost entirely superseded other forms.

The exchequer seems to have been slower than the chancery in adopting the new phraseology. I have found no mention of *temporalia* on the vacancy accounts on the Pipe Rolls of Henry III. At the beginning of Edward I's reign (from 1272–1284) the phrases 'antequam liberaret episcopatum . . . electo' and 'antequam liberaret temporalia episcopatus . . . electo' in the heading of the accounts are used with roughly equal frequency, but after 1284 there is only one use of the shorter phrase (in the heading of the account for the Salisbury vacancy of 1286–87 on Pipe R. 133, m.28d) during the whole of the rest of the reign. The inclusion of the word *temporalia* had by this time become standard.

pressed it hard, though with gradually diminishing success. Throughout the thirteenth century the church was steadily widening the connotation of the term *spiritualia*. Items which were common in the vacancy accounts of the twelfth-century Pipe Rolls disappear one by one from those of the thirteenth century. Peter's Pence is a payment commonly found among the temporalities in the first half of the thirteenth century[1] and lingers until 1263 in the London accounts[2] and until 1264 in those of Bath,[3] but after this it seems to vanish.[4] As late as 1236 the king was still in the habit of regarding the episcopal share of the offerings at the shrine of St. Wulfstan as a part of the temporal revenues of the see of Worcester.[5] However in 1266, on the next vacancy account for the temporalities of that see, an entry for the keeper's account from the offerings at the shrine is prepared; but never filled in.[6] In the account for the Worcester vacancy of 1268 there is no entry at all for this item.[7] However, the final settlement of the question is not mentioned until 1302. On 9 April 1302 Edward I addressed a writ to Humphrey de Walden, keeper of the temporalities of the bishopric, to deliver the oblations from the shrine of St. Wulfstan to the prior and convent because the king had granted them to the prior and

[1] For example in the Winchester accounts of 1238–44 (Pipe R. 85, m.3, Pipe R. 87, m.3d and Pipe R. 88, m.12); in the account for Lichfield, 1238–40 (Pipe R. 85, m.3); and London, 1242–4 (Pipe R. 87, m.3).

[2] Pipe R. 108, m.15d.

[3] *Ibid.*, m.15.

[4] In the early fourteenth century in the see of Worcester Peter's Pence are found, as one might expect, on the accounts of the keepers of the spiritualities (*Reg. Worcs. Sede Vacante*; General Introduction, p. xvii); the pope received £9.15.0 and the surplus, which went to the bishop *sede plena* and to the keeper of the spiritualities *sede vacante*, was £24.7.7½.

There is an apparently curious anomaly in the detailed vacancy account for the temporalities of York, 1304–6 (Pipe R. 152B, m.16) where 'denarii Sancti Petri' are mentioned along with customary works among the receipts from the manors of Bishop Wilton and Wetwang.

[5] This amounted to £3.0.0¾ (Pipe R. 81, m.15d), of which all but the ¾d. was paid into the wardrobe (*ibid.*). There may perhaps be some significance in this, since the rest of the issues went to Walter de Burgh for the stocking of the king's demesnes and in a payment to the bishop-elect.

[6] Iidem J. et R. (reddunt compotum) de oblacionibus ad feretrum Sancti Wulfstani de parte episcopi per idem tempus sicut continetur in compoto J. Maunsel et Thome de Lech de episcopatu Wigorniensi in Rotulo xxj in Rotulo compotorum' (Pipe R. 110, m.13; the account of John de la Moyne and Richard de Compton).

[7] Pipe R. 112, m.2d.

convent whenever a vacancy should occur.[1] The king character-
istically made a virtue of necessity by placing the right of the
prior and convent on the footing of a royal grant.

It was not without a little *fracas* that some items of borderline
income were reluctantly yielded by the king. This happened, for
instance, in the case of prestations. On the vacancy accounts of
the twelfth century these payments from archdeaconries were
regularly harvested for the king *sede vacante*.[2] But in 1223 there
was trouble about prestations in the vacant diocese of Coventry
and Lichfield. The king rebuked the archbishop of Canterbury
because the archbishop's officials had not allowed the royal
keepers to receive 'redditus quosdam provenientes ex archi-
diaconatibus Coventrensis Diocesis'.[3] The king pointed out that
the exchequer rolls had been searched and that the payment
of these sums to the king was clearly customary. The interference must stop immediately. It is a pity that there is no Pipe
Roll account for this vacancy; when Lichfield next fell vacant in
1238 archdeaconry payments have made a discreet disappearance[4] and they never appear on Lichfield vacancy accounts at
the exchequer again.[5]

It was the same in other dioceses. In John's reign the Lincoln
archdeacons had duly paid their prestations to the royal custodians *sede vacante*.[6] In 1235 Lincoln fell vacant again. The exchequer clerk records that the royal keepers are not to be held
accountable for the archdeaconry payments because they have
not received them, but the archdeacons themselves ought to

---

[1] *Reg. Worcs. Sede Vacante*, p. 3. There is an entry to the same effect in the vacancy
account on the Pipe Roll which makes it clear that the king is referring in this writ
to the bishop's share of the offerings: 'De oblacionibus provenientibus ad feretrum
Sancti Wolstani in Wygorn' non respondet quia Rex per cartam suam concessit
priori et conventui Beate Marie Wygorn' hujusmodi oblationes durante vacacione
predicta' (Pipe R. 147, m.25 and *Red Book of Worcester*, p. 542).

[2] See above, p. 38.

[3] *Rot. Litt. Claus., 1204–24*, p. 629a.

[4] Pipe R. 85, m.3.

[5] The struggle appears to have continued behind the scenes, for on the Memoranda Roll of 1244 (L.T.R. Mem. R. 15, m.5) there is this entry of a writ directed
to the keeper of the bishopric of Chester: 'Mandatum est eidem quod venire faciat
coram Baronibus . . . omnes archidiaconos episcopatus Cestrensis in ballia sua ad
respondendum Regi de portione archidiaconatuum suorum de qua solebant
respondere episcopo Cestrensi dum vixit.'

[6] *Pipe R. 3 John, 1201*, p. 173; *Pipe R. 4 John, 1202*, p. 278; *Pipe R. 9 John, 1207*,
p. 13.

I

pay them.[1] It seems doubtful whether the archdeacons ever did. Certainly the payments never appear on any future Pipe Roll accounts of the issues of Lincoln vacancies.

The church found it much more difficult to wrest from the crown the revenue from appropriated churches. When a church had been appropriated to the bishop's use, both temporal and spiritual guardians considered it rightfully theirs *sede vacante*. In the parliament of London in 1280 the clergy set forward among their grievances:

> Item vacantibus archiepiscopatibus, episcopatibus, abbathiis, prioratibus, illi qui per dominum regem ad eorum custodiam deputantur non solum temporalia sed eciam ecclesiastica beneficia appropriata eisdem cum omnibus decimis et oblacionibus occupant, cum hec ad personam laicam non valeant pertinere.[2]

The biggest single dispute in this matter was in connection with the see of Carlisle. This bishopric had such a sparse endowment of ordinary temporal revenue that the issues of its appropriated churches were much more important proportionately than in other sees. It would seem that in a Carlisle vacancy in 1223 some at least of these churches, those in the diocese of Coventry, were in the care of the archbishop of Canterbury.[3] However, on the Pipe Roll account for the vacancy of 1246 there is this provocative entry: 'Compotus debetur de ecclesiis appropriatis episcopatui.'[4] The bishop of Durham, it seems, believed that the fruits of those Carlisle churches that lay in the diocese of Durham belonged *sede vacante* to him.[5] The dispute dragged on

---

[1] Idem R. et J. (reddunt compotum) de redditibus archidiaconorum de tempore pasche. Sed de precepto Regis non debent summoneri quia non receperunt redditus illos sed remanent super archidiaconos qui inde debent respondere' (Pipe R. 78, m.16d; account of Ralph de Warvill and John de Burgh).

[2] *Reg. R. Winchelsey*, p. 1017.

[3] A writ of 7 Dec. 1223 addressed to the archbishop of Canterbury directs him to give seisin of the churches pertaining to the bishopric of Carlisle in the diocese of Coventry to the bishop-elect of Carlisle (*Rot. Litt. Claus., 1204–24*, p. 578a). It may be therefore that the churches which were within the diocese of Durham were in the custody of the archbishop of York, or more probably in that of the bishop of Durham, who certainly claimed them later. The see of Coventry and Lichfield was vacant in 1223 which may well explain why the writ quoted above was addressed to the metropolitan and not the bishop of Coventry.

[4] Pipe R. 97, m.9d.

[5] *Close R., 1242–47*, p. 510; 1 May 1247. The writ orders the safe keeping of the issues until an inquiry is made into the rights of the king and the bishop of Durham.

through two more Carlisle vacancies.[1] Eventually it was agreed that the bishop of Durham who was evidently the ecclesiastic who had most to lose in this matter should pay the king a fine of 1,000 marks for the issues of the appropriated churches during the previous two vacancies and for the confirmation of the right of himself and his successors to enjoy these issues in future vacancies of the see of Carlisle.[2]

However, even as late as the early fourteenth century, appropriated churches are found in the accounts for the temporalities of some vacant sees.[3] The churches of Waltham, Bexhill, Hooe and Ninfield paid pensions to the keeper of the temporalities of Chichester in 1305,[4] and in the Worcester vacancy of 1302 Humphrey de Walden accounted to the king for fourteen shillings and tenpence from the assized rent of the church of Hillingdon 'que annexa est Episcopatui Wigorniensi'.[5] A writ concerning this Worcester vacancy gives a glimpse of the struggle that was still being fought between church and crown over this kind of revenue. The king ordered the keeper of the spiritualities of Worcester to cease to implead the holder of the church of Berkeley for the pension of five marks which was payable from this church to the bishop *sede plena*. The king added that the five marks had been paid already—to the keeper of the temporalities.[6] No doubt, the prior of Worcester was very well aware of this; but by no means satisfied. At Winchester, as late as the end of Edward II's reign, the keepers accounted to the king for the revenues of the church of East Meon,[7] and it was

It seems however as though the king did in fact take the issues during this vacancy since there is an entry among the Memoranda for the Easter term, 1248, ordering the sheriff of Northumberland to pay into the exchequer £85.13.4 '. . . qui Regi a retro sunt de cc li. quas idem vicecomes recepit de sequestris ecclesiarum in Episcopatu Carliolensi dum fuit vacans . . .' (L.T.R. Mem. R. 20, m.9d).

[1] Those of 1254 and 1256–8. See *Close R., 1253–54*, pp. 59, 102–3, 415–6; *ibid., 1256–59*, pp. 105, 141, 285, 313; and cancelled entries: *ibid.*, pp. 460–1; 6 Nov. 1258, and p. 479; 20 May 1259.

[2] *Cal. Pat. R., 1258–66*, p. 86; 3 Aug. 1260. In the vacancy of 1278 the issues from these churches were duly paid to the bishop of Durham (*Cal. Close R., 1272–79*, p. 543; 2 Nov. 1279).

[3] It is always on a very much smaller scale than had been the case with the Carlisle churches. The latter were really valuable.

[4] Pipe R. 152B, m.8. These pensions were a long-standing item on the Chichester accounts. Compare the account for the vacancy of 1244–6 on Pipe R. 90, m.9.

[5] Pipe R. 147, m.25.   [6] *Reg. Wores. Sede Vacante*, p. 36.

[7] Pipe R. 161, m.22 and Pipe R. 169, m.43.

only by special concession that Edward III granted to Bishop John of Stratford in 1331 that the issues of the churches of East Meon and Hambledon should in future be reserved to the use of the priory *sede vacante*.[1] In short it was a stiff struggle, but a struggle in which the church was slowly winning its way. It is interesting to find that in 1324 the king ordered the keeper of the see of Hereford, which was in the king's hand, though not vacant, not to meddle further with a certain church in that see 'as it was not and is not the king's intention that the spiritualities of the bishopric, to wit, ecclesiastical benefices or other such spiritualities should be taken into his hands. . . '.[2]

One by one these various items which the church claimed as *spiritualia* were wrested from the crown as ecclesiastical opinion matured. The king, however, had no great cause for alarm, for even the narrowed interpretation of *temporalia* would have left the crown in control of the great bulk of episcopal property in almost every see *sede vacante*.[3]

The purely temporal wealth accruing to the king from episcopal vacancies may now be broken down into sections. Of the first of these, the rents and the profits of agriculture, little need be said here. They probably formed the largest single element in the wealth which was drawn from vacant sees,[4] but for the present purpose it is not an element which raises many problems. It would be of interest to know whether during a vacancy the king exploited this source of revenue more or less fully than the bishop *sede plena*. But in most cases, in the thirteenth century,

---

[1] *Chartulary of Winchester Cathedral*, ed. A. W. Goodman (Winchester, 1927), p. 181.

[2] *Cal. Close R., 1323–27*, p. 92.

[3] This seems pretty clear from the estimates given in the *Taxatio Ecclesiastica Angliae et Walliae Auctoritate P. Nicholai IV* (Record Commission 1802), pp. 295–6. See for example the preponderance of temporalities over spiritualities in the income of the bishops of Chichester, Bath and Wells, Coventry, Worcester, Hereford, Norwich. In some of the small Welsh sees, however, the spiritualities seem to have formed the more substantial part of the prelate's income, for example in the case of St. Asaph and Bangor.

[4] Mr. Miller makes an interesting analysis of the income from the temporalities of the bishopric of Ely based on the Pipe Roll accounts for the vacancies of 1256–1258 and 1298–9; *Abbey and Bishopric of Ely*, p. 94. For the period of 1256–7 Mr. Miller gives £80 as the estimated figure for 'issues of courts etc.' On the Pipe Roll the comprehensive sum given as receipts 'de placitis et perquisitis finibus terrarum et quibusdam parvis releviis' is £561.9.3 for the period 29 Oct. 1256 to 15 Jan. 1258 which would give a proportional yearly figure of about £460.

there is no material to make such a comparison. From the evidence that does exist it would seem that the issues which were customarily paid at a fixed rate *sede plena* continued at the same figure *sede vacante*. This, at any rate, is suggested by a comparison of the figures for assized rents at Canterbury during one year of the vacancy of 1270 to 1272 and during the year 1273–4 near the beginning of Archbishop Kilwardby's pontificate.[1] This is what one would expect. As far as agricultural profits were concerned one may surmise that the king would on the whole encourage a policy of quick returns, but how far this endangered the future prosperity of the see, it is perhaps impossible to estimate.[2] The complaint of the clergy was that the keepers did not cultivate or sow the soil sufficiently well, and that the incoming bishop was, nevertheless, compelled to pay for the harvest at a rate based on the assumption that the land had been well sown and cared for.[3]

The clergy complained much more frequently and more bitterly about certain other items in the royal exploitation of vacancies. These are listed in their *gravamina antiqua* submitted in the parliament of 1309:

[1] In some cases the figures for assized rent given on the roll of particulars for the year 1270–71 of the vacancy (P.R.O. Min. Acc. 1128/1) vary slightly with those on the Canterbury manorial account roll for 1273–4 (B.M. Additional MS. 29794). Boughton for example, pays £24.13.5½ in 1270–1 (m.1) and £35.0.4 in 1273–4 (m.8d). Usually however the figures are either identical or very close. Reculver pays £62.18.3½ (Min. Acc. 1128/1 m.1 and B.M. Addit. MS. 29794, m.3d), Burne £33.0.5½ (Min. Acc. 1128/1 m.1 and B.M. Addit. MS. 29794, m.6), Bexhill £16.18.2¼ (Min. Acc. 1128/1 m.1 and B.M. Addit. MS. 29794, m.7d) in each case. Westgate pays £26.10.4½ in 1270–1 (m.1) and £26.15.4½ in 1273–4 (m.3); Northfleet £38.8.2 in 1270–1 (m.1) and £38.17.2 in 1273–4 (m.7d).

[2] The king's determination to extract as good a return as possible from the land of a vacant see is seen in a writ addressed to the keepers of the bishopric of Winchester in 1238 'quod provideant qualiter dominice terre episcopatus Wintoniensis seminentur de alio blado quam de illo quod habent in maneriis ejusdem episcopatus, usque in xv dies a festo Sancti Michaelis anno xxij. ita quod caruce non jaceant et quod predicte terre non remaneant interim seminande; et alter eorum ad predictum terminum sit coram rege vel aliquem loco suo ad regem mittant ad ipsum certificandum utrum magis expediat regi quod terras predictas seminari faciat dominus rex de bladis in horreis predictorum maneriorum adunatis an de blado empto vel alio modo perquisito; . . .' (*Close R., 1237–42*, p. 105).

[3] 'Terras eciam arrabiles ecclesiarum ipsarum sic vacancium male coli ac seminari faciunt [i.e. the keepers] tam ad domini regis dispendium quam ad prelati futuri grave dampnum, qui pro fructibus terrarum ipsarum ac si bene culte et seminate forent certum precium solvere compellitur' (*Reg. R. Winchelsey*, p. 1018), in the *gravamina antiqua*.

Vacantibus ecclesiis cathedralibus vel collegiatis custodes per dominum regem deputati nemora ipsarum ac eciam parcos, vivaria et piscarias earundem destruunt tenentes eciam ecclesiarum ipsarum tallagiis et exaccionibus indebitis multipliciter gravant, domos et molendina et stagna, necnon libertates ecclesiarum ipsarum sic vacancium male custodiunt et defendunt.[1]

It is interesting to set this side by side with the two passages from the chronicle of St. Albans relating to the royal treatment of vacancies in the eleventh century.[2] William the Conqueror, it seems, on the death of Abbot Frederick in 1077 treated the vacant abbey of St. Albans very harshly 'extirpatis sylvis et depauperatis hominibus'.[3] Rufus was no better:

coenobium . . . immisericorditer depauperavit, nemora complanando, hominibus . . . pecuniam causis cavillatoriis adinventis extorquendo.[4]

The list in the *gravamina antiqua* of 1309 is more elaborate but the similarity to these earlier complaints is striking. What the clergy mainly complained of, both in the eleventh century and still in the fourteenth was the depreciation which the king's custodians caused in the capital wealth of the vacant see or abbey.[5] The royal defender did not confine himself to taking the fruits of the see, to which presumably he had some equitable right even in the eyes of the church,[6] but he actually reduced

[1] *Ibid.*, p. 1018. See also the complaints made by the Barons in 1264; P. Walne, 'The Barons' Argument at Amiens', *Eng. Hist. Review*, lxxiii (1958), pp. 455–6.

[2] Above, pp. 8–9, and p. 12.

[3] *Gesta Abbatum Mon. S. Albani*, i, 51.

[4] *Ibid.*, p. 65. This passage refers to the vacancy of 1093–7.

[5] In the Constitutions of Archbishop Boniface the same charges are brought: 'ballivi tamen regis vel magnates tutelam sive custodiam exercentes, praeter tallagia immoderata, quae imponunt hominibus et tenentibus ecclesiarum vacantium minus juste, bona mobilia et immobilia plerumque hominum et tenentium praedictorum sic vacantis ecclesiae, in tali custodia, seu cruciatu potius constitutae, consumunt prodigaliter, ac dirimunt violenter parcos, nemora, et vivaria destruentes, et domos habitationes, et grangias, caeteraque aedificia, quae sustineri deberent in bono statu, ex negligentia, vel malitia quandoque dissipari, et ruere permittentes' (Wilkins, *Concilia*, i, 752).

[6] This seems to be the principle underlying the defence of Pope Boniface VIII's articles on this matter, which is found in Bishop John de Pontissaria's register: 'Item quod guardia et custodia ecclesiarum Cathedralium quas vacant regalia per abusum non abutatur nec vacacionis tempore extendantur manus ad cedendas silvas non ceduas, vel ad vacuanda seu destruenda vinaria (*rectius* vivaria) et alia illicita ecclesiis ipsis dampnosa. Quodque habitaciones, domus et maneria non

the permanent value of the bishopric by denuding forests and emptying fishponds, allowing buildings to fall into disrepair and impoverishing the tenants of the see.

Through the complaints of the clergy we may conveniently distinguish two kinds of wealth which the king enjoyed from vacancies and which in the opinion of the church were taken by the king at the expense of serious depreciation in the value of the episcopal property. In the first place there were the 'undue exactions and tallages' which the king extorted from the tenants, and in the second place there was the plunder of the property itself, the timber and the stock.

In considering the complaint made about the extortions from the tenants we may retain the order in the *gravamina* and deal first with 'undue exactions' and then with 'tallages'. Undue exactions is a rather unspecific term, but it seems likely that it relates in part at least to unjust extortions of the kind that Richard de Clifford and his bailiffs made in the vacant archbishopric of Canterbury in 1270–2.[1] According to the complaints in the Hundred Rolls the fines levied by Clifford on the tenants were not always accounted for at the exchequer. This, therefore, was a question of peculation by the keepers and not of deliberate spoliation by the king, and it may well be that it was unrecorded exactions by the keepers which the clergy had mainly in mind when they spoke of 'indebitis exaccionibus'.[2] However the misdeeds of keepers is a matter already dealt with.[3] What is of immediate interest here is the question whether the crown deliberately encouraged a policy of extortion in its own financial interest. If it did, then that policy might be expected to show some reflection in the accounts rendered by the keepers at the

---

depereant, set in statu congruo conserventur, et massarie ovium et aliorum animalium debito teneantur in statu et, deductis expensis oportunis necessariis et moderatis ad custodiam seu guardiam et perceptionem proventuum, quod residuum fuerit reservetur futuris prelatis fideliter resignandum . . .' (*Reg. J. Pontissaria*, II, 548).

The distinction seems to be between the 'necessary and moderate expenses' to which the king has a right (and which perhaps in practice the clergy would have extended to include all actual *revenue*) and inroads on episcopal capital.

[1] See above, pp. 106–7.

[2] The fact that the whole of the complaint quoted above, p. 118, is an attack on the misdeeds of keepers does not *in itself* prove that the clergy did not consider the king responsible for the policy which his servants executed.

[3] Above, pp. 104–9.

exchequer. In this particular case the relevant item in the accounts would be the entry 'de placitis et perquisitis'. If pleas and perquisites were levied at a peculiarly heavy rate during a vacancy it would seem to imply deliberate impoverishment of the tenants and thereby lasting damage to one source of episcopal wealth. A comparison of the Canterbury vacancy accounts of Richard de Clifford for the year 1270-1,[1] with the accounts for the first year of Kilwardby's pontificate 1273-4,[2] suggests that the *official* rate of the levy of pleas and perquisites in this particular case was heavier *sede vacante* than it was *sede plena*—but not dramatically heavier. Over a group of nineteen manors in which comparison is possible, Clifford accounted in one year for £159.17.6½ in pleas and perquisites, whereas the reeves and bailiffs of Kilwardby accounted for only £116.13.1, an increase *sede vacante* of 37 per cent approximately.[3] Furthermore, out of a total amount of £3,514.14.2 accounted by Clifford in the Pipe Roll for 1270-1, £365.4.8 comes under the heading, 'fines, pleas and perquisites, heriots and small reliefs', making a proportion of just over 10 per cent of the total issues.[4] That proportion is a fairly usual one over the whole range of thirteenth-century vacancy accounts. For Canterbury in 1228-9 the proportion was between twelve and thirteen per cent.[5] At Salisbury, 1291, it was a little under eleven per cent.[6] There are a few cases where the proportion was considerably higher. In the 1247 vacancy account for St. David's, for instance, this item forms over fifty per cent of the total receipts,[7] and over forty-six per cent in the account for the Norwich vacancy of 1257.[8] However, there is no need to

[1] P.R.O. Min. Acc. 1128/1.

[2] B.M. Additional MS. 29794.

[3] These figures do not include any payments of a similar nature to pleas and perquisites (such as reliefs) which are separately classed in these detailed accounts.

[4] Pipe R. 119, m.21d. The various items enumerated in this comprehensive entry of £365.4.8 suggest the possible pitfalls in dealing with these figures. Some accountants may include much more under the heading 'perquisites' than others. Heriots, *small* reliefs and fines which are in this case specifically mentioned may elsewhere be covered by the simple term 'perquisites'.

[5] £151.6.6 out of a total gross receipt (minus tallage) of £1,171.6.9½ (Pipe R. 73, m.1).

[6] £79.10.11 out of a total receipt of £740.8.3¾ (Pipe R. 137, m.26d).

[7] £38.14.9½ out of total receipt of £66.12.10 (Chancellor's R. 45, m.20d),

[8] £112.14.2 out of total receipt of £242.3.3½ (Pipe R. 101, m.4).

infer wild extortion whenever the figures seem high. In the case
of St. David's in 1247 the account seems a very condensed one
and more than usual may have been classed under the somewhat elastic heading of pleas and perquisites.[1] The Norwich
figure on the other hand invites some suspicion. £112.14.2 is
a large sum to have extracted from the profits of justice in
twelve weeks, especially in view of the much more moderate
rate implied by the sum of £42.5.4 which was received from
pleas and perquisites in the two months of the vacancy of
1278.[2] However, the figures for St. David's in 1247 and for
Norwich in 1257 are exceptional. In most vacancies the proportion of pleas and perquisites to total gross receipts was between five and twenty per cent.[3] The inference seems to be that
although there are occasional instances of what seem to be very
high figures, and although there may well have been some illicit extortion, especially in judicial exactions, on the part of
some of the keepers, nevertheless as far as the *official* accounts
go they do not serve to reconstruct a picture of general or widespread oppression countenanced by the exchequer.

In the *gravamina antiqua* of 1309 the 'undue exactions' are
very closely associated with the levy of tallages *sede vacante*.
In fact the word 'indebitis' itself in the phrase 'tallagiis et exaccionibus indebitis' may perhaps qualify both substantives. In
any case, the sense is clear. By virtue of their inclusion of
the levy of tallages among the *gravamina*, the clergy evidently
considered the tallages levied by the king on the tenants of the
vacant see as in some way 'undue'. Unfortunately, it is difficult
to go further than this and determine whether the clergy objected to the levy of tallages during vacancies in itself, or
whether they were protesting rather against the unduly heavy

---

[1] There are no expenses mentioned in the account at all and the keeper pays
all the issues plus sixpence into the wardrobe.

[2] Chancellor's R. 74, m.2.

[3] It was less than 5% at Hereford in 1268–9; £9.13.4 of total of £243.19.2½ (Pipe
R. 119, m.21); between 6% and 7% at York 1285–6; £125.12.7½ of total of
£1,860.7.0¾ (Pipe R. 133, m.28); between 8% and 9% at Lincoln, 1258; £22.15.2
of total of £284.14.10½ (Pipe R. 104, m.2); between 10% and 11% at Durham,
1239–40; £451.7.8 of total of £4,366.18.5 (Pipe R. 84, m.2); between 13% and
14% at York 1279; £183.18.4½ of total of £1,357.2.7½ (Chancellor's R. 74, m.7);
and between 16% and 17% at Bath 1242–4; £183.3.3 of total of £1,120.0.8½ (Pipe
R. 91, m.14d). The last figures however include the farms of two private hundreds.

amounts of tallage.[1] In either case the king's tallaging of a vacant see constituted a grievance in the thirteenth century, and since this was the century that saw royal tallage both at its peak and in its dramatically sudden decline,[2] the tallage of vacant sees, as a particular aspect of royal tallage, deserves consideration.

First, by way of recapitulation. Tallage was levied on vacant sees in the reign of Henry II, and as far as the inadequate evidence goes in that of Richard I too, concurrently with the levy of tallage on the royal demesne and the boroughs. Normally it was only when an episcopal vacancy happened to coincide with the levy of a general tallage, that tallage would be demanded from a vacant see. John's reign saw a sharp change. After a period of practically annual levies of tallages on the royal demesne, John reverted to the practice of occasional but heavy tallages as being more profitable. But this intelligent financier saw no reason, it would seem, to forgo any chance of taxing vacant sees. And every vacant bishopric paid John a tallage at least once during each vacancy. Moreover, in his fairly short reign John levied some unprecedentedly heavy tallages: that at Canterbury in 1206 and that at Durham in 1208–9, each being over £1,000.[3]

This was the heritage of Henry III, and he apparently valued it. During the whole of his fairly long reign tallage was levied on a vacant bishopric, with very occasional exceptions, once during each vacancy.[4] It was never levied twice during the same vacancy however, as had sometimes been the case in his father's

---

[1] In Boniface's Constitutions the complaint was against 'tallagia immoderata' (Wilkins, *Concilia* I, 752). Perhaps this suggests on the whole that it was the amount of the tallage rather than the levy of tallage in itself that roused indignation. See also the complaint in the Council of Merton 1258; '[Rex] pauperes tenentes importabilibus gravat tallagiis' (*Annales de Burton*, in *Annales Monastici* I, ed. H. R. Luard (Rolls Series, London, 1857), p. 423).

[2] Mitchell, *Taxation in Medieval England*, p. 237, and *Studies in Taxation*, p. 14.

[3] See above, p. 49.

[4] The only vacancy accounts on the Pipe Rolls which have no entry for tallage (or its obvious equivalent, a 'common aid' or 'recognitions') during the whole period 1216–1327 are those for short parts of the Norwich vacancy of 1214–22 (Pipe R. 63, m.4d) and of the Ely vacancy of 1215–20 (Foreign R. 1, m.3d); and the accounts for Hereford in 1234 (Pipe R. 80, m.2d), for London in 1241–4 (Pipe R. 87, m.3), for Lichfield in 1241–2 (Pipe R. 95, m.6d), for Carlisle in 1246 (Pipe R. 97, m.9d), for St. David's in 1247 and 1280 (Chancellor's R. 45, m.20d and Pipe R. 124, m.24, respectively) and for Winchester in 1260–2 (Pipe R. 106, m.21 and 21d)). All these vacancies except those at St. David's in 1247 and 1280 cover a year or part of a year when a general royal tallage was levied. It *may* possibly

reign.[1] In fact, the tallage of vacant bishoprics had now become largely distinct from the general tallages of the royal demesne. The right to levy a single tallage on a vacant bishopric emerged in Henry III's reign as a right incidental to the king's temporarily immediate lordship over the see. The king himself made it clear that he regarded his right in this light. He frequently tallaged vacant bishoprics in years in which there was no general tallage.[2] In October 1244 the see of Exeter fell vacant and in January 1245 a writ was issued to the keeper of the vacant see of which we have the following enrolment:

Mandatum est custodi episcopatus Exoniensis quod pro consuetudine tenenda de tallagio assidendo super homines episcopatuum vacancium in Anglia assideri faciat racionabile tallagium super homines Episcopatus Exoniensis in manu regis existentis. Ita quod predicti homines non sentiant se inde gravatos.[3]

be therefore that a tallage was levied in some of these instances on the vacant see, but accounted for among the accounts for the general tallage. In the London vacancy of 1241–4 the exchequer's instructions to the keeper Ralph Dayrell do seem to envisage the possible levy of a tallage since Dayrell is told to produce particulars of the tallage 'si fuerit assisum' (L.T.R. Mem. R. 15, m.5). For a list of general tallages levied during Henry III's reign see Mitchell, *Taxation in Medieval England*, p. 330 and in the index to the same writer's *Studies in Taxation*, p. 406. The two lists are not identical.

[1] The vacant see of Durham paid tallage twice to John during the period 1208–12 (see above, p. 54). The vacant abbey of Ramsey paid tallage in 1210 (*Pipe R. 12 John*, p. 214) in 1211 (*Pipe R. 13 John*, p. 270) and again in 1212 (Pipe R. 58, m.1d). Peterborough paid it in 1210 (*Pipe R. 12 John*, p. 215) and in 1211 (*Pipe R. 13 John*, p. 271), and when for the following year the prior fined with the king to have the custody of the vacant abbey the prior was to be allowed to take an aid from the free tenants, except the knights 'pro habendo auxilio de libere tenentibus suis exceptis militibus . . .' (*ibid.*, p. 65).

[2] For example in December 1228 Henry III ordered tallages to be levied in the bishoprics of Canterbury, London and Salisbury (and in Feb. 1229 of Ely also) (Fine R. 28, m. 11; 25 Dec. 1228). There was no general levy of tallage at the time. The last had been taken in 1226–7 (Mitchell, *Studies in Taxation*, p. 172) and the next was taken in 1230 (*ibid.*, p. 190).

[3] Fine R. 42, m.14; 20 Jan. 1245. There are also two references to the granting of an *aid* as being customary during a vacancy. These may be taken as corroborative evidence in view of the connection between aids and tallages *sede vacante* (see below, pp. 130–5). The tenants of York in 1255 were requested to make the king a competent aid 'as the custom has been in the times of the king's progenitors for the tenants of archbishoprics and bishoprics to do' (*Cal. Pat. R.*, 1247–58, p. 412), and in 1238 the tenants of the bishopric of Winchester are informed that 'Whereas the king may rightly, according to the custom observed hitherto in void cathedral churches, assess a reasonable aid upon the lands belonging to such churches he wills that upon the lands of the void bishopric of Winchester a moderate (*mersurabile*) aid be assessed . . .' (*ibid.*, 1232–47, p. 225).

The words 'pro consuetudine tenenda' are significant. Not only did the king regard as customary his right to tallage a vacant see just because it was vacant, it was a right which must not be allowed to lapse through disuse.

The clergy considered that Henry III's tallages were unduly heavy. There is no denying that they were substantial. In the vacancy of 1228–9, the archbishopric of Canterbury paid 1,000 marks.[1] The aid and tallage together at Durham in 1226-8 amounted to nearly £800.[2] Winchester paid over £500 in 1250–1[3] and York over £660 in 1255–6.[4] Although there are no figures quite as high as the sums extorted from Canterbury and Durham in vacancies of John's reign, Henry III's tallages were not light. Moreover they varied considerably in amount from one vacancy to another. Although Canterbury paid 1,000 marks in the vacancy of 1228–9, in the next vacancy the tallage of this see only amounted to £333.7.2.[5] Perhaps the king had been advised to refrain from too harsh an exaction in this particular case, for the writ of 1231 by which the levy of this tallage was ordered, was worded mildly. The keeper was instructed to assess the tallage moderately:

non habito respectu ad magnam summam tallagii alias assisi in archiepiscopatu Cantuariensi . . .[6]

Similarly Ely was tallaged at £450.15.10 in the vacancy o1 1228–9,[7] but the figure dropped to £189.0.2 in the vacancy of 1254.[8] On the other hand the tallage of Salisbury at £50.9.4 in 1246–7[9] and at £79.6.8 in 1271[10] shows an upward trend in the course of the reign. On the whole, however, there is a tendency to achieve equilibrium in the latter part of Henry III's reign. Thus at Salisbury the figures for 'recognitions and tallage'[11] in

---

[1] Pipe R. 73, m.1.   [2] *Ibid.*

[3] Pipe R. 95, m.6.   [4] Pipe R. 101, m.4d.

[5] Pipe R. 76, m.5d. This includes the tallages of Harrow and Hayes which are accounted for separately.

[6] *Close R., 1227–31,* p. 574. The tallage in the vacancy of this see in 1270–2 amounted to £294.19.0.

[7] Pipe R. 72, m.10d.   [8] Pipe R. 101, m.4.   [9] Pipe R. 92, m.16.

[10] Pipe R. 116, m.2d. This is the figure given for the tallage of villeins only, without the 'recognitions' paid by the freemen. Compare p. 125, n. 3, below.

[11] The 'recognitions' and 'tallage' paid in these Salisbury vacancies are simply parts of a single levy. The distinction is in the status of the men who paid. The relation between recognitions and tallage in general is considered below, pp. 136–41.

the vacancies of 1256, 1262–3 and 1271 were £104.18.2,[1] £96.5.10[2] and £95.4.8 respectively.[3] This tendency towards a steadier level of payment becomes even clearer in the reigns of Edward I and Edward II. Canterbury paid £254.3. 4 in tallage in the vacancy of 1278–9,[4] and £259.4.1½ in 'recognitions' in that of 1292–5.[5] Ely paid £245.10.0 in the vacancy of 1286,[6] £248.12.3¾ in 1290,[7] £258.11.1¼ in 1298–9,[8] £253.0.0½ in 1302–3,[9] £250.10.0½ in 1310[10] and £245.10.0½ in 1316.[11] The figures for tallages and later for recognitions at Winchester maintained a marked equilibrium from as early as 1238, always keeping within the range of £551.7.3½[12] to £487.16.10,[13] and in the last two vacancies of Edward II's reign the payment from Winchester recognitions was exactly £501.4.2 on each occasion.[14] To sum up: during Henry III's reign there was greater variation in the sums paid in tallage than during the two subsequent reigns, and speaking generally, tallage was being paid at a rather lower level at the end of Henry III's reign than it was at the beginning. It may be noted in passing that the tendency to much steadier figures in the reigns of Edward I and Edward II roughly coincides with the increasing use of the term 'recognitions' and the gradual disappearance of the term tallage which was taking place in the reign of Edward I and which will be considered more fully later.

[1] Pipe R. 100, m.19.   [2] Pipe R. 112, m.1d.

[3] Pipe R. 116, m.2d. This figure includes the £15.18.0 paid in recognitions by the freemen as well as the £79.6.8 referred to on p. 124, n. 10, above.

[4] Pipe R. 124, m.23d.

[5] Pipe R. 141, m.28d. In this and the following examples in this paragraph 'recognitions' may be understood as interchangeable with 'tallage' for the present purpose.

[6] Pipe R. 144, m.34 and 34d. The entries are given manor by manor.

[7] Pipe R. 135, m.1.

[8] Pipe R. 144, m.29. The entries are given bailiwick by bailiwick.

[9] Pipe R. 150, m.34 and 34d.

[10] Pipe R. 155B, m.6.

[11] Pipe R. 162, m.36. The payment is said to be less this time 'propter pauperitatem quorundam custumariorum apud Walpol, Walton et Hatfeld . . .'

[12] This was the figure of the tallage in the 1238–44 vacancy; it includes the tallage of the manors of Taunton and Rimpton (£150.3.4) in addition to the sum of £401.3.11½ from the rest of the bishopric (Pipe R. 85, m.3).

[13] The figure for 'aids and recognitions' in the vacancy of 1268 (Chancellor's R. 61, m.27d).

[14] Pipe R. 165, m.29d (for the vacancy account of 2 Nov. 1319 to 17 Apr. 1320) and Pipe R. 169, m.43 (for the vacancy account of 13 Apr. 1323 to 30 Sep. 1323).

Some of the figures which have been mentioned were round sums, others were not. This is of interest because a figure which is not a round sum may indicate an assessment of individuals *per capita*, instead of a levy of a round sum *in commune*. In the general history of royal tallage, assessments *per capita* were, it seems, very unusual between 1227 and 1252, although in the latter year the method of individual assessment was revived in an attempt to make tallage more lucrative for the crown.[1] The assessment of tallage in vacant sees does not seem to follow such neat lines. There seems to be considerable diversity of procedure throughout the reign of Henry III. Very occasionally the whole bishopric was tallaged at a round sum. The Canterbury payment of 1,000 marks has already been mentioned[2] and this is a striking example of a levy *in commune* on the bishopric as a whole. The payment of £93.0.0 by London in 1228–9[3] and of £64.0.0 by Norwich in 1257[4] might possibly be further examples of the treatment of the whole bishopric as a single unit of assessment. No other bishopric during Henry III's reign paid a round number of pounds or marks, and the instances of London and Norwich may well have been accidental. Nor was there any noticeable movement towards round figures in the two succeeding reigns.[5]

Where the total payment of the tallage levied on a vacant bishopric is clearly not a round sum, there remain two possibilities. Either the individual tenants were assessed *per capita* or else the manors within the bishopric were assessed as units. Both methods seem in fact to have been employed. A sum such as £51.11.0½ which was levied on the see of Worcester in 1236,[6] or the sum of £352.17.5 levied on Lincoln in 1253–4,[7] seems to indicate an assessment which *originally* at least was levied on the individual and not on the manor. The qualification 'originally' is necessary because a complex amount, received from a manor, which presumably originated in an assessment on individual tenants, might develop in course of time into a fixed customary payment from the manor as a whole. This may have been what

---

[1] Mitchell, *Taxation in Medieval England*, p. 340.
[2] Above, p. 124.
[3] Pipe R. 72, m.10d.
[4] Pipe R. 101, m.4. This levy was called an 'aid'.
[5] See Appendix A for Edward I's tallages.
[6] Pipe R. 81, m.15d.
[7] Pipe R. 101, m. 4.

happened in some Winchester manors: in successive vacancies
the same amount was levied in 'recognitions' on an individual
manor although that amount was not a round sum.[1] But perhaps, more frequently, each manor or even each bailiwick was
assessed at a round sum. Thus at Ely in the vacancy of 1302–3 all
the manors paid round sums,[2] and most did at Worcester in
that of 1302–3.[3] In the case of Lincoln in 1299 wherever the
sums for recognitions are given separately on the Pipe Roll
account they are in round figures for each bailiwick,[4] and in the
Canterbury account for 1292–5 the totals for the recognitions
in each bailiwick are evidently based on round figures except
in the case of South Malling.[5] Evidently there was no uniformity in this matter, but perhaps the most usual unit of
assessment was the manor.

From the actual sums which the vacant sees paid in tallage
it is difficult, as so often when attempting to consider medieval
statistics from the standpoint of absolute value, to determine
whether they were unduly heavy or not. Certainly a swift
succession of vacancies as in the case of Ely in the three decades
from 1286 to 1316,[6] might bear hard on an individual see, but
it seems doubtful whether in the ordinary course of events
these levies were more than the see could reasonably sustain.
The sums which Peter des Roches levied on the manors of his
bishopric of Winchester, *sede plena* in the early thirteenth century seem to be comparable in amount to those levied later in
the century during vacancies of the see.[7] Moreover, as in the

---

[1] Thus Ecchinswell paid the king £4.19.7 in recognitions in the vacancy of 1268
(Eccles 2/15928, m.6) and the same in that of 1280 (Min. Acc. 1142/1) and
also in 1323 (Min. Acc. 1142/4); the manor of East Meon paid £22.4.5½ in the
vacancies of 1268 and 1304 (Eccles 2/159298, m.12d and Min. Acc. 1142/5,
respectively). Bitterne paid £4 in the vacancy of 1268 (Eccles 2/159298, m.10) and
again in that of 1304 (Min. Acc. 1142/15) and again in that of 1323 (Min. Acc.
1141/12).

[2] Pipe R. 150, m.34 and 34d. The total figure of £253.0.0½ is due to the inclusion
of the payment of £6.11.0½ from the freemen of Wisbech. The payments from the
freemen of Ely and Witchford and those from the customaries of the various vills
are in each case in round figures.

[3] Pipe R. 147, mm.24 and 25.

[4] Pipe R. 150, m.36 and 36d.

[5] The figure for South Malling was £34.7.5½ (Pipe R. 141, m.28d).

[6] Ely fell vacant in 1286, in 1290, in 1298, in 1302, in 1310 and again in 1316.

[7] *Pipe Roll of the Bishopric of Winchester*, 1208–9, ed. H. Hall (London, 1903).

case of the levy of tallage generally the king was not deaf to complaints of incapacity to pay the amount originally assessed on the vacant see. In 1229 the tenants of Somersham in the bishopric of Ely complained that they were burdened beyond measure by the tallage assessed on them. The keepers were ordered to adjust their assessment so that these men should not have cause to complain of an unjust and intolerable charge.[1] The tallage on the see of Lincoln in 1235 was to be assessed reasonably 'in such a way that men should not feel themselves unduly burdened by it',[2] and we have already seen that at Ely in 1316 there was a slight modification in the amount of recognitions paid because of the poverty of some of the tenants.[3]

In the case of boroughs within the bishopric, the bargaining as to the amount of tallage to be paid might be referred to the central government and not settled by the keepers. In the York vacancy of 1255–6 the burgesses of Beverley offered the king 200 marks in tallage and the king accepted the offer 'if they would add two marks of gold as well'.[4] In 1236–7 the burgesses of King's Lynn fined with the king for £100 for their tallage,[5] and it was paid into the wardrobe, separately from the rest of the issues;[6] nor did the keepers of the bishopric account for it. However, to bargain as to the amount of tallage to be given was one thing, to attempt to evade it altogether was quite another matter. The burgesses of Durham tried to do this in the vacancy of 1311. In June 1312 the king allowed them respite until the matter had been investigated.[7] In May 1313 he orders the immediate levy of the tallage.[8]

---

[1] *Close R., 1227–31*, p. 171.

[2] *Ibid., 1234–37*, p. 53. The note of warranty of this writ: 'per J. Bathoniensem episcopum' is perhaps significant. Bishop Jocelin was superior keeper of Lincoln in this vacancy which followed the death of his brother Hugh of Wells and the writ may show his restraining influence with the king.

[3] See above, p. 125, n. 11.

[4] *Close R., 1254–56*, p. 98.

[5] Pipe R. 81, m.13. Here it is described as an 'aid' but on the wardrobe account it is called a 'tallage' (*ibid.*).

[6] 'c li. de taillagio Burgensium episcopi de Len eo quod episcopatus fuit in manu Regis'; *ibid.*; Brother Geoffrey's account for the receipts of the wardrobe, 1236–7.

[7] *The Register of Richard de Kellawe Lord Palatine and Bishop of Durham, 1314–1316*, ed. T. D. Hardy (Rolls Series, London, 1874), II, 863–4. There is a further respite granted 3 Apr. 1312 (*ibid.*, pp. 920–1).

[8] *Ibid.*, pp. 934–5.

In short tallage was levied on a vacant see at the king's will and normally there could be no refusal,[1] but its assessment as in the case of general royal tallage was not necessarily completely arbitrary. Bargaining was sometimes allowed and there seems to have been some regard for capacity to pay. The real difficulty of determining whether an individual levy of tallage was unduly heavy or not is neatly illustrated in the records of an inquiry which was made by the archbishop of York into the levy of a tallage on the vacant bishopric of Durham in 1226.[2] Witnesses were called upon to state on oath whether the tallage had been *ultra modum*. On the whole, witnesses called to give evidence on behalf of the monks were inclined, as one would expect, to think that the tallage was too heavy.[3] Walter de Melsanby, for instance, said, 'quod homines ultra modum gravantur ut creditur'. Thomas Anglicus claimed that he knew well that the men of the bishopric gave the tallage unwillingly,[4] and William of Weardale was of the same opinion. But the king's witnesses took a different view. Peter de Bedington, asked whether the freemen and 'rustics' gave the tallage willingly or unwillingly, replied that the freemen gave willingly but the rustics unwillingly, 'quia semper consueverunt inviti dare'. No doubt there was much in this! The chaplain of Howden was sure that the rustics had been tallaged 'satis moderate'.

At one moment the court seems on the verge of making William of Weardale, one of the monks' witnesses, commit himself to definite figures. He was quite sure that the tallage was too heavy, and he was apparently asked to say by how much it was too heavy. 'Sed quantus fuerat excessus ignorat.' It is

[1] The only instance I have found of the total remission of a tallage on a vacant see is in the London vacancy of 1259. The writ is interesting:

'Quia rex non vult quod tenentes episcopatuum et abbaciarum vacantium et in manu regis existentium extra debita et consueta anni tempora et terminos consuetos quos [sic] talliari consueverunt, ad presens tallientur, mandatum est Ade de Greynvil, custodi episcopatus Londoniensis quod tallagium, quod nuper extra tempus debitum et consuetum ut dicitur assideri fecit super tenentes episcopatus predicti eis de gracia regis remittat' (*Close R., 1256–59*, p. 410; 29 June 1259). It seems possible that this concession was really baronial and not royal in inspiration.

[2] Durham MS. 5520.

[3] The whole document turns on the various points at dispute between the monks of Durham cathedral priory and the royal custodians of the bishopric.

[4] 'Set bene scit quod homines episcopatus inviti dant tallagium domino regi' (*ibid.*).

K

disappointing that William did not know, but even the most seemingly inconclusive evidence recorded in these documents is far from valueless. It is perhaps impossible to decide now as between king's witnesses and monks' witnesses but the very restraint of the remarks on both sides perhaps indicates that even if the king had been rather harsh, this levy had not been ruinous. Moreover, the figure of this Durham tallage was fairly typical of the amount levied on other sees of roughly comparable wealth,[1] so that the inferences suggested by the evidence of these Durham rolls may, with reasonable caution, be applied more widely.

But the interest of the levy of tallages *sede vacante* is not merely a matter of their size and frequency. In speaking of tallage it is essential to know what kind of tallage is meant. In its origin, of course, the tallage of vacant sees was royal tallage as distinct from seignorial tallage,[2] and it retained many of the characteristics of royal tallage even when its levy had ceased to be coincident with the levy of general royal tallage on the demesne and boroughs. In particular it retained some of the characteristics of an 'aid'. Not infrequently it was called an aid, as for instance in the accounts on the Pipe Rolls for the vacancies at Durham in 1237–41[3] and in 1249,[4] at London in 1262–3[5] and at Worcester in 1236 and in 1266.[6] Professor Carl Stephenson has spoken of the 'official identification' and 'unofficial differentiation' of the terms 'aid' and 'tallage' for the levies made by the Angevin kings on the royal boroughs.[7] Certainly the government frequently used the two different terms as applied to a single levy on a vacant see in the thirteenth century. The tallage

---

[1] See tallage figures in the tables in Appendix A.

[2] Professor Mitchell carefully distinguishes 'ordinary' tallage which was an annual levy paid to a lord from his demesne, payable at a certain date in the year, fixed in amount 'and so commonly limited to villeins that its payment became one of the tests of villeinage'; and on the other hand 'the tallage levied by the king on his demesne, from time to time, paid by freemen usually but occasionally by villeins, and based on bargaining between royal commissioners and the men of the area' (*Taxation in Medieval England*, pp. 236–7). Professor Hoyt makes a similar distinction although he does not describe seignorial tallage as an annual levy but rather as a levy taken by the lord at will (*The Royal Demesne*, p. 108).

[3] Pipe R. 84, m.2   [4] Pipe R. 94, m.18.   [5] Pipe R. 108, m.15.

[6] Pipe R. 81, m.15d and Pipe R. 110, m.13 respectively.

[7] C. Stephenson, 'The Aids of the English Boroughs', *Eng. Hist. Review*, xxxiv (1919), pp. 473–4.

of £100, paid by the men of King's Lynn into the wardrobe in
the Norwich vacancy of 1236–9 is entered 'de tallagio' in the
wardrobe account of 1236–7,[1] but the same levy is referred to as
an aid in an entry on the Patent Rolls,[2] and also on the Pipe
Roll account for this vacancy.[3] In both 1237 and 1249 the writs
ordering the assessment of a tallage in the vacant see of Durham
use the word 'tallagium',[4] yet the corresponding entry in the
vacancy account in the Pipe Roll is in each case 'de communi
auxilio'.[5]

These variations, however, are all intelligible, if it is understood that royal tallage was one kind of aid. An aid could not
always be called a tallage, but a tallage, especially a royal
tallage, might always be called an aid.[6] It seems clear that this
convention extended beyond government practice, and therefore beyond what may be called 'official identification' in the
sense intended by Mr. Stephenson. In the course of the proceedings before the archbishop of York's court, already referred to, concerning the affairs of the Durham vacancy of
1226–8, the questioner or questioners of the king's witness,
Peter de Bedington, seem to have used the words tallage and aid
quite interchangeably for the levy that the king had made on
those who held by unfree tenure:[7]

Petrus de Bedington . . . Requisitus de causa tallagiorum per
episcopatum factorum per regem dicit quod causa assignata est in
litteris domini regis lectis coram examinatoribus. Requisitus utrum
moderatum auxilium exigatur per ballivos domini regis in maneriis
episcopatus dicit quod in Hovedenescir positum est satis moderatum
auxilium et credit quod idem faciant ballivi domini regis in allis
maneriis episcopatus.

Another witness, Richard, the chaplain of Durham castle, also
used the two terms without distinction when he spoke of this

---

[1] The entry is quoted above, p. 128, n. 6.
[2] *Cal. Pat. R., 1232–47*, p. 173.
[3] Pipe R. 81, m.13.
[4] *Cal. Pat. R., 1232–47*, p. 185, and Fine R. 46, m.9 (10 Apr. 1249) respectively.
[5] Pipe R. 84, m.2. and Pipe R. 94, m.18.
[6] In the vacancy account for the bishopric of Exeter in 1211 even the annual
customary levy from the manors as distinct from the special vacancy levy which
the king made, was called an *auxilium* (*Pipe R. 13 John, 1211*, p. 272).
[7] Durham MS. 5520.

levy made on all those below the rank of freeholders.[1] This apparently indifferent use of the words is all the more significant because at some points in the inquiry it had been necessary to make a very careful distinction between this tallage levied on rutiscs and another levy made on the knights and freeholders of the bishopric and never called anything but an *auxilium*.[2] Yet even so it was possible for cross-questioners and witnesses to refer to the tallage on the rustics, by the names *tallagium* and *auxilium* within a single sentence. This seems less surprising in view of the witnesses' incidental explanation of how the keepers set about levying the tallage. They said that the reason for this levy was stated in letters which were read in the presence of examiners,[3] and it was then arranged between the men of the bishopric and Stephen de Lucy that they should give the king an aid,[4] (that is a tallage). It is no doubt true that the rustics of Durham could not well refuse to pay a tallage to the king, but the king's approach does not seem to have been wholly arbitrary. He at least explained the reasons for making the levy.

Perhaps the most revealing example of 'official identification' of *tallagium* and *auxilium* appears in a writ addressed to the keepers of the vacant see of Ely in 1229 concerning the complaint of the men of Somersham about the heavy tallage which had been levied on them.[5]

Venientes ad nos homines de Sumeresham graviter conquerendo robis monstraverunt quod ultra modum graviti sunt per tallagium quod nuper assisum erat super eos, licet vobis injunximus, si bene recolitis, quod auxilium moderatum et tolerabile ab eis et aliis hominibus episcopatus Elyensis caperetis, ita quod inde non gravarentur ultra modum . . .[6]

This is a clear instance of the interchangeable use of 'tallage'

[1] 'Ricardus capellanus de castro Dunelm' juratus dicit quod nescit utrum tallagia imposita hominibus episcopatus Dunelm' sponte data fuerunt vel non quia animos eorum non novit set bene scit quod ita convenit inter ipsos et magistrum Stephanum [i.e. Stephen de Lucy, the royal custodian] quod auxilium darent domino regi.'

[2] Whereas the levy on the 'drengs, thanes and villeins' is referred to in the Pipe Roll account as a tallage, the levy on the knights and freeholders is styled an aid (Pipe R. 73, m.1).

[3] See Peter de Bedington's statement, above, p. 131.   [4] See above, note 1.
[5] The writ is that referred to on p. 128, above.
[6] *Close R.*, 1227-31, p. 171.

and 'aid' for what is obviously an entirely compulsory levy. But
the use of the words in this writ is not indiscriminate. The men of
Somersham complained bitterly of a heavy 'tallage'. One would
not expect them to call it an 'aid', for the associations of the
word tallage were more forceful and oppressive. On the other
hand the king said that he had ordered a moderate and bearable
'aid' to be taken from them. The use of *auxilium* rather than
tallagium, in this latter case, did not imply the slightest difference in the kind of levy, the method of its assessment, or its
compulsory nature. Yet the use of the synonym seems to have
been due to something more than literary elegance. When the
king wrote of an *auxilium* rather than a *tallagium* he immediately
heightened the force of the two qualifying adjectives *moderatum*
and *tolerabile*. The men of Somersham were emphasizing their
grievances and they used *tallagium*. The king was emphasizing
his own benevolent intentions and used *auxilium*.

The word 'aid', therefore, when used to describe a vacancy
exaction may mean a royal levy of tallage. But it may, on the
other hand, mean something different though still connected.
At Durham in 1226–8 in addition to the tallage which was
levied on the *rustici*, there were two other levies, an aid of the
burgesses and an aid of the knights and freeholders. There are
thus three separate entries in the Pipe Roll:[1]

£405.5.6 de tallagio drenggorum theinorum et villanorum episcopatus[2]

£42.6.8 de auxilio burgorum episcopatus[3]

£351.13.7½ de auxilio militum et libere tenencium gratis concesso.

There is here a definite distinction between the tallage of the
drengs, thanes and villeins (the *rustici* of the Durham Rolls),
and the 'aid' willingly given by the knights and freeholders of
the see. Whereas the *tallagium* of the rustics was assessed by the
keepers, the *auxilium* of the knights and freetenants had all the
characteristics of a gracious aid. On receiving the king's re-

---

[1] Pipe R. 73, m.1.

[2] It is interesting to compare this with the payment which Henry I exacted
'de Tainis et Dreinnis et Smalemannis' in the vacancy of Durham in 1130 (*Pipe R.
31 Henry I, 1130*, p. 132). The similarity of the wording perhaps strengthens the
hypothesis that Henry I may have been levying something comparable with a
tallage on that occasion. See above, pp. 28–9.

[3] There is no information in the Durham MS. as to how this was levied.

quest the knights and freeholders held a discussion and then granted the king an aid *'spontanea voluntate'* at a rate of four marks on the knight's fee.[1] Among all those whose witness is recorded in the Durham MS. there is not one dissentient voice as to the willingness with which this aid was granted. The disagreements arose entirely over the tallage.

This composite Durham levy of both tallage and aid does not stand alone. Similar levies are found in other vacancies. In the Lichfield vacancy of 1238–40 there was an aid paid by knights and freeholders and a tallage by burgesses and *rustici*,[2] and similarly at York in 1255–6.[3] Sometimes there is no mention of knights but simply a distinction between the tallage of the villeins or customaries and the aid of the freeholders, as in the Ely vacancy of 1256–8,[4] and in the Lincoln vacancies of 1253–4[5] and 1279–80.[6] These composite levies, though they are far from being an invariable feature of vacancy accounts,[7] are perhaps one sign of the differentiation that was emerging between general royal tallage and the special levies which the king now made on a vacant see simply by reason of its vacancy and not by reason of a general tallage of the royal demesne. A levy which extended to knights was not a tallage, not even a

---

[1] This is the statement of Hugh Devon, one of the king's witnesses in the case before the archbishop's court: '. . . ipsi milites et libere tenentes diliberacione habita concesserunt domino regi spontanea voluntate de quolibet scuto quatuor marcas' (Durham MS. 5520).

[2] £82.5.4 is entered in the account 'de auxilio militum et libere tenentium rusticorum et tallagio burgorum et rusticorum' (Pipe R. 85, m.3).

[3] The Pipe Roll entry in this case is perfunctory and unhelpful: £661.8.10 is entered 'de auxiliis tallagiis per maneria archiepiscopatus' (Pipe R. 101, m.4d) but the distinction between the tallage and the aid levied in this vacancy is brought out clearly in the Close Roll entry of 20 June 1255 (*Close R., 1254–56*, p. 203).

[4] £249.17.4 is accounted for 'de auxilio libere tenencium et tallagio villanorum per maneria' (Pipe R. 101, m.4).

[5] £352.17.5 is accounted for 'de auxilio libere tenencium et tallagio villanorum et recognitionibus quorundam' (*ibid.*).

[6] Here the sum was £111.8.8 'de auxilio libere tenencium et tallagio custumariorum' (Pipe R. 125, m.3d).

[7] Very often a tallage only was levied. This would never extend to knights but perhaps in some cases it may have covered all who could not claim to hold their land by military tenure. This at any rate seems to be the implication of the king's order to the keepers of the vacant see of Lincoln concerning a claim to exemption from tallage in 1235: '. . . si Thomas filius Rannulfi terram suam teneat per servitium militare,. . . tunc nullum ab eodem Thoma capiant tallagium . . .' (*Close R., 1234–37*, p. 62).

royal tallage. Moreover, though royal tallage was paid by freemen on the king's demesnes, it was ordered that in a vacancy of the see of Canterbury in 1231 the royal custodians should assess the tallage:

super villanos et eos qui per archiepiscopum possent talliari et non super liberos homines.[1]

In short, the king's levies on vacant sees although they seem in origin to have been an extension of general levies of royal tallage were in the thirteenth century developing along their own lines. They might, as in the case of Canterbury in 1231, be more narrow in their incidence than ordinary royal tallage,[2] or they might, on the other hand, be large composite exactions which threw their net more widely than royal tallage ever did.

Where a distinction was made in vacancy levies between aid and tallage the division seems to have been drawn along lines of tenure. It was those who held by free tenure who paid the aid, and the others paid tallage. This had obviously caused some resentment at Durham in 1226. Several of the witnesses for the monks considered it a grievance that freemen had been obliged to pay tallage,[3] but they nowhere say that freeholders, *libere tenentes*, paid tallage. The government was evidently not prepared to make distinctions in regard to personal status in this matter, but only in regard to tenure. In some cases indeed even those who held by free tenure had to be watchful of their rights. In the vacancy of the see of York 1255–6 the freeholders of Sherburn informed the king that although they were willing, along with other freeholders of the archbishopric, to give the king a reasonable aid, they had been unjustly assessed for the payment of a tallage and distrained for payment by the keepers. The king ordered that the keepers should not proceed in this matter 'nomine tallagii'.[4]

---

[1] *Close R.*, *1227–31*, p. 574.

[2] There seems to have been no levy at Canterbury in this vacancy other than this tallage on the unfree.

[3] Walter of Selby for instance said 'quod tam liberis quam rusticis imponit dominus rex tallagia et graves exactiones' (Durham MS. 5520). Thomas Anglicus corroborated this: 'De tallagiis impositis hominibus episcopatus tam liberis quam rusticis concordat cum eodem [i.e. Walter of Selby] (*ibid.*).

[4] *Close R.*, *1254–56*, p. 203.

The death of royal tallage has been variously explained. Professor Mitchell has pointed out that by the second half of the thirteenth century the tax had become very stereotyped and the government was unable to transform it into a flexible expansible levy.[1] Moreover, there was now a more productive tax to replace it. After the accession of Edward I taxes on movables were levied with increasing frequency, whereas royal tallage was not levied between the death of Henry III and the opening of the fourteenth century, and thereafter it was only levied twice, in 1304 and 1312.

In the accounts for vacant sees too the word tallage has almost disappeared in the late thirteenth century, persisting only in the accounts for the see of Durham. Whether this was the result of the practical abandoning of royal tallage in general would be difficult to determine, but one thing is certain that in the case of vacancies the levy sometimes named tallage did not, in practice, meet with extinction in the way that general royal tallage did. Rather it underwent a change, of name and of nature.

In order to understand what royal tallage of vacant bishoprics became by the later thirteenth century it may be helpful to examine more closely an incident already mentioned in an earlier discussion,[2] the various payments exacted by Abbot Samson when he succeeded to the abbey of Bury St. Edmunds in 1182. In the first place, having received homage from his knights he asked them for an aid, and they promised him twenty shillings each.[3] Shortly afterwards he visited all his manors,

poscens ab omnibus et a singulis auxilium et recognicionem secundum consuetudinem regni.[4]

Abbot Samson, therefore, on the occasion of his accession to the abbey levied an aid on his knights and recognitions on his lesser tenants *per maneria*. These were payments *mutatio domini*, and they were already customary in 1182.

---

[1] *Studies in Taxation*, p. 14 and *Taxation in Medieval England*, p. 359.
[2] See above, pp. 17–18.   [3] Jocelin of Brakelond, p. 27.
[4] *Ibid.*, p. 31 It may be as Professor Butler has suggested in the footnote that the two words *auxilium* and *recognitionem* should be taken together, or it seems just possible, in view of later practice that there is an implied distinction between a payment made by the freeholders and one made by those who held by unfree tenure.

The custom continued and in the thirteenth century there is more evidence. At Hereford in 1241, the free tenants of the bishopric were requested to make an aid to the new bishop at his entry into the see 'such as they have been accustomed to make to his predecessors when they entered therein'.[1] Whether this was accompanied by a levy on those holding by unfree tenure as well, we do not know for certain but the two not infrequently went together. However that may be, at Winchester in 1251, Aymer de Valence, on his accession to the temporalities of the see made a levy on the men of the episcopal manors, both free and unfree.[2] In some instances this was referred to as an 'aid', 'the lord's first aid'.[3] More often, however, it is called a *recognition*,[4] but it is quite distinct from those small annual recognitions which appear on all the Winchester rolls. It is a payment in recognition of a new lord. Similarly, recognitions were paid to Bishop John Gervais when he succeeded to this bishopric in 1262[5] and to Nicholas of Ely who became bishop in 1268.[6] Moreover, the amounts paid by each manor show on the whole a marked steadiness. East Meon paid £22.4.5½ in 1251, 1262 and 1268 and was still paying it in 1316.[7] Hambledon paid £11.2.3 in 1251 and £11.2.2½ in 1262 and again in 1316.

But has this anything to do with the tallaging of vacant

---

[1] *Cal. Pat. R., 1232–47*, p. 248.

[2] Eccles 2/159447. The roll is that of Mich. 1251 to Mich. 1252.

[3] Among the receipts of the manor of Fonthill Bishop there is the entry of £2.2.0 'de primo auxilio domini' (*ibid.*, m.14). At Waltham £30 is accounted for 'de auxilio villanorum' (*ibid.*, m.17d).

[4] For example in the manors of Downton (*ibid.*, m. 15) Ivinghoe (m.7), Adderbury (m.7d) and Bishop's Sutton (m.22).

[5] Eccles 2/159294. For specific examples see below, p. 138, n. 6.

[6] Eccles 2/159450A. In one case, in the entry for the manor of Adderbury (m.5) the scribe has written 'tallag.' in the margin instead of 'recognitiones' but he uses the latter term for the same payment in the text of the roll.

[7] The list of recognitions paid to John Sandale in this first year of his pontificate is printed in the Appendix to *The Registers of John de Sandale and Rigaud de Asserio, Bishops of Winchester, 1316–1323*, ed. F. J. Baigent (Hampshire Record Soc., London and Winchester, 1897), p. 627.

It is interesting to notice that in the see of Worcester too recognitions to a new bishop seem to have been paid at fixed rates in the late thirteenth century. Thus among the many obligations of one Elias de Meleberwe was this: 'et dabit etiam cuilibet episcopo de novo creato ij s. de recogniscione.' The reference occurs in an extent of the lands of the bishopric of 1299 (*Red Book of Worcester*, p. 283).

bishoprics? On the Pipe Roll vacancy accounts for Winchester the last account to record a tallage (*eo nomine*) of the see is that of 1250–1.[1] In the Winchester vacancy of 1268 the Pipe Roll records no tallage, but does mention £487.16.10 received from 'aids and recognitions'.[2] It so happens that the Winchester Roll for the last year of John Gervais and the first year of Nicholas of Ely also covers the whole of the short period of the 1268 vacancy (25 February to 2 May according to the Pipe Roll dates) and it therefore records the amounts paid to the king in recognitions. East Meon paid £22.4.5½[3] and Hambledon paid £11.2.2½[4]—exactly the same amounts as they customarily paid in recognition to an incoming bishop.[5] Indeed, there are at least seventeen manors which pay to the king in 1268 just the same amount as they had paid in recognition to Bishop John Gervais on his first entry into the see in 1262.[6] Royal tallage in Winchester vacancies, then, had disappeared to be replaced by recognitions, which were in most cases identical in amount to the recognitions customarily paid to an incoming bishop. Would it perhaps, be more accurate to say that tallage was not so much replaced by recognitions as that it was transformed into recognitions? At least there is no very great gap between the £510.18.6½ paid to the king in tallage in the vacancy of 1250–1[7]

---

[1] Pipe R. 95, m.6.

[2] 'de auxiliis et recognicionibus regi factis' (Chancellor's R. 61, m.6d).

[3] Eccles 2/159298, m.12d.

[4] *Ibid.*, m.13d.

[5] See above, p. 137.

[6] The list is as follows: in 1262 Burghclere paid £8.17.9 (Eccles 2/159294, m.8d); Ecchinswell £4.19.7 (*ibid.*, m.8); Highclere £3.13.4 (m.8d); North Waltham £2.0.0 (m.7); Bitterne £4.0.0 (m.14d); East Meon £22.4.5½ (m.17d); Hambledon £11.2.2½ (m.18d); Bentley £3.0.0 (m.22); Ivinghoe £10.13.4 (m.10); Witney £18.13.4 (m.9); Adderbury £13.6.8 (m.9d); Bishop's Sutton £13.6.8 (m.19); Rimpton £5.0.0 (m.2d); Twyford with Marwell £12.6.8 (m.15d); Alresford £3.6.8 (m.20d); Cheriton £7.6.8 (m.19d); Downton £29.13.0 (m.4).

In 1268 *sede vacante* the same amounts were paid by Burghclere (Eccles 2/159298, m.6); Ecchinswell (*ibid.*, m.6); Highclere (m.6d); North Waltham (m.5); Bitterne (m.10); East Meon (m.12d); Hambledon (m.13d); Bentley (m.16); Ivinghoe (m.7b); Witney, leaving aside three payments separately accounted for (m.7); Adderbury (m.7b); Bishop's Sutton (m.14); Rimpton (m.2); Twyford (m.9d); Alresford (burgh) (m.15); Cheriton (m.14d.) Downton (m.2d).

The eighth membrane of this roll is, by a slip, unnumbered. For convenience of reference the present numbering is preserved in this footnote and the eighth membrane has been called '7b'.

[7] Pipe R. 95, m.6.

and the £487.16.10 paid in 'aids and recognitions' in the vacancy of 1268.[1]

There are three other sees in which the word 'recognition' appears on the vacancy accounts before the end of Henry III's reign. In the case of the Lincoln vacancy of 1253–4, the entry is obscure but suggestive. £352.17.5 was paid:

de auxilio libere tenencium, de tallagio villanorum et recognitionibus quorundam.[2]

Might the 'quorundam' possibly denote men of free status but of unfree tenure?[3] At least in the Salisbury vacancies of 1256, 1262–3 and 1271, 'recognitions' is the term used for the payments of freeholders in the first case[4] and of freemen in the two latter cases,[5] in contrast each time to the tallage levied on the villeins. Finally, in the Bath vacancy of 1266–7 there is no tallage *eo nomine*, but simply 'recognitions' of burgesses and villeins.[6]

In Edward I's reign, the movement away from tallage and towards recognitions gathered speed. Later than about 1280 the use of the word tallage on the vacancy accounts became exceptional. A few bishoprics still used the term, notably Chichester,[7] York[8] and Durham.[9] The Salisbury accounts still distinguished between recognitions of freemen and tallage of

[1] Chancellor's R. 61, m.6d. When the recognitions paid *sede vacante* reach complete equilibrium in the early fourteenth century they stand at £501.4.2. See above, p. 125.   [2] Pipe R. 101, m.4.
[3] This is of course mere speculation. The phraseology is repeated in the Lincoln vacancy account for 1258 (Pipe R. 104, m.2).
[4] 'de recognicionibus libere tenentium et tallagio villanorum . . .' (Pipe R. 100, m.19).
[5] 'de recognicionibus liberorum hominum et tallagio custumariorum' (Chancellor's R. 61, m.6d); and on the account for 1271 the two items are entered separately: 'de recognicionibus liberorum hominum' and 'de tallagio villanorum' (Pipe R. 116, m.2d).   [6] Pipe R. 101, m.28.
[7] There are two Chichester accounts in Edward I's reign. In that of 1287–8 £66.6.8 was paid in tallage; Chancellor's R. 81, m.17d.
In the vacancy account for 1305 the figure for tallage is £63.13.4 (Pipe R. 152B, m.8). The two figures are interestingly close.
[8] When York was vacant in 1285–6 the keepers accounted for a 'tallage' (Pipe R. 133, m.28). In the account of 1299–1300, however, 'recognitions' is the term used throughout (Pipe R. 150, m.30–31d). In the account of 1304–6 'tallage' is the term generally used but in a few cases 'recognitions' appears instead (Pipe R. 152B, mm.16–19).
[9] The account is for the 1283 vacancy (Pipe R. 127, m.2d).

villeins.[1] In Edward II's reign Durham alone retained the now antiquated term 'tallage', and on the account for the Durham vacancy of 1316–17 there is a note of explanation. The tallage was levied 'loco recognicionum tempore seisine Regis . . .'.[2] In all the other sees, as far as the evidence goes, tallage had by this time disappeared, and in every case recognitions were levied instead.

There can be little doubt that the 'recognitions' which appeared immediately tallage disappeared in any particular see were essentially the same in kind as the recognitions which the men of the manors of the bishopric of Winchester paid to each new bishop on his entry into the see. The *sede vacante* payments were recognitions of the king's lordship. On several Pipe Roll accounts of Edward I's reign 'recognitions' are said to be taken 'tempore seisine Regis'[3] or 'tempore capcionis seisine Regis'[4] or in one case 'in principio seisine Regis'.[5] Like the recognitions paid to a bishop in the first year of his pontificate these were recognitions on change of lordship.

Here we may pause to look back, first as far as the reign of Henry II, who levied tallage on vacant sees on those occasions when he levied it on his demesne and boroughs. It is a fairly far cry from this royal tallage of the twelfth century, a tax which was 'public rather than seignorial',[6] to the recognitions of the late thirteenth and early fourteenth centuries which were levied in each vacancy 'in principio seisine Regis'. When did

[1] Pipe R. 133, m.29 (Apr. 1284 to Aug. 1285); Pipe R. 137, m.26d (Oct. 1291 to Dec. 1291); Pipe R. 143, m.25d (May 1297 to Aug. 1297). There was a tendency for a repetition of the same phraseology in the successive vacancy accounts for a particular bishopric. However, the account of the 1286–7 vacancy breaks the continuity at Salisbury, for in this one instance the villeins as well as the freemen paid 'recognitions' (Pipe R. 133, m.28d). This break in an otherwise perfect sequence corroborates the idea that tallage and recognitions had become essentially the same thing.

[2] Pipe R. 164, m.34.

[3] In the vacancy accounts for Canterbury in 1292–5 (Pipe R. 141, m.28d), for Carlisle in 1292 (Pipe R. 142, m.29d) and for Worcester in 1302 (Pipe R. 147, mm.24–25). See also the roll of particulars for this last account printed in the *Red Book of Worcester*, pp. 498–547, *passim*.

[4] This is the definition of the payments made by the freemen of the hundred of Witchford in the Ely account for 1298 (Pipe R. 144, m.29).

[5] See the entries for the manor of Bibury in the Worcester account referred to in n. 3, above (Pipe R. 147, m.24 and *Red Book of Worcester*, p. 504).

[6] Hoyt, *op. cit.*, p. 115.

this vital change take place? It would be quite artificial to give a date, but an interesting stage is seen in the levies made in the Durham vacancy of 1226–8.[1] In some ways the king's levy on this occasion had marked similarities with Abbot Samson's levy at Bury St. Edmunds in 1182.[2] Like his, it consisted of an aid demanded from the knights and another payment, called, in this case, by the names 'aid' and 'tallage', from the lesser tenants. Moreover the levy was made fairly near the beginning of the vacancy. If we stopped there it might seem that the change was already complete. But that would be a hasty conclusion. The king, it would seem, did not in this case demand either the aid or the tallage completely as a matter of course, *mutatio domini*. He asked the knights for an aid 'ad terram suam recuperandam',[3] and even in the case of the tallage it was thought advisable to give a reason for the levy (presumably the same as that given to the knights), and the reason was accordingly stated in the king's letters.[4] We may safely assume that by the end of the thirteenth century no such explanation would have been required; recognitions were then levied as a matter of course, 'in principio seisine Regis'.

The story of the development of vacancy tallages is one of gradual transition. If a significant turning-point is demanded then it must probably be found in the reign of John when tallages first came to be levied once in each vacancy. If an ultimate inspiration be sought may we not look back (with due caution) to William Rufus who demanded a relief from the military tenants of the see of Worcester in 1095 when the *honor* came into his hand?[5]

Be that as it may, the gradual transition from the occasional levy of a tallage on a vacant see when a general tallage was being levied, to the practice of tallaging in each vacancy, and finally to the levy of recognitions 'in principio seisine Regis' is an impressive tribute to the inventiveness of Angevin government. The crown's financial administration in the thirteenth century was controlled by a flexibility of thought and a power of

[1] See above, p. 133.
[2] See above, pp. 136.
[3] Durham MS. 5520 in the evidence given by Stephen de Lucy's clerk, Hugh Devon.
[4] *Ibid.*; see above, p. 131.   [5] See above, pp. 16–18.

invention and adaptation which belied the apparent sluggish-
ness of its formal surface.

From this necessary diversion on the nature of the tallages
levied by the king on vacant sees we must now return to the
main argument of this chapter. The clergy in complaining of
the king's ruinous practices in vacant bishoprics had on the one
hand charged him with impoverishing the tenants of the see by
'undue exactions and tallages'. This has been discussed; it
remains to consider the second charge which they brought, the
alleged spoliation of the woods, parks and fishponds of the
bishopric and the failure to maintain the capital equipment
in houses and other buildings.

For a colourful commentary on the abuses which the clergy
condemned there is no need to look further than the chronicle
of Matthew Paris. At Winchester in the vacancy of 1250-1, the
king ordered woods to be cut down and sold 'et inde pecuniam
aerario suo addi accumulandam'.[1] At Bath in 1248 the king laid
greedy hands on the goods of the bishopric.[2] The see of York
was kept vacant by the king in 1256 'ut diutius et liberius bona
diriperet archiepiscopatus',[3] and on the property of Ely from
1256-8, the woods were cut down, the streams were emptied
of fish and the parks of wild boars.[4] Finally, the see of London
in the vacancy of 1241-4 was not allowed a new bishop until
the king had first ruined the episcopal property.[5]

The keeper in this London vacancy of 1241-4 was Ralph
Dayrell who, as we have already noticed, was officially suspected of bad stewardship.[6] He held the custody of the abbey
of Evesham as well as the see of London and the king had
ordered the regents in England to remove him if he was not
satisfactory.[7] This suggests that the main responsibility for the
harsh treatment of the bishopric of London between 1241 and
1244 may have lain chiefly with the keeper rather than the
king. And there are other instances where the bishopric may
have suffered a good deal from unscrupulous custodians.[8]
Where the king was angry with the chapter, on the other hand,

---

[1] *Chron. Majora*, v, 198.   [2] *Ibid.*, p. 3.   [3] *Ibid.*, p. 516.
[4] *Ibid.*, p. 619.   [5] *Ibid.*, iv, 170.   [6] See above, p. 105.
[7] '. . . si super hujusmodi inveniatur culpapilis [*sic*] et suspectus, statim ab ad-
ministratione sua amoveatur . . .' (*Close R.*, *1242–47*, p. 33; 11 July 1243).
[8] See above, pp. 104–9.

it may well be that he deliberately encouraged dilapidation of the bishopric.[1] It is certainly difficult to apportion the blame as between king and keepers in any particular case.[2]

Many of the writs on the Close Rolls and Liberate Rolls lead one to suspect that the king was pretty free with episcopal property when it came into his hand. His very large order for luce, bream, and eels from Ely in 1256 when he was entertaining prelates and magnates from overseas has already been mentioned.[3] Three months later he was again making demands on an impressive scale from the same bishopric[4] and the orders to seek out fowl in the archbishopric of Canterbury and in the bishopric of London in 1243 sound suspiciously comprehensive.[5]

The king's huntsmen were frequent visitors to vacant sees. In 1226 Master Guido 'our huntsman' was commended to the keepers of Durham for help in his elastic mission to hunt 'in hac saisona in foresta episcopatus Dunholm'.[6] In December 1245 the king sent Robert de Stopham and Robert de Mares with the more specific order to take thirty does in the parks of the vacant bishopric of Chichester.[7] Eighty does were sent to the

---

[1] As in the case of the Winchester vacancy of 1238–44 referred to above, p. 105.

[2] Matthew Paris for instance suggests that in the Ely vacancy of 1256–8 the king gave the keeper a fairly free hand to despoil the see but that he went even further than the king would have authorized: 'Rex . . . permisit ut Johannes Walerannus cui custodiam episcopatus illius commiserat ut silvas explanans omnia devastaret, quod et ipse plenius quam permissum fuerat vel concessum [fecerat], episcopatum suis bonis graviter viduaret' (*Chron. Majora*, v, 589). Robert Walerand was the chief keeper in this Ely vacancy (Pipe R. 101, m.4) but his brother John seems to have been associated with him (*Cal. Pat. R.*, 1247–58, p. 612. The incoming bishop of Ely made complaint as we have seen (above, p. 105, n. 4), of the 'immense trespasses and damages' done in his bishopric by the royal custodians (*Cal. Pat. R.*, 1258–66, p. 48).

[3] Above, p. 91, n. 1.

[4] *Close R.*, 1256–59, p. 39; 27 Feb. 1257: 'Mandatum est Johanni Waler' custodi episcopatus Eliensis quod cum omni festinacione provideat regi de 1ª luciis trium pedum, 1ªluciis ij pedum et dimidii, 1ªluciis ij pedum et aliis pikerellis, cc esteiling', 1ª stikis anguillarum que vocantur shastel', mmmm pimpernellis, de redditu predicti episcopatus vel de vivariis, aut piscariis ejusdem episcopatus, vel de empto.'

[5] The order to the keeper of Canterbury is referred to above, p. 91. The keeper of London, in the previous month, was ordered to seek out for the king's use 'de dono et empto et alio modo, sicut poterit, omnes cignos et omnes pavones et alia volatilia que per totam ballivam suam querere poterit . . .' (*Close R.*, 1242–47, pp. 47–8). Rabbits were in demand too: 'In ccc cuniculis capiendis et cariandis usque Westmonasterium xxxiij s. per breve Regis'; Chichester account 1244–6 (Pipe R. 90, m.9).

[6] *Rot. Litt. Claus.* 1224–27, p. 134b.　　　　　　　　[7] *Close R.*, 1242–47, p. 380.

king from the lands of the see of York in the vacancy of 1255–6[1] and one hundred in the vacancy of 1299–1300.[2] Perhaps royal policy is most aptly illustrated by a writ addressed to William of Wilton, the keeper of the vacant see of Lincoln in 1253. Wilton is to hunt in the parks of the bishopric 'tot damas quot in eis capi poterunt sine vasto et destructione eorundem parcorum'.[3] This sounds very reasonable: but perhaps the king thought that there might have been too few does sent to him as a result. Anyway, there is an addendum to the writ:

Postea mandatum fuit eidem W. quod in eisdem parcis capi faceret usque ad summam lx dammarum, si sine destruccione fieri posset.[4]

There would presumably be few king's clerks so scrupulous about episcopal property that they would risk the king's displeasure by deciding that sixty does would in fact cause waste and destruction.

Henry III seems to have found particular temptation to be generous to his clerks and friends at the expense of episcopal wealth. The oaks in the forests of the vacant see of Winchester (1238–44) fell fast as Master Simon the carpenter received forty,[5] Imbert Pugeys twenty,[6] Robert de Lexinton ten 'ad quandam domum faciendum apud Sarrisburiam';[7] the Earl Marshal twenty 'ad se hospitandum apud manerium suum de Hamsted'[8] and the archbishop of York twelve.[9] A few months later the archbishop of York received a further four whole shiploads of wood from this see,[10] and Walter Cantilupe 'two good shiploads'.[11] These are only a few instances, and there are

---

[1] Pipe R. 101, m.4d.

[2] Pipe R. 150, m.31. There are many such entries on the Pipe Rolls: for example, 'In venacione capta in parcis et boscis predicti archiepiscopatus salandi et cariandi ad Regem usque Eboracum et Lincoln'. xij li. iiij s. iiij d.' (York account 1255–6; Pipe R. 101, m.4d).

'In iij cervis ij bissis cxx damis captis in predicto episcopatu salandis cariandis ad Regem . . . ij li. vj s. vj d.' (continuation of Ely account 1256–8; ibid., m. 4d).

[3] Close R., 1253–54, p. 3.

[4] This might, of course, be a separate order, but it seems more naturally interpreted as a further elucidation of the original writ.

[5] Ibid., 1237–42, p. 200.

[6] Ibid., p. 201.

[7] Ibid., p. 300.

[8] Ibid., p. 378.

[9] Ibid., p. 394.

[10] Ibid., p. 426.

[11] Ibid., p. 452.

other vacancies too where trees were hewed in very quick succession.[1] Nor was it only a matter of trees. Fulk Fitz Warren restocked one of his parks to the extent of ten does from the vacant see of Canterbury in 1233 'de dono regis'[2] and in 1242 Master Ralph Neketon received:

viij matrices bremias in vivario de Rehnes ad quoddam vivarium suum instaurandum de dono regis.[3]

This was at the expense of the bishopric of London.

Did the king's policy and practice amount to spoliation? That he took too much we may be fairly sure. Trees in the forests of vacant bishoprics seem to be hewed down at a considerably higher rate than trees in royal forests. On the other hand Matthew Paris's scenes of complete devastation may be treated with reserve. The resources were considerable, and the king did not as a rule deliberately set out to despoil episcopal property. More often he simply took what he required, just when he required it, with too little regard for the consequences.

The complement of the royal tendency to take too much from the bishoprics was apparently a tendency to do too little to conserve the property. In every bishopric there were buildings which were the bishop's property and their maintenance was the obligation of the king during vacancy. Here at least *official* royal policy was irreproachable. The keepers of vacant sees were constantly receiving mandates to maintain the buildings in a proper state of repair, or at any rate in as good a condition as they were in when the late bishop died. The keeper of Durham in 1238 was ordered to re-erect a mill that had been blown down in Northallerton and to see to the maintenance of the houses of the see.[4] The next year he was again ordered to 'cause the castles, houses, chapels, parks and mills of the bishopric to be

---

[1] In the archbishopric of Canterbury, for example, in 1242 (*ibid.*, p. 415, Apr. 1242; p. 420, 1 May 1242; p. 422, 3 May 1242; p. 424, 5 May 1242; pp. 426–7, 6 May 1242; and p. 427, 6 May 1242).

In the next reign in the Salisbury vacancy of 1284 the dean and chapter wrote to both Edward I and Robert Burnell urging that the king should order his escheator Henry de Bray to refrain from cutting down trees which he intended to cut, since this would cause grave damage to the episcopal property (*Charters and Documents Illustrating the History of the Cathedral City and Diocese of Salisbury*, ed. W. D. Macray (Rolls Series, London, 1891), pp. 359–61).

[2] *Close R., 1231–34*, p. 331.

[3] *Ibid., 1237–42*, p. 386.   [4] *Cal. Liberate R., 1226–40*, p. 308.

L

maintained and to cause those things that are out of repair in his custody to be repaired'.[1] The keepers of Canterbury in 1241 were instructed to have buildings and mills repaired, parks enclosed and vineyards tilled.[2] The king evidently considered himself fully responsible for the maintenance of the capital equipment of the vacant see, but it remains very possible that in some cases the keepers were negligent.

It is not surprising from this brief survey that the chapters of cathedral churches should have pressed for the right to farm episcopal vacancies from the crown themselves.[3] Their chief aim was to avoid the loss which the church incurred through the unscupulousness of some of the royal keepers. This was the reason expressly stated in those grants of self-custody which Edward II made to the church of Lincoln,[4] London,[5] Salisbury[6] and Exeter,[7] between 1316 and 1320.

It might perhaps be thought that the church itself was perhaps not without an eye to a little profit in pressing these arrangements. It is interesting then to examine the account rendered by Richard de Carleton to the chapter of Lincoln in 1320.[8]

[1] *Ibid.*, p. 368.

[2] *Ibid., 1240–45*, p. 43. There are many other examples of similar writs relating to vacancies in other sees. The keeper of the bishopric of Chichester in 1246 was ordered 'quod omnes domos episcopatus Cycestr' que sunt in custodia sua sustineat et emendet ita quod non corruant vel deteriorentur et terras dominicas ejusdem episcopatus excoli faciat et seminari sicut debent et solent' (*Close R., 1242–47*, p. 385). The same mandate was sent to the keeper of the vacant bishopric of Lichfield. Directions for the upkeep of the property in the bishopric of Winchester may be seen *Cal. Liberate R., 1226–40*, p. 488; 13 Aug. 1240, and Liberate R. 35, m.6; 25 Feb. 1259.

[3] This solution was suggested by the clergy in 1309 in their petition to the king: . . . petitur quatinus pro indempnitate ecclesie et commodo vestro pociori capitulis et conventibus ecclesiarum vacancium pro tempore vacacionis ipsarum et pro certo solvendo juxta quod conveniri poterit custodia concedatur' (*Reg. R. Winchelsey*, p. 1018).

[4] *Cal. Fine R., 1307–19*, p. 272; 1 Feb. 1316. The bishopric was to render to the king for each voidance £1,000 a year, 'at which the bishopric is yearly taxed'.

[5] *Ibid.*, p. 349; 25 Dec. 1317. This bishopric was also to render for each voidance £1,000 a year 'at which the bishopric is yearly taxed'.

[6] *Ibid.*, pp. 348–9; 19 Dec. 1317. The bishopric was to render for each voidance £1,021.7.11 a year 'at which the bishopric is yearly taxed'.

[7] *Ibid., 1319–27*, pp. 38–9; 2 Nov. 1320. This arrangement applied to the one vacancy only and was not a grant in perpetuity, as the three foregoing grants were. Again the chapter was to pay to the exchequer 'the taxation of the bishopric, if the voidance last for a whole year . . . '.

[8] Lincoln Cathedral, Dean and Chapter Archives Bj/2/5, ff. 28d.–30.

Carleton acted as keeper of the temporalities of the vacant bishopric of Lincoln on behalf of the dean and chapter in the first vacancy following the grant just cited.[1] His total receipts from 12 January 1320 to 5 August 1320 amount to £443.7.9¾,[2] and his expenses are £44.14.10[3] thus leaving a net receipt of £398.12.11¾. But the amount due to the king is £563.3.8½, as is stated in the transcript of the Pipe Roll entry at the end of Carleton's account:

Iidem Decani et capitulum reddunt compotum de dlxiij li.iij s. viij d. ob. de rata mille li. per annum de temporalibus predicti episcopatus Lincolniensis vacantis et in manu Regis existentis per mortem Johannis nuper Episcopi eiusdem loci a duodecimo die Januarii anno terciodecimo quo die dicta temporalia per mortem eiusdem Johannis capta fuerunt in manu Regis usque quintum diem Augusti proxime sequentem quo die Rex cepit fidelitatem H. Episcopi eiusdem loci et temporalia predicti episcopatus ei restituit.[4]

Richard de Carleton duly paid £563.3.9 [sic] into the treasury of the exchequer[5] but only by dint of borrowing. His account shows where the money came from. He accounts to the chapter for £100, 'receptis ex mutuo de custodibus beati Johannis'; for £40, 'ex mutuo de custodi beati Hugonis' and for £26, 'de custodi beati Roberti'. From his net receipt of £398.12.11¾ from the temporalities of the bishopric and £166 from the keepers of the various shrines, Carleton was able to pay £563.3.9 to the king and leave himself with a surplus of £1.9.2¾.[6]

In the course of the fourteenth century the practice of farming the custody of the temporalities to the dean and chapter of a vacant cathedral became increasingly common. In 1340 it was ordered by statute that if a vacant church should offer to the king the value of the voidance,

as other will reasonably yield, then the Chancellor and Treasurer shall have power to let [to] the said Dean and Chapter . . . the said voidances by good and sufficient surety, so that they shall have the same before all other.[7]

---

[1] Above, p. 146, n. 4.   [2] Lincoln Bj/2/5, f. 29.
[3] *Ibid.*, f. 30.   [4] *Ibid.*   [5] *Ibid.*   [6] *Ibid.*
[7] Statute 4, 14 Edward III c.4 (*Statutes of the Realm*, 1, 294). The king promised that even if this arrangement was not made in any particular case, his escheators should not commit waste and that they should 'sell no underwood nor hunt in the parks or warrens, nor fish in ponds nor free fishings . . .' (*ibid*).

The value of the voidance 'as other will reasonably yield' was a sufficiently indefinite term to give the king an opportunity for not allowing the chapter to farm the voidance unless he so wished. It is interesting, however, to notice that in the case of the four sees already mentioned which had made arrangements for farming by the chapter in Edward II's reign, the rate of the farm was related to the valuation of the temporalities in the *Taxation* of Pope Nicholas.[1] A similar arrangement had also been made with the chapter of Llandaff in Edward II's reign,[2] and after the statute of 1340 this was apparently the rate at which the sacrist of Ely farmed that see too.[3] There can be little doubt, I think, that the valuation of the temporalities of English sees in the *Taxation* of Pope Nicholas was on the whole rather lower than the net income which the king had been taking from the vacant sees when he had exploited them directly in the thirteenth century.[4]

Why then did the king permit this apparently less profitable arrangement in the fourteenth century? There may be several strands of explanation. The absolute value of the bishoprics may have been on the decline in the early fourteenth century.[5] Moreover, if an estimate of the value of temporalities for the purpose of the farming of vacancies was to be made at all then the figures of the *Taxation* of Pope Nicholas had the advantage of

[1] See above, p. 146, nn. 4, 5, 6 and 7. A comparison of the figures given in these notes leaves no doubt that the 'taxation' referred to is the taxation of Pope Nicholas.

[2] *Register of Edward the Black Prince* (P.R.O., 1930–3), I, pp. 41–2; 20 Jan. 1347. This writ refers to an agreement made between Edward II and the bishop and chapter of Llandaff by which the chapter were to farm the bishopric 'at a rent for each voidance of a year's duration of £93.9.8, at which sum the bishopric is taxed . . .'. Compare *Taxatio Ecclesiastica*, p. 280.

[3] *Sacrist Rolls of Ely*, ed. F. R. Chapman (Cambridge, 1907), I, 54. Mr. Miller uses this figure as corroborative evidence, independent of the evidence of the *Taxation* itself, in his suggestion that £2,500 is probably too high a figure for the net income of the bishops of Ely in the thirteenth century (*Abbey and Bishopric of Ely*, p. 81). The sum £2,500 is the figure which Mr. Miller calculates as the net income of the bishopric from the evidence of the vacancy accounts whereas the valuation in the *Taxation* is only £2,000 (*Taxatio Ecclesiastica*, p. 270b). However, in view of the existence of other examples of farming a vacancy at the rate given in the *Taxation* it would seem that the evidence of the Ely Sacrist Rolls on this point cannot be regarded as evidence independent of the evidence of the *Taxation* itself.

[4] See tables below, Appendix A.

[5] Miller, *op. cit.*, p. 81.

being already widely used and comparatively acceptable to both clergy and crown. Moreover, the arrangement seems to have been an equitable one, and perhaps the pressure of clerical opinion in favour of self-custody became increasingly strong. Yet, despite all these considerations, it would seem unlikely that this solution would have seemed acceptable to the crown a century earlier. Vacant abbeys were quite frequently farmed by their convents in the thirteenth century, but the only bishopric to be farmed by its chapter was Salisbury in 1271. Bishoprics were in general wealthier than abbeys, and were vacant longer and were, therefore, more likely to repay direct exploitation. By the fourteenth century, however, when episcopal vacancies were shorter, and other more expansible sources of royal income were being developed the importance of vacancies as a source of revenue fell on a fairly steep decline.

It remains to be discovered what use the government was able to make of vacancy revenues during the thirteenth century. Sir James Ramsay cautiously remarked with regard to Henry III's reign that, 'vacant sees, at any rate in the latter part of the reign, still figured in the revenue'.[1] We must try to estimate their significance a little more exactly.

Matthew Paris has a relevant anecdote. In 1237 Henry III demanded the grant of a thirtieth.[2] In reply, Richard of Cornwall, the spokesman of the baronial element in the council, sternly rebuked the king for his misgovernment and extravagance:

Addidit etiam comes, quod ipse [i.e. the king] infinitos proventus et innumerabilem pecuniam in suo tempore collegerat nec erat in Anglia archiepiscopatus vel episcopatus praeter Eboracensem, Bathoniensem et Wintoniensem, qui non vacaverit suo tempore. Similiter intulit de abbatibus et comitatibus et baroniis, custodiis et aliis excaetis;[3]

This reflects a contemporary view, whether that of Richard of Cornwall or of Matthew Paris, of the importance of the income which the crown drew from vacant bishoprics. It is put in a position of some importance in regard to the other items of revenue mentioned; it appears at the head of the list.

[1] *Revenues of the Kings of England*, I, 360.
[2] *Chron. Majora*, III, 410.   [3]*Ibid.*, p. 411.

We can judge the value which the king himself attached to the revenue from episcopal vacancies more particularly by discovering what he did with it. In the first place it was very rarely indeed that the crown yielded the profits of a vacancy even to a highly favoured bishop-elect. Henry III made this gesture twice only.[1] The issues of the short London vacancy of 1259 were given as we have seen to Henry Wingham 'by counsel of the nobles of the council',[2] and those of Worcester in 1268 were conceded to Godfrey Giffard, the king's chancellor.[3] There seems to be no evidence that Edward I ever made a similar concession.[4] Normally the king showed his appreciation of vacancy revenues by exploiting them directly to his own use.

For the most part, the wealth which the king drew from vacancies was taken in the form of money. The corn harvest and other agricultural issues were either sold on the manors, or in the case of a short vacancy sold to the bishop-elect, or sometimes, in a long vacancy sold *in grosso*.[5] Occasionally, however, the harvest of a large and wealthy see could be of use to the king as it was, for the provisioning of an army for instance. In the course of 1242 the king made two distinct demands for large food supplies for his Gascon campaign, from the vacant sees of Winchester and Canterbury. In March, when the campaign was still at the stage of preparation the keepers of Winchester were ordered to send 1,000 carcases of

---

[1] That is in respect of English bishoprics. He did grant the issues of a Dublin vacancy to Luke, dean of St. Martins, London, one of his chief wardrobe clerks, in 1229 when Luke was elected to that see through Henry's influence (*Pat. R., 1225-32*, p. 326, 23 Jan. 1229). However, it appears later that with 500 marks of the 700 marks which seem to have formed the main bulk of the issues Luke was obliged to pay his debts to the king. He was allowed to keep the remaining 200 marks as a gift (*ibid.*, pp. 329-30; 7 Mar. 1230).   [2] Above, p. 100, n. 5.

[3] *Cal. Pat. R., 1266-72*, p. 238. It so happened that the keeper of this vacancy rendered an account at the exchequer even though the issues went to the bishop-elect. The gross income from the vacancy amounted to a mere £66.11.9; Pipe R. 112, m.2d.

[4] Edward II, however, conceded the issues of the Worcester vacancy of 1307-8 to Walter Reynolds (*Cal. Pat. R., 1307-13*, p. 44).

[5] The corn from the vacant archbishopric of Canterbury in 1271 was sold *in grosso* to the archbishop of York (Walter Giffard) in order that the king's creditors might be paid from the proceeds (*Cal. Pat. R., 1266-72*, p. 571). (Compare *ibid.*, p. 603 and also *Reg. W. Giffard*, p. 140 and Pipe R. 119, m.21d.) The corn of Ely in the vacancy of 1298-9 was sold *in grosso* to a certain Reginald of Thunderley for 1,000 marks (Pipe R. 144, m.31).

bacon, 1,000 quarters of wheat and 1,000 quarters of oats, from the manors of the bishopric to Portsmouth 'by Easter at the latest against the king's voyage beyond seas'.[1] Most of the corn of the Canterbury manors was to be sold to provide money for the campaign.[2] The second demand came in October. The regents in England were required to send to the king in Gascony 3,000 quarters of wheat and 3,000 quarters of oats from the bishoprics of Canterbury and Winchester.[3] The regents made out writs to the keepers of the bishoprics[4] who were directed to send the corn to Portsmouth where it would be shipped to Gascony 'ac si esset Anglia puteus inexhaustus' as Matthew Paris bitterly remarks.[5] A similar use of the rich harvests of Winchester was made by Edward I to help in the provisioning of his army in the Welsh war of 1282–3. One thousand quarters of wheat, 300 quarters of barley and 600 quarters of oats were bought for the king in the manors of Winchester in the early summer of 1282 and sent by his order to Chester.[6]

These arrangements were dictated by special circumstances. Apart from occasional liveries of food to the royal household[7] the king seems to have preferred to let the keepers sell the

[1] *Cal. Liberate R., 1240–45*, p. 109. By the same writ a further 700 quarters of wheat and 300 quarters of barley were to be sent to Windsor for the provisioning of the castle.

[2] *Ibid.*, p. 110. 700 quarters of wheat and 500 quarters of oats were reserved for the provisioning of Dover castle. On 12 Mar. 1242 a further 700 quarters of wheat, 200 quarters of barley and 100 quarters of oats were ordered to be sent to 'the nearest harbour of Pageham' (*ibid.*, p. 112).

[3] *Close R., 1237–42*, p. 518.

[4] *Cal. Liberate R., 1240–45*, p. 161, and p. 163 (*bis*). In all, Winchester was ordered to produce 2,000 quarters of wheat and 2,500 quarters of oats and Canterbury 1,000 quarters of wheat and 500 quarters of oats, on this occasion.

[5] *Chron. Majora*, IV, 230. The Winchester Pipe Roll account for 1241–43 (Pipe R. 87, m.3d) is very much coloured by the king's wartime requirements: 'In MCCCLXVj baconis emptis et missis ad Regem in Wasconia CLV li. xvij s. iij ob. Et in eisdem caritandis *sic* usque Portesmue et cariandis per naves iiij li. iij ob. . . . Et in portagio mm qr. frumenti et MM et CCCLij qr. avene de granariis usque ad naves lxxiij s. v d. ob. . . . Et in C et vij baconibus resaliandis et portandis ad naves iiij s. x d. ob . . . Et in MMMMxxvij cleis D et LXij pontibus faciendis de meyremo et cariandis usque mare contra transfretationem Regis C. et ij li. i js. viij d. ob.'

[6] Pipe R. 128, m.28.

[7] For examples see above, pp. 90–1. It was chiefly fish and game which the king required and the latter, and for the most part the former too, would not in any case have appeared among the keeper's receipts. Game would only be taken by the keepers in answer to royal writs.

agricultural produce of the vacant sees and send him money rather than issues in kind. The money sent to the king was normally paid either into the exchequer or into the wardrobe, and in either case it usually lost its identity in the pool of revenue into which it was received. But some of the issues from vacancies never reached either wardrobe or exchequer, they were paid out by the keepers direct to the payee and it is chiefly from these payments that we form some idea of the way in which the profits of vacancies were spent.

Especially on the earlier Pipe Rolls of Henry III's reign the expenditure side of the vacancy accounts tends to be long, comprising numerous comparatively small payments. Some throw light on the king's interests and on the projects which he had in hand. Payments to friars are very numerous in the middle period of the reign[1] and various building projects, both religious and secular, were partly financed from the issues of vacancies. The keepers of the works at Westminster abbey, at the castles of Windsor and Winchester, and at the Tower of London all received vacancy revenue from time to time. These payments were sometimes fairly substantial, rarely less than £100 at a time and sometimes considerably more.[2] The expenses of those who contested an episcopal election on the king's

---

[1] See for example the Winchester vacancy account, 1241–3 (Pipe R. 87, m.3d): 'Et fratribus minoribus Winton' ad fabricam ecclesie sue L marcas per breve Regis. Et in xxxj fratribus predicatoribus et xxiij fratribus minoribus Winton' vestiendis per duos annos xl li. xvj s. ij d. per ij brevia Regis.'

There are similar entries on other accounts:

'Et fratribus minoribus de Lichefeld x marcas de dono Regis . . . Et fratribus predicatoribus de Dereby ad operationes ecclesie sue xx marcas de dono Regis.'; Lichfield account, 1238–40 (Pipe R. 85, m.3). 'Et fratribus predicatoribus morantibus apud Novum Castrum et fratribus minoribus apud Hertepoll ad tunicas singulorum . . . xj li. xj s. Et fratribus predicatoribus de Beverlaco ad se sustenandos in capitulo suo provinciali x marcas de dono Regis.'; Durham account 1240–1 (ibid., m.6d). 'Et fratri Waltero priori fratrum predicatorum ad robas emendas xx li. per breve Regis.'; Chichester account, 1244–6 (Pipe R. 90, m.9).

[2] The keepers of the works on the Tower of London for example received £200 from the issues of the vacant see of Winchester (1240–1; Pipe R. 85, m.3) and on the same account a total of £716.13.4, in five payments, was paid to the keepers of the works on Windsor castle (ibid.). The keepers of the works at Windsor castle also received two payments (one of £223.6.8 and another of £200) from the issues of the vacancy of the bishopric of Chichester, 1244–6 (Pipe R. 90, m.9); and the keepers of the works at Winchester castle received in all over £2,000 on three Winchester accounts for the vacancy of 1238–44 (Pipe R. 85, m.3 and 3d, Pipe R. 87, m.3d. and Pipe R. 88, m.12). See also the table in Appendix B, below.

behalf were sometimes paid, with a slightly comical appropriateness, out of the issues of the bishopric concerned. Thus in the Canterbury vacancy of 1228–9 £100 in all was paid to three king's clerks 'euntibus ad curiam Romanam in nuncium Regis'.[1] Their business at Rome as explained in a royal letter to the pope was the cause at issue between the king and 'the monk Walter de Eynsham, whom the monks of Christ Church, Canterbury have chosen—so they say—to be their archbishop'.[2] A similar entry is to be found on the Canterbury account of 1270–2,[3] and in the Durham vacancy of 1226–8 the king had spent over £350 of the issues of the vacancy in the expenses of his proctors, acting for the king both in England and in Rome in the cause of the Durham election.[4]

All these payments were of the kind that the king would make as need arose. They do not necessarily reveal any conscious budgeting of the income from vacancies as a distinct source of revenue. But in February 1241 the king issued a writ which showed that he had planned to set aside temporarily certain sections of his revenue to be stored separately for a special object (perhaps the Gascon campaign of the following year?). Among the revenue specially treated were all the issues derived from vacant sees and from wardships. The money was to be kept in the Tower of London and 'in nullos alios usus convertantur'.[5] This was perhaps the first sign of a planned use of the issues of episcopal vacancies.

In 1249 when the wealthy see of Durham fell vacant Henry III followed up the precedent of 1241 by again making a block grant of the revenues of this vacancy to a special object, the payment of a royal debt of 5,000 marks to Richard, earl of

[1] Pipe R. 73, m.1.

[2] Pat. R., 1225–32, p. 204.

[3] £18.6.8 to two king's clerks going to Canterbury 'pro negocio electionis loci eiusdem' (Pipe R. 119, m.21d).

[4] Pipe R. 73, m.1. This does not include the annual fees of Walter Crespin and William Greenlaw which were also paid out of these issues. Crespin and Greenlaw, together with Stephen de Lucy, went from Durham to London and back three times on the business of the election 'pro causa contra magistrum W. Scotum et monachos'. On the fourth occasion Crespin and Greenlaw went on to Rome, while Stephen de Lucy returned alone to Durham to his task of administering the vacant bishopric.

[5] Close R., 1237–42, p. 277; 20 Feb. 1241.

Cornwall.[1] The procedure was not exactly the same as in 1241. Then the money had passed through the exchequer. In 1249 the issues of Durham were to be paid direct to Richard of Cornwall.[2] As financial pressure grew more stringent Henry III turned to the bishoprics again to repay the debts he had contracted. On 13 September 1254 the king ordered that all the issues of the vacant sees of Ely and Carlisle (together with the issues of Jewry) should be kept in a safe place until the king's return to England:

ut inde satisfacere possit quibusdam creditoribus suis quibus dictos exitus per sacramentum suum obligavit pro quibusdam debitis in quibus eis tenetur.[3]

A few weeks later it became clear that this assignment of the issues of Ely and Carlisle was part of a more general plan that the issues of all bishoprics, abbeys and priories either vacant or to become vacant should be placed under the special custody of John Chishull, Robert de Manneby, and William of Axmouth (three royal clerks) until a sum of 5,000 marks had been raised by them and repaid to the citizens of Bordeaux.[4] The issues of these vacancies were accounted for by Chishull, Manneby and Axmouth before the barons of exchequer and the deputies of the citizens of Bordeaux, but the issues themselves were not paid *in thesauro*. They were paid to the three royal clerks and by them presumably to the citizens of Bordeaux.[5] As in the case of the issues of the Durham vacancy in 1249, the treasury of exchequer had been by-passed.

Vacancy issues had become a financial asset which the king used freely as a surety for the loans that he was now contracting with alarming speed. On the 6 February 1256 he empowered

---

[1] *Cal. Pat. R.*, *1247–58*, p. 38; 9 Mar. 1249.

[2] 'R. comiti Cornubie fratri Regis in partem solutionis debitorum in quibus Rex ei tenebatur MMXX li.' (Durham account, 1249; Pipe R. 94, m.18.)

[3] *Close R.*, *1253–54*, p. 272; 13 Sep. 1254.

[4] *Cal. Pat. R.*, *1247–58*, p. 359; 29 Sep. 1254.

[5] For example £709.8.6 from the issues of the vacant bishopric of Ely were paid by the sub-keeper of that bishopric, William Breton, to Manneby, Axmouth and Chishull (Pipe R. 101, m.4). It is stated at the end of this account that Axmouth should answer for this £709.8.6 on behalf of the three. There is a cross reference to the dorse of the membrane (i.e. *ibid.*, m.4d) but there it is merely restated that Axmouth *owes* the money.

the treasurer Philip Lovel to raise a loan of 1,000 or 800 marks 'from merchants or others' and to give security on the issues of the archbishopric of York, the bishopric of Salisbury and the abbey of Evesham, 'now void and in the king's hands'.[1] Four months later Henry required 2,000 marks for the expenses of his proctors at Rome 'on the business of Apulia', and he committed the issues of those vacancies, that were not already pledged for the payment of other debts, to Robert Walerand for this special purpose.[2] Walerand thus became keeper of the Ely vacancy of 1256–8. By the time 2,000 marks came to be paid from this see, many complications in the system of credit had arisen, but certainly 2,000 marks from this Ely vacancy by-passed the treasury and were paid to various royal creditors.[3] In June 1257 all vacancy issues, except those of Ely and Carlisle

[1] Cal. Pat. R., 1247–58, p. 461.

[2] Ibid., p. 480; 10 June 1256.

[3] The sale of the corn of the bishopric was granted to the executors of the late bishop of Ely for a sum of 2,000 marks of which the executors were to pay 1,000 marks to Thomas Count of Savoy and 1,000 marks to Edward the king's son (Fine R. 54, m.2; 14 Sep. 1257). Edward in his turn had bound himself to satisfy the citizens of Bordeaux, out of the custom of Bordeaux, for the 1,000 marks which was his share of the Ely issues (Cal. Pat. R., 1247–58, pp. 563–4; 28 June 1257). Eventually this 1,000 marks was sent, at Edward's order, to Robert Walerand 'and other knights going with him to the war of Wales', (ibid., p. 605; 8 Nov. 1257).

The carry forward of Robert Walerand's account for this Ely vacancy (Pipe R. 101, m.4d) corroborates the evidence cited above by the following entry:

'Et executoribus testamenti Willelmi quondam Elyensis episcopi de venditione bladorum dicti episcopatus de autumpno anni xlij quam Rex eis fecit MM marcas per breve Regis, de quibus MM marcis iidem executores solverunt pro Rege Edwardo filio suo apud novum templum Lond' in festo S. Martini anno eodem M marcas quas Rex ei assignavit pro M marcis quibus eum adquietavit versus maiorem et cives Burdegalenses in parte solucionis debitorum in quibus Rex eis tenebatur et M marcas solverunt iidem executores Thome de Sabaudia comiti loco predicto.'

It is tempting to identify the sum of 2,000 marks paid by the executors and the 2,000 marks which the king needed for his proctors' expenses 'in the business of Apulia'. This, however, presupposes that the Count of Savoy and the citizens of Bordeaux had meanwhile advanced the money for the proctors' expenses, and I know of no evidence for this. On the other hand the only other bishopric of which Robert Walerand became custodian at this time was Lichfield from 29 Oct. 1256 (Fine R. 54, m.14), to a date not later than 17 Feb. 1257 (Cal. Pat. R., 1247–58, p. 542; a writ which was addressed in fact to Robert Walerand's brother and frequent associate, John). This short Lichfield vacancy, for which unfortunately there is no Pipe Roll account, is unlikely to have yielded much more than £100 (compare figure for vacancy of 1241–2, Appendix A, p. 222, below).

were pledged (along with several other sections of royal revenue) for the repayment of a loan of 10,000 marks to the merchants of Florence.[1]

The practice of assigning the money of a vacancy wholesale to the payment of a royal creditor and, in some cases at least, by-passing both the exchequer and the wardrobe except as places of account was, in 1258, a development of the previous decade. It is natural to wonder whether it was an unpopular development or not from the baronial point of view. In the Provisions of Oxford the barons stated their principles about the financial supremacy of the exchequer: 'et la vengent totes les issues de la tere, et en nule part ailurs'.[2] This has in general been assumed to be an expression of baronial dislike of the wardrobe. No doubt it was. But what exactly did the barons dislike about the wardrobe? Professor Treharne has suggested that the barons had no need of concern as long as the keepers of the wardrobe presented accounts regularly at the exchequer: the danger being that on the precedents of Rivaux and of Aigueblanche, they might not present accounts.[3] This may, of course, be the whole truth. On the other hand it does seem possible that the barons might still have wished all the issues of the land to come to the exchequer and not to the wardrobe even if they could have been certain that future keepers of the wardrobe would invariably render accounts at the exchequer for the whole period of their office. The barons speak of *issues*, not of accounts. When the keeper of the wardrobe presented his account at the exchequer the issues which he had received had, for good or ill, been spent. Not much could then be done; but if a baronial treasurer were to be assured that all the issues of the land would pass through his hands, then the prospects for baronial 'control' would be brighter. The income of the wardrobe would then, of course, derive from the exchequer, and not from independent sources.

If the barons were, in fact, concerned as it has just been suggested, not merely that all issues should be accounted for at the

---

[1] *Cal. Pat. R.*, *1247–58*, p. 562.

[2] Stubbs, *Select Charters*, p. 382.

[3] R. F. Treharne, *The Baronial Plan of Reform, 1258–63* (Manchester, 1932), p. 29. For the gaps in the series of wardrobe accounts see *P.R.O. Lists and Indexes*, XI, 102.

exchequer, but also that all issues should actually go through the treasury of exchequer, then, the phrase 'et en nule part ailurs' may possibly have been intended in a wider sense than 'and not into the wardrobe'. Some at least of the large sums which the king had paid to his creditors out of the issues of certain vacant bishoprics had not touched the treasury of the exchequer. They had in most cases been accounted for at the exchequer, but by that time the payments had been made. If the king was to be free to contract heavy loans and pledge away the issues of the land for their payment in such a way that those issues never flowed into the treasury at all, there was little chance of restoring the government to a state of comparative solvency. It may have been, therefore, that the barons disliked all by-passing of the treasury of the exchequer, that they were thinking in terms of hard cash rather than in terms of accounts, and that they had in mind other diversions of revenue in addition to diversion through the wardrobe.

However, this suggestion must necessarily be tentative if only for the fact that in the period of baronial control of the supposedly 'vacant' see of Winchester, Nicholas de Haudlo, the keeper, was ordered to pay 1,000 marks of the issues of the see to Richard de Clare, earl of Gloucester, so that Richard in turn might pay it to the merchants of London in payment of the king's debts.[1] Later, Haudlo was ordered to pay a further 2,000 marks direct to these merchants.[2] This baronial keeper therefore was also by-passing the treasury of exchequer. But these writs do not necessarily invalidate the interpretation suggested above. As is well known, the barons, once in power, made few changes in the machinery of administration. When they were themselves in a controlling position they could afford to use methods which they had considered dangerous in the hands of the king.[3] For instance, they did not altogether stop payments '*de forinseca*' into the wardrobe. Thus the baronial keeper of Winchester paid £1,213.6.8 into the wardrobe from the issues

[1] *Cal. Pat. R.*, *1258–66*, p. 22; 18 May 1259. Aymer, the king's brother, was at this time bishop-elect of Winchester but the barons a little later chose to regard the see as vacant none the less.

[2] *Ibid.*, p. 30; 17 July 1259.

[3] See S. B. Chrimes, *An Introduction to the Administrative History of Mediaeval England* (Oxford, 1952), p. 125.

of the see between Michaelmas 1258 and Christmas 1260.[1] Similarly, the payments of money direct from the keeper of Winchester to the merchants of London might well have commended itself by its obvious convenience, and when the payments had the sanction of the barons, and the keeper of the see was a trusted baronial servant,[2] then there was no immediate risk in not insisting that the issues should first pass through the exchequer.

In the latter part of Henry III's reign, after the Barons' Wars, there does not seem to have been any general pledging of vacancy issues on the scale of the few years before 1258. But occasional instances occur. In 1271 the chapter of Salisbury fined with the king for the custody of the vacancy of their see and the king assigned the 3,000 marks to his brother in repayment of a loan.[3] Indeed, the amount of the fine may have been determined by the amount of the loan.

It is clear from the use that Henry III made of the issues of vacancies in the second half of his reign that he had come to regard this source of income as having a distinct part to play in his financial administration. In particular it was outstandingly suitable to use as a security for the repayment of loans. It was perhaps a sign of the king's planned use of vacancy revenue that he should have required to know in June 1261 exactly how much money had been received at the exchequer from various

[1] Pipe R. 104, m.2; Nicholas de Haudlo's account. Some money was evidently paid into the wardrobe from the vacant see of Durham too in the vacancy of 1260-1 (see entry on P.R.O. Enrolled Accounts, Wardrobe and Household, I, m.1; 'mcc li. de exitibus episcopatus Dunolm annis xliij et xlv per manus magistri Johannis Maunsell et Thome Penroz'). There was no Pipe Roll account for this Durham vacancy.

On the other hand the barons may have discouraged such payments into the wardrobe on occasion. Tout suggests that this may be the reason for the cancelling and surrender of a writ of 5 Mar. 1259 (*Cal. Pat. R., 1258-66*, p. 13) by which the king ordered Nicholas de Haudlo to pay 300 or 400 marks from the money of the bishopric to the king's servants, to be paid by them into the wardrobe (*Chapters in Admin. Hist.*, I, 301, n. 2). Perhaps the baronial alternative to this writ is another, of 8 Mar. 1259, made 'by counsel of the nobles of the council', and ordering £120 of the money of the king's brother Aymer to be delivered in the wardrobe for the king's expenses (*Cal. Pat. R., 1258-66*, p. 14). The barons may have preferred the king to draw on Aymer's private income for his expenses than to take the money from the issues of the vacant bishopric.

[2] For Haudlo's appointment see above, p. 90, n. 2.

[3] *Cal. Pat. R., 1266-72*, pp. 543-4.

sees recently vacant.[1] The information was evidently wanted for a specific purpose, although that purpose is not revealed. The writ issued for this purpose is in many ways baffling but it deserves quotation:

Mandatum est Johanni abbati de Burgo Sancti Petri, thesaurario regis, quod scrutatis rotulis scaccarii regis sine dilacione scire faciat regi sub sigillo suo quantum receptum fuerit ad scaccarium regis de exitibus et proventibus archiepiscopatus Eboracensis in duabus ultimis vacacionibus eiusdem, dum fuit in manu regis, et de exitibus et proventibus episcopatus Wintoniensis a tempore quo idem episcopatus extitit in manu regis post recessum A. quondam Wintoniensis episcopi fratris regis ab Anglia; et similiter quantum receptum fuerit ad idem scaccarium de exitibus et proventibus episcopatus Dunelmensis de tempore quo ultimo vacans fuit et in manu regis; ut rex inde distincte et aperte certiorari possit citra diem Jovis in instanti septimana Pentecostes; et a quo tempore dicte ecclesie vacaverunt et in manu regis fuerunt. Et hoc sicut regem diligit nullo modo omittat.[2]

The writ is characteristic of that atmosphere of financial sophistication that distinguished the later from the earlier part of the reign of Henry III. In the first half of the reign the income from vacant sees seems to have been simply a welcome addition to an invariably needy royal treasury. The king would dip into the wealth from the bishoprics to pay his proctors, to finance building operations on a castle or on a church, to make gifts to his friends or benefactions to religious causes. It was only when financial stress became severe that Henry was forced into a new expedient of assigning the issues of vacancies in large block grants to pay his creditors. This development reached its peak in the period 1254–8. Only on two further occasions, after the troubled period of the Barons' War, does Henry seem to have assigned the whole revenues of a vacancy to a single object; in the case of Norwich in 1266,[3] and of Salisbury in 1271.[4]

Edward I too used the revenue of vacancies to pay his debts, but not at the beginning of his reign, or at least not on a big

---

[1] This of course was the period when the king was gradually re-establishing his power.

[2] *Close R., 1259–61*, p. 388; 4 June 1261.

[3] *Cal. Pat. R., 1258–66*, p. 528. This was the occasion on which the issues were assigned to the king's son Edmund and the exchequer was ordered not to intermeddle. See above, p. 101.   [4] Referred to above, p. 158.

scale. It is true that £1,467.0.0 of the £2,668.19.10½ accounted
for from Durham in the vacancy of 1274 was spent in paying off
loans to three merchants,[1] but this is an isolated example, and a
good proportion of the issues of this vacancy still remained when
the merchants had been paid, and this was delivered into the
wardrobe.[2] It is from 1299 to the end of the reign that echoes
of the decade before the Barons' War ring loudly. This again
was, of course, a period of great financial pressure. On 21
August 1299, the king granted to Edmund, earl of Cornwall,
'the custody of the first archbishopric or bishopric which falls
void until he has fully raised from the issues thereof 2,000 marks
lent by him to the king'.[3] The see was to be the archbishopric of
York.[4] The parallel with the assignment of the issues of the
Durham vacancy to Richard, earl of Cornwall in 1249, which
inaugurated Henry III's use of vacancies for paying large debts,
is an interesting one. At the same time as the assignment of the
issues of the York vacancy to Earl Edmund, practically the whole
of the issues of the vacant see of Lincoln 1299–1300 were spent
in the release of Peter de Mauley, who had incurred debt in
the king's service in Gascony and was being held hostage in
London,[5] and a substantial part of the issues of the vacancy of
Ely in 1298–9[6] and at York in 1304–6[7] were paid to the king's

---

[1] Pipe R. 118, m.18d: 'Et Donasio Donanti mercatori pro mutuo regi facto ad
negocia sua inde expedienda ccccliij li. xiij s. iiij d . . . Et Edoni de Gaske mercatori pro eodem dxlvj li. xiij s. iiij d. Et Tegro Amato mercatori pro eodem
cccclxvj li. xiij s. iiijd.'

[2] £912.6.0 (ibid.).   [3] Cal. Pat. R., 1292–1301, p. 431.

[4] In fact York had already fallen vacant a few days earlier, 16 Aug. 1299
(Pipe R. 150, m.30). £1,206.14.0 was paid in all to the earl and his executors from
the issues of this vacancy (ibid., m.31d).

[5] The order to Walter of Gloucester to receive the necessary amount for Mauley's
release, from the keeper of the vacant bishopric of Lincoln, for payment to the
merchants of Bayonne, is dated 21 Nov. 1299 (Cal. Pat. R., 1292–1301, p. 479).
On the Pipe Roll account for this Lincoln vacancy it is stated that £540.5.6
has been paid to Walter of Gloucester (Pipe R. 150, m.36d). The cross reference to
Pipe R. 155, m.2d is quite unhelpful. However a Close Roll entry of 25 Apr.
1305 acquits Walter of Gloucester of £540.5.6 which had been handed over in
payment for the release of a hostage, Peter de Mauley (Malo Lacu) (Cal. Close R.,
1302–07, p. 262).

[6] The order for the payment of 2,000 marks of the issues of the bishopric of Ely
to John of Brittany was issued 1 Sep. 1299 (Cal. Pat. R., 1292–1301, p. 435). This
sum was duly paid according to the vacancy account on the Pipe Roll (Pipe R.
144, m.31).

[7] In June 1305 the king granted to John of Brittany 'in further payment of the

nephew John of Brittany who, like Peter de Mauley had incurred heavy expenses in the king's service in Gascony. The ball was gathering speed. In 1302 the king contracted a heavy loan of 10,000 marks with Amadeus of Savoy and pledged the issues of vacancies at Ely, Worcester and Bath for repayment.[1] Later the revenue from the vacancies of London, 1303–4,[2] and of Winchester 1304–5[3] were also drawn into the task of repaying Amadeus. It would seem that by this time the issues of vacancies were being pledged further than was financially healthy, for in April 1303 the king granted to the 'commonalties, inhabitants and merchants of certain Gascon towns— the issues of bishoprics, abbeys and priories void, as soon as 5,000 marks have been paid to Margaret queen of England and to Ametz count of Savoy'.[4] By the end of the reign Amadeus had drawn in the region of £4,000 from episcopal vacancies towards the repayment of the loan he had made to the king.[5]

The use of episcopal vacancies as a security for royal loans was in one sense a sign of a planned financial administration, but it was also a sign of approaching insolvency when it reached the pace that it did in the last five years of Edward I's reign. A

king's debts to him . . . all the corn in the lands of the archbishopric of York, which is void and in the king's hands . . . ' (*Cal. Pat. R., 1301–07*, p. 366; 19 June 1305).

[1] The keepers in each of the three sees were ordered on 18 July 1302 'to pay Amadeus, count of Savoy, all the issues of the bishopric received from the day when this order was made, as the king has granted to him all the issues of the bishopric, until he shall be satisfied for 10,000 marks from those and other issues, which sum the king lately granted to him, as contained in the king's letters patent.' (*Cal. Close R., 1296–1302*, p. 540).

[2] *Cal. Close R., 1302–07*, p. 357; 22 Nov. 1305. Walter of Gloucester was to be allowed 675 marks in his account for the vacant see of London for a payment of that sum made to Amadeus.

[3] 1,600 marks were paid to Amadeus's attorney according to the Winchester account on Pipe R. 152B, m.20.

[4] *Cal. Pat. R., 1301–07*, pp. 136–7.

[5] £621.11.9 from the bishopric of Worcester (account of 1302–3; Pipe R. 147, m.25); £260.8.1½ from Bath (continuation of account of 1302; Pipe R. 151, m.7d); £1,983.6.8 from Ely(account of 1302; Pipe R. 150, m.34d); £1,066.13.4 from Winchester (account of 1304–5; Pipe R. 152B, m.20) and £450 from London. See n. 2, above. On the Pipe Roll account for this vacancy the keeper is left with a credit balance of £506.19.3¾, when agricultural expenses have been deducted. However, as the keeper is accounting as escheator this balance is grouped with many other sums for which he is accounting and any further payments which may have been made from the issues of the bishopric of London are not separately classified (Pipe R. 149, m.37).

M

more healthy phase in the planned use of vacancy issues occurs earlier in that reign, roughly between 1278 and 1285. The king was building castles in North Wales and for nearly a decade a large proportion of the revenue from vacancies flowed into this investment. In 1279 both archbishoprics were vacant and the greater part of the issues from York were paid to William de Perton 'ad operaciones castri Regis de Rothelan'.[1] The keepers of Canterbury made a more modest contribution of 500 marks 'for the furtherance of the king's works in Wales'.[2] From the very profitable Winchester vacancy of 1280–2 a substantial proportion of the issues was eventually delivered to Perton to help in the building of the castles of Flint and Rhuddlan. In this case, however, the payments were not all made direct to Perton. Some were; but others reached him through the wardrobe or through the treasury of the exchequer. These different strands are perhaps worth disentangling because although the details are both tedious and complicated they do produce some impression of the kind of relation the official accounts bore to what was really happening. In the first place, £1,850 of the issues from Winchester seem to have been paid direct to William de Perton.[3] A further 4,800 marks appear to have been paid into the wardrobe while the wardrobe was in Wales or at Chester,[4] and since Perton was drawing on wardrobe reserves

[1] £1,042.1.2, was the exact sum paid; Chancellor's R. 74, m.7. Perton was in charge of the building at Flint and Rhuddlan (Pipe R. 131, m.26).

[2] 'Radulfo de Broketon custodi operacionum Regis Wall' ad operaciones Regis ibidem faciendas D marcas' (Pipe R. 124, m.23d).

[3] This total was allowed to the keepers of the vacant bishopric by three separate writs of *allocate* ordering the barons of exchequer to allow the keepers of the bishopric of Winchester six separate payments which they made to Perton (Liberate R. 57, m.3, 28 Oct. 1281, Liberate R. 58, m.2, 20 July 1282 and Liberate R. 59, m.8, 6 Dec. 1282). In every case except the last mentioned, each of these writs of *allocate* find their complement in a recorded payment or payments direct to Perton on the Pipe Roll account for this vacancy (Pipe R. 128, m.28). But in the one exceptional case, a payment of 400 marks authorized by the writ of *allocate* on Liberate R. 59, m.8, the corresponding entry on the vacancy account was *originally* a payment direct to Perton, but has been altered to a payment 'Willelmo de Luda' (William of Louth was at the time keeper of the wardrobe). Perton himself however accounts for all six payments, that is the whole £1,850, without any differentiation as to the way in which he received the sums. They are all described as 'received from the keepers of the bishopric of Winchester' (Pipe R. 130, m.1d).

[4] This figure is calculated from a correlation of the payments *in garderoba*, and carriage expenses 'in partibus Wallie' as given on the account for the Winchester vacancy (Pipe R. 128, m.28).

at the time it may be that *some* though not all of this money reached him too.[1] Furthermore, at least £1,000 of the money which was paid by the keepers of Winchester into the treasury of the exchequer was subsequently paid to Perton in obedience to a writ of *liberate* addressed to the treasurer and chamberlains.[2] These complexities are quite absent from the account which perhaps shows the perfecting of the allocation of the revenue from a vacancy to the work of castle building. When the archbishopric of York fell vacant in 1285 Otto of Granson, justice of Wales was given superior custody of the see, 'on condition that he apply the issues thereof to the construction of the castles in Wales'[3] with the result that £1,264.13.4 was paid in five instalments to the king's chamberlain of Caernarvon.[4]

Admittedly the amounts contributed from the issues of vacancies to the building of castles in Wales were not startlingly great, but they were appreciable. And they were significant. This allocation of the profits of vacancies to a large constructive project was perhaps the most purposeful and discriminating use of casual revenue that had been achieved. As far as the issues of vacancies were concerned it was a phase that never recurred. By the end of his reign, Edward I had been driven, like his father, to pledging his revenue from vacant bishoprics to royal creditors even before the vacancies had occurred, and in

[1] According to the account rendered by Perton's executors (Pipe R. 131, m.26) Perton appears to have received £1,489.7.1½ from the wardrobe which might have included some sums received from the Winchester vacancy. (See the entry of this outpayment of £1,489.7.1½ on the wardrobe account on Pipe R. 130, m.5; 20 Nov. 1282 to 20 Nov. 1284).

[2] Liberate R. 57, m.11; 26 Nov. 1280. 'Rex eisdem (thesaurario et camerariis) salutem. Liberate dilecto clerico nostro magistro Willelmo de Perton custodi operacionum nostrarum de Rothelan et de Fflynt M li. videlicet de illis denariis qui nuper liberati fuerunt in thesauro predicto de exitibus episcopatus Wyntoniensis.'

It seems possible that a further £800 followed these same lines. Perton accounted in his account for Rhuddlan (1279–80; Pipe R. 124, m.29) for £800 'receptis Willelmo de Hamelton tunc custode episcopatus Wyntoniensis sede vacante'. There is no record of such a sum of money being paid direct to Perton at this period of the Winchester vacancy on the vacancy account on the Pipe Roll, but there *is* a record on that account of £800 being paid into the exchequer at Westminster, and there is a writ of *liberate* directing the treasurer to pay Perton £800 which may possibly be connected (Liberate R. 56, m.6; 14 May 1280).

[3] *Cal. Pat. R.*, *1281–92*, p. 193; 15 Sep. 1285.

[4] Pipe R. 133, m.28.

the reign of his son there is no sign of the recurrence of this phase, nor of any originality in the treatment of this source of income. However, while it lasted this brief constructive phase has a further interest. It provides a convenient standard of reference against which to measure the value which episcopal vacancies still held for the king in the late thirteenth century. Vacancies were in general becoming shorter, and the interregnum at Winchester 1280–2 was longer than most, lasting two and a half years. In that time the crown drew a net profit of £11,332.5.8 from this see. Harlech castle was probably built for less than this,[1] and the great fortress of Conway for less than twice as much.[2] Admittedly, Winchester was an exceptionally wealthy bishopric but even considerably smaller sums were far from negligible.[3]

It has already been pointed out that normally it was only when the revenue from a vacancy was paid direct to the payee that we know on what it was spent. But a large proportion of vacancy profits was paid straight into the treasury of the exchequer or into the wardrobe, and in these cases there is usually no means of knowing what happened to it subsequently. However, there is some interest in seeing how the proportionate relation between the amounts paid into these two royal treasuries varied from time to time. Until quite near the close of the thirteenth century it is doubtful whether one could select a single decade in which the issues of vacancies were paid exclusively into either the wardrobe or the exchequer. The lines were never drawn completely rigidly. But there were perceptible changes of emphasis.

[1] See J. G. Edwards, 'Edward I's Castle-Building in Wales', *Proceedings of the British Academy*, XXXII (1946), pp. 62–3. 'At Harlech the recorded total of £8,184.10.9 suggests a notional figure of £9,000 for that castle.'

[2] Professor Edwards suggests a notional figure of about £19,000 for the cost of Conway, the largest of Edward I's Welsh fortresses (*ibid.*, p. 63).

[3] Henry III had drawn a net profit of over £10,000 from Winchester, 1258–60 (Pipe R. 104, mm.1–2). York 1279 yielded a more modest net total of £1,503.2.4½ (Chancellor's R. 74, m.7) and in 1304–6 £3,301.6.6¼ (Pipe R. 152B, mm.16–19). The net total from Durham in 1283 was £2,540.18.0¼ (Pipe R. 127, m.2d) and from Ely in 1302–3 £2,718.9.2¾ (Pipe R. 150, m.34 and 34d).

Canterbury however in the vacancy of 1292–5 approaches the large figure for the Winchester vacancy of 1280–2 with a net yield of £10,136.7.5¾ (Pipe R. 141, mm.28d–29d). The figures for smaller bishoprics such as London, Bath, Norwich or Chichester fluctuate at a lower level, around £500. See Appendix A, below.

Between the beginning of Henry III's reign and 1237 payments into the wardrobe from vacant sees are very moderate. Most of the money is paid *in thesauro*.[1] However about the year 1237 there is a noticeable swing of the pendulum. In the long Durham vacancy of 1237–41, by far the greater part of the issues go to the wardrobe and only very small payments are made *in thesauro*.[2] The same general pattern is found in the vacancy accounts for Lichfield 1238–40,[3] for Winchester in the earlier part of the vacancy of 1238–44,[4] and also the earlier part of the London vacancy of 1241–4.[5] Broadly speaking it might be said that between 1237 and 1242 vacancy issues flow in full spate into the wardrobe, and in a comparative trickle into the exchequer.[6] There follows a period during which the issues are much more evenly apportioned between the two treasuries, and then in 1255–8 there is another period of marked emphasis on the wardrobe.[7]

Here we may take stock. The two peak periods in the payment of vacancy issues into the wardrobe were from 1237 to 1242 and from 1255 to 1258. These correspond with two distinctive phases in the history of the wardrobe finance itself. During each period the proportion of wardrobe receipts *de forinseca* to total wardrobe receipts was particularly high,[8] whereas in the intervening period 1242–55, roughly the period of Chaceporc's keepership, the proportion of foreign receipts was

---

[1] See Appendix B, pp. 234–5.

[2] The three Pipe Roll accounts for this vacancy cover the period 19 Apr. 1237 to 10 Feb. 1241 (Pipe R. 84, m.2 and Pipe R. 85, m.6d). Altogether only £208.13.4 is paid into the treasury, whereas the very large sum of £9,933.18.6 is paid into the wardrobe.

[3] Pipe R. 85, m.3. In this case there is no payment at all into the treasury but £334.3.4 is paid into the wardrobe.

[4] Between 1238 and 1241 (Pipe R. 85, m.3 and 3d) £4,737.15.10 was paid into the wardrobe as compared with £1,003.6.8 into the treasury; but the last two accounts for this vacancy (Pipe R. 87, m.3d and Pipe R. 88, m.12) show a more even balance of payments between treasury and wardrobe.

[5] See Appendix B, p. 236.

[6] See Appendix B, pp. 235–6.

[7] In the York vacancy of 1255–6 £1,393.6.8 is paid into the wardrobe, nothing into the treasury (Pipe R. 101, m.4d). From Salisbury in 1256 £340 is paid into the wardrobe and again nothing into the treasury (Pipe R. 100, m.19), and from the Ely vacancy of 1256–8 £1,040 is paid into the wardrobe as against £193.15.6½ into the treasury of exchequer (Pipe R. 101, m.4 and 4d and m.6).

[8] See the figures given by Tout, *Chapters in Admin. Hist.*, VI, 74–7.

appreciably smaller. The coincidence of these trends is perhaps not unexpected, but it is interesting. Vacancy issues were evidently a type of revenue which the king could conveniently divert from the exchequer when he wished to increase the 'foreign' receipts of the wardrobe, and that increase appears therefore to represent deliberate royal policy.

Between the period of the Barons' Wars and the end of Henry III's reign, and again during the early part of Edward I's reign, there was no very strongly preponderating allocation of vacancy revenue to either the wardrobe or to the exchequer, although the emphasis in Edward I's reign was, on the whole, in the direction of the wardrobe. Then comes a marked change. After 1284 there were no more payments of vacancy issues into the wardrobe so far as can be seen from vacancy accounts, and this remained true for the whole of Edward II's reign as well.[1] It seems evident that this change was the direct result of the changed relationship between wardrobe and exchequer which reached its completion about 1290, when the machinery of the exchequer had been taken over by men trained in wardrobe methods, and when the use of tallies as an instrument of credit had made it easy for the wardrobe to draw its revenue direct from the country although formally that same revenue was

---

[1] Moreover, there only seems to be one reference on the vacancy accounts of Edward II's reign to a payment *in camera*. William Beauchamp was custodian of Worcester for a part of the vacancy of that bishopric in 1317, from 28 March, the date of Walter Maidstone's death, to 20 June (Pipe R. 165, m.30). By a writ of privy seal of 13 June 1317 the king ordered a letter close to be sent to the treasurer and barons of exchequer ordering them not to compel Beauchamp to render account at the exchequer for the issues which he had received from this vacant bishopric, as he had paid a certain sum into the king's chamber, and he would pay the rest there. (*Cal. Close R., 1313–18*, p. 415; 15 June 1317.)

The barons however, appear to have thought that Beauchamp should account at the exchequer, and on the Pipe Roll of 1320, on which the account for the rest of the vacancy is enrolled, there is a note that Beauchamp's debt is enrolled on the Exannual Roll:

'Willelmus de Bello Campo debet respondere de exitibus temporalium episcopatus Wigorniensis de tempore quo habuit custodiam sicut supra continetur . . . Et respondit in Rotulo Exannuale inter debita extracta de compotis forinsecio post Rotel.' (Pipe R. 164, m.30).

On Exannual R. 3, m.15 is the unhelpful entry:

'Willelmus de Bello Campo de exitibus temporalium espiscopatus Wigorniensis de tempore quo habuit custodiam sicut continetur . . . in rotulo xiij° rotulo compotorum.'

being paid *in thesauro* and not *in garderoba*.[1] This sufficiently explains the apparently uniform flow of money from vacant sees *in thesauro* after 1284 and the disappearance of payments *in garderoba*. Here again the administration of vacancy revenue faithfully and speedily reflects an important change in the general history of financial administration.

In conclusion, there is a story from the chronicle of Matthew Paris which raises an interesting point in connection with the revenue which the crown drew from vacant sees in the thirteenth and early fourteenth centuries. When the see of York fell vacant in 1255 the king, according to Matthew Paris, delayed and hindered the election of a new archbishop so that he might the more freely despoil the archbishopric:

Ait enim, 'Nunquam illum archiepiscopatum antea in manu tenui; ideo cavendum est, ne nimis cito elabatur.'[2]

Did Henry III, and Edward I too perhaps, deliberately prolong episcopal vacancies in order to enjoy the revenues? It is certainly true that there were some long vacancies in Henry III's reign, and that the longer vacancies did tend to be in the wealthier sees. Several of those wealthy sees had monastic chapters, Winchester, Durham, Ely and Canterbury for instance. This immediately increased the likelihood of a disputed election, and therefore of a longer vacancy, since monastic chapters were less inclined than secular chapters to elect royal nominees. Moreover, the king was especially anxious that his own nominee should be chosen in the case of a wealthy bishopric. When an episcopal see was both conventual and wealthy therefore the chances were weighted on the side of electoral tension and a long vacancy. It seems quite obvious that both Henry III and Edward I would be well aware of the advantage of prolonging the struggle over an episcopal election in a case where the monks would not elect the royal candidate and where the issues of the vacancy were meanwhile having a bracing effect on royal finance. It is in the fourteenth century that the real decline in the importance of vacancy revenue sets

[1] Tout, *op. cit.*, pp. 95–9. The system of tallies is explained more fully by Sir Hilary Jenkinson in his article 'Exchequer Tallies', *Archaeologia*, LXII, Part II (1911), pp. 367–80.
[2] *Chron. Majora*, V, 516.

in, and by Edward II's reign bishoprics are rarely vacant for as long as a year.

Thomas Madox suggested that 'as the Kings in the Five or Six Successions after the Conquest ordered matters one may guess they made the income from vacancies a "considerable Revenue"'. Perhaps we might not go very far astray if we extended that guess to the seven or eight successions after the Conquest.

CHAPTER VI

The Emoluments of Episcopal Vacancies: (II) Patronage and Feudal Perquisites

Two portions of the emoluments which the king enjoyed by reason of an episcopal vacancy were deliberately excluded from the consideration of vacancy revenue in the last chapter. The first of these portions may for convenience be called feudal perquisites. These were the rights and attendant profits which the king derived from his temporary position as immediate overlord of those tenants who held in chief of the bishopric. Wardships, marriages and reliefs, escheats and the scutage from knights' fees fall into this class. The second is the royal right of patronage *sede vacante*. The king claimed that during a vacancy he might present to all those prebends and other ecclesiastical benefices to which the bishop had a right to collate *sede plena*.

The feudal perquisites do not need much explanation. Those which involved only single payments, reliefs and levies of scutage,[1] were often accounted for by the royal custodians of the temporalities.[2] Wardships and escheats were sometimes

---

[1] Since the king levied scutage from the vacant bishopric as the bishop would have levied it had the king taken a scutage *sede plena* (i.e. from both recognized and unrecognized fees) this payment is properly classed as a 'feudal' perquisite.

[2] For example the receipts from vacant bishoprics for the scutage of Kerry were accounted for by the keepers of the bishoprics of Salisbury, London and Ely in their accounts on the Pipe Roll of 1228 (Pipe R. 72, m.10, 10d and 10d respectively), and by the keepers of Canterbury on the subsequent roll (Pipe R. 73, m.1).

In the next Canterbury vacancy, 1231–4, there is a mandate to the keepers of the archbishopric for the collection of scutage (Fine R. 30, m.2; 27 Sep. 1231) and again in the vacancy of this see in 1242 a mandate is issued to the sheriffs of Essex and Hertford ordering them to allow the keepers of the vacant archbishopric to collect scutage themselves and answer for it at the exchequer (Fine R. 39A, m.2).

Reliefs are frequently classed with pleas and perquisites, as on the Chichester account for 1244–6 (Pipe. R 90, m.9); the Lichfield account 1241–2 (Pipe R. 95, m.6); the Ely account for 1256–8 (Pipe R. 101, m.4); the Bath account for 1302 (Pipe R. 150, m.32). Instances of the separate entry of reliefs are found on the Salisbury accounts of 1228–9 (Pipe R. 72, m.10), 1246–7 (Pipe R. 92, m.16); and

accounted for by the custodians too,[1] but they could lend themselves to an alternative treatment. Not infrequently the king
would grant out wardships and escheats for private exploitation instead of retaining them in the custody of the keeper of the
bishopric.[2] Wardships and marriages were sometimes granted
to the relatives of the heir. Thus, in the Canterbury vacancy of
1240–5, Robert of Canterbury was given the custody of the land
which had belonged to his son, now deceased, during the minority of his son's heir,[3] and Nicholas de Yeland a tenant of the
bishopric of Durham had the custody of his brother's land in
1227.[4] Alternatively the wardship might be conceded to a royal
servant. In 1272, William de Wintreshull, as a reward 'for long
service', received the wardship of the lands and the heirs of
John Gravenel who held of the archbishop of Canterbury.[5]
Stephen de Lucy in the vacancy of the see of Durham 1226–8,[6]
and Bertram de Crioil in the Canterbury vacancy of 1240–5 paid

1256 (Pipe R. 100, m.19), on the Durham account for 1249 (Pipe R. 94, m.18)
and the Winchester account for 1258–60 (Pipe R. 104, m.2).

[1] The keeper of the vacant bishopric of Durham, 1249, accounts for £2.4.10½ 'de
exitibus terre dicti Ricardi (Richard de Brompton) dum fuit in manu Regis'
(Pipe R. 94, m.18); the keeper of Canterbury, 1270–2, for £3.4.9 'de exitibus
terrarum que fuerunt Johannis Gravenel qui tenuit de predicto archiepiscopatu
antequam liberaret easdem terras Willelmo de Wintreshull' (Pipe R. 119, m.21d);
the keeper of Carlisle, 1278–80, for £13.15.9½ 'de exitibus terrarum Ricardi de
Crosseby qui de Episcopo tenuit in capite post mortem ipsius Ricardi captarum in
manu Regis antequam liberaret dictas terras sororibus et heredibus ipsius Ricardi
plene etatis existentibus.' (Pipe R. 128, m.34d).

[2] In some cases where the recipient of the wardship pays a fine the fine may be
accounted for by the custodian of the bishopric on the Pipe Roll. For example, when
the wardship of the land of Richard de Brompton's heir, in the vacant bishopric
of Durham, referred to in the previous footnote, was granted by the king to John
de Romundeby for a fine of 60 marks (Fine R. 46, m.1; 25 Oct. 1249) the keeper
of Durham rendered account for the fine along with the other issues of the bishopric
(Pipe R. 94, m.18). Alternatively the recipient of the wardship might appear as
an independent accountant on the Pipe Roll, as in the case of Adam de Eyvill who
owed £20 for the custody (with marriage) of the lands and heirs of Ralph de
Bakethorp (Pipe R. 118, m.18d; Durham account, 1274).

In other cases there seems to be no entry of any payment on the Pipe Roll and
perhaps no fine was demanded. For examples of grants of escheats or wardships by
letters patent see Cal. Pat. R., 1232–47, p. 204; ibid., p. 338; ibid., 1247–58, p. 583;
and ibid., 1266–72, p. 197.

[3] Cal. Pat. R., 1232–47, p. 269.   [4] Pat. R., 1225–32, p. 117.

[5] Cal. Pat. R., 1266–72, p. 617. The wardship was in the king's gift by reason of
the Canterbury vacancy of 1270–2. See Pipe Roll reference in n. 1, above.

[6] Pat. R., 1225–32, p. 172. It is interesting to note that de Lucy was custodian of
the bishopric of Durham during this vacancy.

fines to the king for similar grants.[1] Escheats might be useful for benefiting lesser royal servants, laymen who could not be rewarded with ecclesiastical benefices.[2]

All these things were the incidental perquisites of the custody of a vacant see. They were as 'casual' in their relationship to the regular income of the vacancy as vacancy revenue itself was casual in relationship to royal income as a whole. They were the windfalls.

In the second place the king took over, *sede vacante*, the bishop's right of patronage. This, like his feudal rights, gave rise to occasional emoluments, windfalls, distinct from the regular income of the see. As the king might reward his serjeants with small escheats from vacant sees, so he could reward his clerks with those ecclesiastical benefices to which the bishop would have presented *sede plena*. Patronage was not a source of wealth which the king, at least as late as the reign of Henry III, could exploit directly for himself,[3] but he could use it to provide incomes for his civil servants. It was of vital importance to the king that he should have a sufficient reserve of benefices at his disposal for this purpose. As Miss Edwards has said, 'in the absence of banks and ready money, kings, popes and bishops would have been hard put to find any means other than prebends with which to provide for the busy clerks in their service'.[4] The king's ordinary rights of patronage were by no means sufficient to meet the needs of his clerks, and he had to rely very largely on the rights which came to him through the wardship of lay and ecclesiastical fiefs.[5] Mr. Hartridge has

[1] Bertram de Crioil paid 20 marks for the wardship of a fief of the archbishopric of Canterbury at the time when he was keeper of the temporalities of that see; Fine R. 40, m.9; 11 Nov. 1242.

[2] William Chubbe, king's serjeant, was granted for the term of his life 'a carucate of land which Adam le Drake held in Bissopestun, and another carucate which Peter de Camera held in Bedon, which are the king's escheats by reason of the voidance of the bishopric of Salisbury' (*Cal. Pat. R., 1232–47*, p. 494).

[3] Henry II seems to have kept both churches and prebends vacant in the archbishopric of York, near the end of his reign and to have drawn the revenues. (See above, pp. 37–8). The following typical entries are from the York vacancy account of 1188 (*Pipe R. 34 Henry II*, p. 10) The keepers account, 'de xxxviij li, ij s. ij d. de ecclesiis vacantibus', and 'de xv li. xij s. iiij d. de prebendis vacantibus'.

[4] K. Edwards, *The English Secular Cathedrals in the Middle Ages* (Manchester, 1949), p. 7.

[5] In reference to the reign of Edward I, Mr. R. A. R. Hartridge has written, The principal means by which the king acquired presentations not *pleno jure* were

estimated that of the royal presentations to benefices which appear in the Patent Rolls of Edward I (nearly a thousand in all), certainly not more than one in twelve would have come into the king's gift *pleno jure*.[1] The rest came from his rights of wardship over lay fiefs and from the custody of vacant sees and abbeys.

Here it is important to make a distinction between prebends and churches. It is true that wardship over lay fiefs contributed a larger number of benefices to the pool of royal patronage than did vacant bishoprics,[2] but the value of patronage could not be measured on a purely quantitative basis. From the point of view of a royal clerk a cathedral prebend, generally speaking, was far more useful to him than the rectorship of a church. A prebend was a benefice without cure of souls and very often it was of superior financial value.[3] No wardship of a lay fief would give the king the right to present to vacant cathedral prebends. But a vacancy in a bishopric attached to a secular cathedral did give him that right, and therein lay the peculiar importance of the *jus regale* as a source of patronage.

The king valued his right to present to both prebends and churches *sede vacante* very highly, and as far as the evidence goes he used the right very largely for the promotion of royal clerks.[4]

by the vacancy of a bishopric, by the concurrent vacancy of an abbey, and by the minority, idiocy, or other incapability of a tenant-in-chief. The last of these causes was by far the most frequent, although the voidance of a see always meant a large windfall for the crown.' ('Edward I's Exercise of the Right of Presentation to Benefices as shown by the Patent Rolls', *The Cambridge Historical Journal*, II, no. 2 (1927), p. 171.) It should perhaps be noted in addition that whenever an abbey of royal patronage fell vacant, the king presented to those benefices which were in the gift of the abbot *abbatia plena*.

[1] *Ibid.*
[2] See above, p. 171. n. 5.
[3] Prebends were very unequal in value. The cathedral churches of York, Salisbury and Lincoln had some very rich ones, and Wells was well endowed too, but the prebends at Exeter and Hereford were not sufficiently substantial to be in such great demand for royal and papal clerks (K. Edwards, *op. cit.*, pp. 39–41, and pp. 74–6).
[4] Names which may be those of kings' clerks cannot always be identified as such because it is only in Edward I's reign, and still more in Edward II's reign that the addition of 'king's clerk' after the name of a candidate in the writ of presentation becomes common form. Grants of churches, though rarely of prebends, are made to chaplains too. A chaplain of the queen was presented to Ivychurch in the Canterbury vacancy of 1240–5 (*Cal. Pat. R., 1232–47*, p. 274). For other examples of the king's presentation of chaplains to livings in vacant sees see *ibid., 1247–58*, p. 39; *ibid., 1258–66*, p. 326; *ibid., 1266–72*, p. 575; *ibid., 1281–92*, p. 5; *ibid., 1301–07*, p. 230 and p. 303.

A few examples will suffice. When the see of London was vacant in 1228–9 two prebends came into the king's gift, both were given to wardrobe clerks.[1] At least five royal clerks benefited by the York vacancy of 1265–6.[2] In the Lincoln vacancy of 1279–80 and in that of 1299–1300 the presentations, mostly prebends, went to the king's clerks.[3] Between 1304 and 1307, Edward I presented to nineteen prebends or similar livings in the diocese of York, of which at least six are specified as being in the cathedral church, by reason of the vacancy of the see. Seventeen of those presented were king's clerks and the other two were chaplains.[4] As a final example, in the Durham vacancy

[1] Ralph Breton (Pat. R., 1225–32, p. 231) and Walter Brackley (ibid., p. 243). For Breton's association with the wardrobe see Tout, Chapters in Admin. Hist., I, 198. Brackley appears as an accountant on the first extant wardrobe account of Henry III's reign (Foreign R. 1, m.4).

[2] They were John Chishull (Cal. Pat. R., 1258–66, p. 404); Bogo de Clare (ibid., p. 498; Godfrey Giffard (ibid., pp. 498–9); William de Fiscampo (ibid., p. 532 and p. 562); Theodosius de Camilla (ibid., p. 573).

[3] In the 1279–80 vacancy two prominent wardrobe clerks benefited: William of Louth (Cal. Pat. R., 1272–81, p. 356; 30 Dec. 1279) and Thomas Bek (ibid., p. 361). Louth followed Bek as keeper of the wardrobe in Nov. 1280, shortly after the end of this vacancy. (The temporalities were restored 28 Feb. 1280.)

The following presentations were made in the vacancy of 1299–1300: John de Lacy (Cal. Pat. R., 1292–1301, p. 479); John Lovel (ibid., p. 481); William de Chosey (ibid., p. 484); John Brouward (ibid., p. 491); Gilbert of Navenby (ibid., p. 491); Roger of Ashridge (ibid., p. 508). All these presentations, except the last, which was to a church, were to prebends in the cathedral church of Lincoln. The presentations of Chosey and Navenby, however, were both to the treasurership of the church.

[4] The list of presentations of king's clerks to prebends was as follows: John Droxford (ibid., 1301–07, p. 263); Maurice de Pissiaco (ibid., p. 290); John de Kenley (ibid., p. 306); William de Melton (ibid., p. 307); Richard de Havering (ibid., p. 333); John of Nassington (ibid., p. 365); Ralph de Stokes (ibid., p. 375); Poincardiis de Monte Martini, (ibid., p. 375); John de Hedon (ibid., p. 377); Robert de Cotingham (ibid., p. 378); Robert de Bardelby (ibid., p. 381); Adam de Blyda (ibid., p. 414); Roger Droxford (ibid., p. 499); John de Merkingfeld (ibid., p. 525). There were apparently two reshuffles in the above list. The presentation of Richard de Havering mentioned above followed rapidly on his presentation to a different prebend (that of Weighton, ibid., p. 316; 7 Mar. 1305). The prebend of Weighton however was presumably already full since John de Kenley had already been presented to it 29 Dec. 1304 (see above).

In the second place Poincardiis de Monte Martini who had been presented to the prebend late of Philip of Willoughby in the church of York (see above) was later given the prebend of Laughton in that church (ibid., p. 414; 11 Feb. 1306)— presumably to enable the king to confer Philip of Willoughby's prebend on Adam de Blyda, the next day (see above).

In addition to the above presentations to prebends two other king's clerks were given similar offices: Walter Reginald was granted the provostship of the church

of 1316–18 six royal clerks were presented by Edward II to livings in that see.[1]

Both Henry III and Edward I seem to have been determined that the royal prerogative of patronage should not lose its character as a personal privilege of the king. When Henry was abroad in Gascony in 1243 he was careful to define the exact limits of the regents' powers in this matter:

Mandate to the Archbishop of York, and W. bishop of Carlisle, to provide for the king's clerks Robert Passelewe and Peter Chaceporc in some prebend in the church of St. Paul, London, and for John le Maunsell, king's clerk, in the church of Wells, as soon as opportunity occurs.[2] And because the king wishes to benefit his clerks who serve him well, he reserves all collations to benefices, whether prebendal or other, and they are not to confer any without his special mandate, except upon king's clerks for whom the king has already directed letters patent to them.[3]

A similar wariness was shown by Edward I when he revoked a presentation made by the chancellor to the church of Winwick in the vacant see of Lincoln, 'especially as that presentation from the beginning was not made with the king's knowledge, nor after it was made was it confirmed by the king'.[4]

of St. John, Beverley (*ibid.*, p. 421), and Walter de Bedwynd was given the treasurership of the cathedral church of York (*ibid.*, p. 467). Finally Roger Sutton, king's clerk, was granted the hospital of St. John, Nottingham for life (*ibid.*, p. 266).

Two chaplains received prebends: Ralph de Stanford, styled king's chaplain, (*ibid.*, p. 372) and John de Dynyeton (*ibid.*, p. 380). Another chaplain, Martin of Grimsby, was presented to the vicarage of Felixkirk, York (*ibid.*, p. 370) and on his resignation the vicarage was granted to another chaplain, William of Grimston (*ibid.*, p. 416).

[1] The clerks presented were: Simon de Eycote (*Cal. Pat. R., 1313–17*, p. 556); William Airmyn (*ibid.*, p. 573); Richard Airmyn (*ibid.*, p. 625); William of Salford (*ibid.*, p. 626); Robert de Woodhouse (*ibid.*, p. 635); Edmund of London (*ibid.*, p. 640). Of these the last five were presented to prebends and the first to the custody of a hospital.

It is interesting to note the comment of the Abbé Mollat on the extent to which royal officials were beneficiaries of royal patronage *sede vacante* in France, 'L'application du droit de régale spirituelle en France du XIIᵉ au XIVᵉ siècle', *Revue d'histoire ecclésiastique*, xxv (Louvain, 1929), p. 675.

[2] Both sees were vacant at the time.

[3] *Cal. Pat. R., 1232–47*, p. 354.

[4] *Ibid., 1292–1301*, p. 508; 13 Apr. 1300. The chancellor had certain responsibilities in regard to appointments to smaller livings in the king's gift (B. Wilkinson, *The Chancery under Edward III* (Manchester, 1929), pp. 30–1), but in this case he had gone too far.

As might be expected from this watchful attitude the king discriminated carefully as to the value of the prebends which he granted. In 1242 Henry III instructed the archbishop of York, who was then acting as regent in England, that the king was willing that Robert Passelewe should have a moderate prebend in the church of Lichfield:

but if the prebend in Lichfield be good and fat the king wills that it be conferred upon Philip de Sabaudia.[1]

In 1255 the king's kinsman Simon de Rupe Chiwardi was seeking a benefice, but there was at least one more privileged competitor in the field. Simon had to rest content with the assurance that the king would provide for him:

in some ecclesiastical benefice, dignity or prebend, except the treasurership of York if it should fall void or any prebend in that church or elsewhere which Henry de Wengham will accept for his own use.[2]

It is easy to pick out the king's more favoured clerks by the number of benefices that they accumulated, often within a comparatively short space of time. John Mansell was presented to three prebends,[3] together with the chancellorship of St. Paul's[4] and the church of Maidstone[5] between 1241 and 1244, through patronage which came to the king *sede vacante*. Between 1226 and 1228 Ralph Breton, treasurer of the wardrobe, received three churches and two prebends[6] and Master Laurence of St. Martin, the king's confidential clerk and a proctor on important diplomatic missions, increased his income to the extent of an archdeaconry and three prebends in two years.[7]

---

[1] *Cal. Pat. R., 1232–47*, p. 289.   [2] *Ibid., 1247–58*, p. 424.

[3] One was in the church of South Malling in the vacant see of Canterbury (*ibid., 1232–47*, p. 252; 5 June 1241), the second in London (*ibid.*, p. 268; 8 Dec. 1241), and the third in Chichester (*ibid.*, p. 422; 6 Apr. 1244).

[4] *Ibid.*, p. 377; 24 May 1243.   [5] *Ibid.*, p. 260; *c.* 10 Oct. 1241.

[6] Breton was presented to the church of Langham during a Norwich vacancy (*Pat. R., 1225–32*, p. 92; 3 Nov. 1226); to the church of Boughton in a voidance of the see of Canterbury (*ibid.*, p. 225; 31 Oct. 1228); to a prebend in St. Paul's (*ibid.*, p. 231; 7 Dec. 1228); and to a prebend in Salisbury cathedral and to the church of Charing three days later (*ibid.*, p. 231; 10 Dec. 1228).

[7] He was presented to a prebend in Chichester (*Cal. Pat. R., 1232–47*, p. 448; 28 Feb. 1245), to the archdeaconry of Coventry and to a prebend in the church of Lichfield on the same day (*ibid.*, p. 467; 5 Nov. 1245) and to a prebend in the church of Salisbury (*ibid.*, p. 492; 6 Nov. 1246).

Apart from these three, Peter Chaceporc, John Chishull, Guy de la Palude, Theodosius de Camilla, Robert Passelewe, John of Colchester and Guibert of Kent, all received three or more benefices in vacant sees from Henry III during the course of his reign.[1] In the shorter reign of Edward I only four clerks, John Benstead, John of Berwick, John Bush and William de Estden were presented to as many as three benefices from this

---

[1] The references may for convenience be tabulated:

Peter Chaceporc
  Winchester: ch. of Ivinghoe; c. 13 Apr. 1241; *Cal. Pat. R.*, *1232–47*, p. 249.
  Chichester: preb. in ch. of Chichester; 23 Apr. 1244; *ibid.*, p. 423.
  Exeter: preb. in ch. of Exeter; 21 Jan. 1245; *ibid.*, p. 448.
  Winchester: wardenship of hosp. of St. Cross; 6 Nov. 1250; *ibid.*, *1247–58*, p. 79.
  Lincoln: treasureship and preb. in ch. of Lincoln; 22 Mar. 1254; *ibid.*, p. 366.

John Chishull
  Ely: ch. of Upwell; 12 Oct. 1257; *ibid.*, p. 581.
  Bath: preb. in ch. of Wells; 13 May 1264; *ibid.*, *1258–66*, p. 317.
  York: provostship of Beverley; 7 Feb. 1265; *ibid.*, p. 404.

Guy de la Palude
  London: preb. in St. Paul's; 6 Apr. 1243; *ibid.*, *1232–47*, p. 371.
  Canterbury: ch. of Newchurch; 13 May 1243; *ibid.*, *1266–72*, Appendix, p. 722.
              ch. of Lambeth; 18 May 1243; *ibid.*, p. 722.
              ch. of Saltwood; 27 May 1243; *ibid.*, p. 377.
  Chichester: preb. (in ch. of Chichester?); 23 Feb. 1246; *ibid.*, p. 475.

Theodosius de Camilla
  York: archdeac. of York and preb. in ch. of York; 28 Mar. 1266; *ibid.*, *1258–66*, p. 573.
  Hereford: preb. in ch. of Hereford; 9 Dec. 1268; *ibid.*, *1266–72*, p. 306.
  Canterbury: chs. of Tarring and Poling; 16 Mar. 1271; *ibid.*, p. 523.
              ch. of Wingham; 20 Apr. 1271; *ibid.*, p. 532.

Robert Passelewe
  London: preb. in St. Paul's; 20 May 1242; *ibid.*, *1232–47*; p. 298.
          preb. in St. Paul's; 8 Nov. 1242; *ibid.*, *1266–72*, Appendix, p. 718.
          preb. in St. Paul's; 1 Apr. 1243; *ibid.*, p. 721.
  Chichester: archdeac. of Lewes; 5 Mar. 1244; *ibid.*, *1232–47*, p. 421.
  Salisbury: preb. in ch. of Salisbury; 8 Dec. 1246; *ibid.*, p. 494.

John of Colchester
  Norwich: ch. of Bacton; 28 May 1257; *ibid.*, *1247–58*, p. 557.
  Exeter: preb. in ch. of Crantock; 10 Feb. 1258; *ibid.*, p. 616.
  Winchester; ch. of Ebbesborne Wake; 10 Jan. 1261; *ibid.*, p. 136.
  Canterbury; ch. of Monks Eleigh; 15 Mar. 1272; *ibid.*, *1266–72*, p. 636.

Guibert of Kent
  Lichfield; preb. in ch. of St. Chad, Shrewsbury; 11 July 1245; *ibid.*, *1232–47*, p. 456.
  Carlisle: mediety of ch. of Whittingham; 11 Aug. 1257; *ibid.*, *1247–58*, p. 574.
  Exeter: ch. of St. Erme; 16 Feb. 1258; *ibid.*, p. 616.
  Winchester: ch. of Adderbury; 17 Nov. 1259; *ibid.*, *1258–66*, p. 106.

source of patronage,[1] but at least twelve others received two
benefices each as the result of episcopal vacancies.[2]

[1] John Benstead, a controller of the wardrobe, was given a portion of a church
in the see of Canterbury (*ibid.*, *1292–1301*, p. 51; 22 Nov. 1293); a prebend in
Ripon (*ibid.*, p. 248; 12 May 1297) and a prebend in the church of Salisbury
(*ibid.*, p. 249; 21 May 1297).

John of Berwick, a keeper of the queen's wardrobe, 1286, the keeper of the
vacant bishopric of Lincoln in 1279 and a justice in eyre in 1292, received the
church of Droxford during a Winchester vacancy (*ibid.*, *1272–81*, p. 416; 1 Dec.
1280); the deanery of South Malling in a Canterbury vacancy (*ibid.*, *1292–1301*,
p. 58; 27 Dec. 1293) and a prebend in the church of York (*ibid.*, p. 221; 22 Nov.
1296). The last grant however only meant exchange of prebends with William
Pickering.

John Bush, another wardrobe clerk, was presented to a prebend in the church
of St. David's (*ibid.*, *1292–1301*, p. 223; 6 Dec. 1296); to the church of Foxton in
an Ely vacancy (*ibid.*, p. 347; 27 Apr. 1298); and to a prebend in the church
of York (*ibid.*, p. 512; 30 Apr. 1300).

William de Estden, a clerk of Queen Eleanor, Edward I's mother, was presented
to the church of Enford in a Winchester vacancy (*ibid.*, *1272–81*, p. 403; 12 Nov.
1280; to the church of East Lavant, in a Canterbury vacancy (*ibid.*, *1292–1301*,
p. 96; 8 Oct. 1294) and to the church of Orsett in a London vacancy (*ibid.*, *1301–07*,
p. 212; 16 Feb. 1304).

[2] These again may be tabulated:

Bonettus de Sancto Quintino
    Canterbury: parsonage of Aldington and of Smeeth; 1279; *ibid.*, *1272–81*, p. 297
    York: preb. in ch. of Southwell; 1286; *ibid.*, *1281–92*, p. 225.

John de Lacy
    Canterbury; preb. of Deal, 23 Mar. 1293; *ibid.*, *1292–1301*, p. 8.
    Lincoln: preb. in church of Lincoln; 21 Nov. 1299; *ibid.*, p. 479.

John Droxford
    Salisbury: preb. in ch. of Salisbury; 1297; *ibid.*, p. 254.
    York: preb. in ch. of Southwell; 1304; *ibid.*, *1301–07*, p. 263.

Hugh of Nottingham
    Canterbury: ch. of Ivychurch; 10 Dec. 1293; *ibid.*, *1292–1301*, p. 58.
    Ely: ch. of Doddington; 29 Mar. 1298; *ibid.*, p. 336.

Peter de Aimericy
    Canterbury: ch. of Peckham; 27 Jan. 1295; *ibid.*, p. 129.
    York: preb. in ch. of Beverley; 24 Aug. 1299; *ibid.*, p. 436.

William of Louth
    York: preb. in ch. of Beverley; 1 Aug. 1279; *ibid.*, *1272–81*, p. 323.
    Lincoln: preb. in ch. of Lincoln; 30 Dec. 1279; *ibid.*, p. 356.

Thomas Bek
    Lincoln: preb. in ch. of Lincoln; 20 Jan. 1280; *ibid.*, p. 361.
    St. David's; preb. in ch. of St. David's; 17 May 1280; *ibid.*, p. 370.

Robert de Camera
    Winchester: ch. of Esher; 10 June 1280; *ibid.*, p. 378.
              vicarage of Meon; 1 Dec. 1281; *ibid.*, *1281–92*, p. 5.

N

Although the king usually knew which of his clerks he wished to favour, and although he guarded his prerogative jealously, he was, of course, open to influence and supplication. Members of the royal family, of the king's domestic household and of the various government departments had the best opportunity of pressing their own interest or the interests of their relatives and protégés. James of Spain, a kinsman of Queen Eleanor (the first wife of Edward I), who was presented to the church of Crondall in the Winchester vacancy of 1280–2,[1] was a person whose ecclesiastical career the queen had much at heart.[2] In a vacancy of that see in the previous reign, John of Abbotsham, 'kinsman of Master Richard, the king's cook', was presented to the church of St. Mary Rouncivall. In these cases one is inclined to assume that there had been a personal solicitation of the king's favour before the writ of presentation was issued. But it was very rarely, of course, that we have written evidence of how many strings had been pulled before any particular letters of presentation were finally sealed with the great seal and duly enrolled in the chancery archives.

This gives a special interest to an unusually informal letter which is printed by Shirley in the *Royal Letters of Henry III*. It is written by a certain R. of Doncaster on 11 October 1262 from France. He writes to tell John Kirkby, a prominent

Gilbert of Reigate
    Winchester: ch. of St. Faith, Winchester; *c.* 25 Dec. 1281; *ibid.*, p. 7.
               ch. of Overton; 9 Aug. 1282; *ibid.*, p. 32.
Geoffrey de Stokes
    Ely: ch. of Gransden; 27 Sep. 1302; *ibid.*, *1301–07*, p. 63.
    Winchester: ch. of Brightwell; 15 Dec. 1304; *ibid.*, p. 304.
Robert de Bardelby
    Canterbury: ch. of Sandhurst; 7 Oct 1294; *ibid.*, *1292–1301*, p. 96.
    York: preb. in chapel at York; 6 Sep. 1296; *ibid.*, p. 200.
Peter de Colingburn
    Worcester: ch. of Kempsey; 1302; *ibid.*, *1301–07*, p. 63.
    Winchester: ch. of Ivinghoe; 12 Dec. 1304; *ibid.*, p. 303.

[1] *Ibid.*, *1281–92*, p. 32.
[2] In a Salisbury formulary book of the late thirteenth century (B.M. Royal MS. 12D.xi, ff.69–88d) there is a letter from 'J. priest of Ely' conveying to the chapter of Salisbury the queen's recommendation of William de Cornella for their bishop (f.88). The writer says of the queen:
'ecclesie vestre utilitatem et promocionem diligit et affectat pro eo maxime quia dominus Jacobus de Hispania prebendatus est in eadem.'

chancery clerk[1] and later bishop of Ely, about his attempt to carry out a commission which Kirkby had entrusted to him:

Die S. Michaelis sanus et incolumis veni Parisiis, ubi dominum R. de Messenden et Thomam de la Ley in prandio jocose sedentes sanos inveni et hilares. Finito autem prandio illo literas vestras predicto domino directas porrexi, qui postmodum negotium per vos ei demandatum ad opus suum vel etiam clerici sui tepide fuit executus, ita quod per ipsius teporem, vel etiam, ut credo, revelationem negotium illud ad magistrum Thomam Cirugicum devenit; cujus filius Petrus de Weseham nomine, a domino rege ad eandem ecclesiam est praesentatus. Super quo ei praedixi vos fore moturos, nec immerito, cum illud ad opus clerici sui quem intime dilexistis distulit procurare.[2]

John Kirkby had evidently been anxious to press forward the interests of one of the clerks of his chancery colleague Roger de Messenden, and to have the clerk presented to a church which he knew to be vacant. However, through Messenden's lack of interest or lack of discretion, the matter had come to the knowledge of Thomas de Weseham, the king's surgeon, who had apparently lost no time in persuading the king to present his son, Peter de Weseham, to the church in question. The name of the church is not given, nor the reason why it was in the king's gift. But the Patent Rolls help to fill these gaps in the story. On 3 October 1262, four days after Messenden had received Kirkby's letter by the hand of Doncaster, Peter de Weseham was presented to the church of 'Calwesdon' in the king's gift by reason of the voidance of the bishopric of London.[3] There seems little doubt that this is the church which Kirkby had intended for Messenden's clerk. The date of the letter of presentation fits well with the date of Doncaster's letter to Kirkby,[4] and there is no mention of any other presentation of anyone by the name of Weseham on the Patent Rolls for several years on either side of this date. The likelihood is perhaps

[1] He was put in charge of the chancery in 1278 (Tout, *Chapters in Admin. Hist.*, VI, 6.)
[2] *Royal and other Historical Letters Illustrative of the Reign of Henry III*, ed. W. W. Shirley (Rolls Series, London, 1862–6), II, 221–2.
[3] *Cal. Pat. R., 1266–72* (Appendix), p. 732.
[4] Doncaster wrote the disappointing news to Kirkby on 11 October, eight days after the presentation had been made.

strengthened even further by a writ of 5 December of the same year:

> Nomination to the prior of Pritelewell (because by an ordinance made between the sometime bishops of London and the prior, confirmed by the chapter of St. Paul's, London, in the voidance of the bishopric of London it pertains to the king to nominate) of Peter de Weseham, king's clerk for the prior to present to the vicarage of Canewedon.[1]

The original royal letter dated in France had referred to a *presentation* to the *church* of Canewdon instead of more accurately, a *nomination* to the *vicarage* of the church. These slips were understandable if we consider the several stages by which Thomas de Weseham seems to have come to hear of this vacant living.

There seems little doubt that the initiative in royal presentations to benefices would very often come from the clerks who were presented or whose protégés were presented. To discover a vacant living in the king's gift, especially a small one, which did not belong to the king *pleno jure* and which might otherwise have escaped notice was one step towards acquiring it. This, also, may in some cases account for the presentation of keepers of temporalities or of their clerks to benefices within the bishopric temporarily in their custody. There were at least twelve instances of such appointments during Henry III's reign,[2] and at least four during the reign of Edward I.[3] There was perhaps a tendency too for information about vacant

---

[1] *Ibid.*, *1258–66*, p. 237. Canewedon and Calwedon are variations of the same name, *The Place Names of Essex*, ed. P. H. Reaney (English Place Name Society, XII, Cambridge, 1935), p. 179.

[2] Alan Poinant during a Canterbury vacancy (*Pat. R.*, *1225–32*, p. 239); John Mansell in a vacancy of the same see (*Cal. Pat. R.*, *1232–47*, p. 252 and p. 260); in vacancies at Durham William Thornour (*Pat. R.*, *1225–32*, p. 108); Stephen de Lucy's clerk Ralph (*ibid.*, p. 115); Stephen de Lucy himself (*ibid.*, p. 148); John Mansell (*Cal. Pat. R.*, *1258–66*, p. 129); in Exeter vacancies: William Passelewe (*ibid.*, *1232–47*, p. 450); William of Axmouth (*ibid.*, *1247–58*, p. 618); in a Winchester vacancy: Peter Chaceporc (*ibid.*, p. 79); in a York vacancy: John Mansell (*ibid.*, p. 652); and in a St. David's vacancy: a clerk of William Earl Marshal (*Pat. R. 1225–32*, p. 261).

[3] In an Ely vacancy: Richard of Abingdon (*Cal. Pat. R.*, *1301–07*, p. 29); in a St. David's vacancy: Ralph Broughton (*Cal. Pat. R.*, *1292–1301*, p. 32); in a Winchester vacancy: William Hamilton (*ibid.*, *1272–81*, p. 427); and in a York vacancy: Henry Newark (*ibid.*, p. 312).

livings in a particular see to travel fast in one department of government. In the vacancy of Bath and Wells (1264) when the chancery clerk, Godfrey Giffard, exchanged the prebend which he held in the church of Wells for that of a deceased prebendary, it was the chancellor himself John Chishull who stepped into the prebend that Giffard had resigned.[1] And in this same vacancy there is a presentation of Roger of Doncaster to the church of Dinder,[2] who may just possibly have been the R. of Doncaster who had been a friend of John Kirkby's in 1262.[3] Similarly in the London vacancy of 1228–9 the two prebends which fell vacant went to wardrobe clerks[4] and so did the two which fell vacant in Lincoln in the vacancy of 1279–80.[5] In the Ely vacancy of 1298 there were two appointments of men connected with the exchequer.[6] In each case the note of warranty to the enrolment of these Ely presentations was the same: 'By the king on the information of W. bishop of Coventry and Lichfield.' Walter Langton, bishop of Lichfield, was treasurer of the exchequer at this time. Exchanges of benefices during a vacancy were quite frequent too, and these may well have been made on many occasions at the request of the clerks concerned.[7] The total impression is of a complicated network of influence. The power to present rested with the king alone, but the privilege of request lay open to those who would take it.

It is clear enough, then, that the king could ill have afforded to lose the right of patronage which came to him through episcopal vacancies. But sometimes he was faced with a threatened

---

[1] Giffard's appointment to the prebend of Dulcot and Chishull's appointment to the prebend which Giffard had vacated are both dated 13 May 1264 (*ibid., 1258–66*, p. 317).

[2] *Ibid.*, p. 315.

[3] The Doncaster who wrote to Kirkby evidently associated closely with chancery men.

[4] These have already been mentioned above, p173. 1, n.

[5] See above, p. 173, n. 3.

[6] Hugh of Nottingham, late remembrancer of the exchequer (*Cal. Pat. R., 1292–1301*, p. 336); and Thomas de Abbrebury who had gone abroad with the treasurer on the king's service in 1296 (*ibid.*, p. 345).

[7] Walter Merton for example changed his prebend in St. Paul's for the prebend vacated by the death of Richard Talbot (*Cal. Pat. R., 1266–72* (Appendix), p. 732; 6 Oct. 1262) and on 12 Oct. Merton's former prebend was filled by another royal clerk, Ralph de Montibus (*ibid.*, p. 735). John of Berwick and William Pickering exchanged prebends at York in the vacancy of the see in 1296–8 (*Ibid., 1292–1301*; p. 221). Both were king's clerks.

diminution of his right. One such threat was the splitting up of prebends or other benefices into several portions, the ecclesiastical equivalent in some respects of subinfeudation. This the king would not tolerate in the case of a living to which he had the right of presentation *sede vacante*. It appears that the emoluments of the church of St. Michael's Coventry had been split into three parts, thirty marks being paid to the canons of Lichfield, thirty marks to the monks of Coventry and the rest to the stipend of a vicar.[1] Apparently this church had been in the gift of the bishop of Lichfield and this division of the benefice had been made by him; nevertheless in the vacancy of the see in 1241–5 the king ignored the division that had been made and presented one of his clerks to the whole benefice. He then forbade the hearing of the case in an ecclesiastical court:

. . . quia collaciones tam ecclesiarum parochialium quam prebendarum spectantes ad episcopum ipso superstite, ad nos spectant sede vacante, . . .[2]

A similar case arose in 1292 in a Carlisle vacancy. The king presented John Droxford to the church of Dalston, but the vicar-general of the archbishop of York refused to institute him. The late bishop of Carlisle had divided this church into three portions and since the portioners were still living the vicar-general did not consider the benefice vacant.[3] The king, however:

considering that the bishop had not the power to make any division of the church without the king's special assent, which, as the king recollects, he never obtained, for which reason the king is bound to consider the church in the same condition as it was in at the time of the ordinance, to wit, that it is void rightfully, and considering that it would redound to his disinheritance and the prejudice of his crown if he suffered division to be made in it which he will neither do nor ought to do: the king therefore orders the vicar-general to admit the king's clerk aforesaid . . . without delay.[4]

Finally, in 1322 the king defended the rights of Robert Baldock, his nominee to the prebend of Aylesbury in the church of Lincoln. The prebend had been granted to Baldock:

[1] *Close R., 1242–47*, pp. 478–9; 26 Aug. 1246.
[2] *Ibid.*, p. 479.
[3] *Cal. Close R., 1288–96*, pp. 263–4.   [4] *Ibid.*, p. 264.

when the bishopric of Lincoln was in his [the king's] hands during
voidance, in its entirety as it was before it was divided into portions
in the time of [the king's] progenitors without royal assent, as the
king recovered and proved his right in his court against Gaillard de
Mota, incumbent of the church of Milton, one of the portions of the
aforesaid prebend, and against others impeding the king's collation . . .[1]

The king clearly considered that the division of a benefice to
which he might present *sede vacante*, made without the royal
assent, was an infringement of the rights of the crown.

But this dispute over the prebend of Aylesbury has a further
interest. The reference to 'the time of the king's progenitors'
raises a suspicion that it was perhaps a rather long-buried
royal claim that was being brought to the surface in the Lincoln
vacancy of 1322. In the first half of the fourteenth century the
king was not merely defending his right of patronage *sede
vacante*; he was extending it. This was in part the culmination of a
development which had begun in the thirteenth century, during
which the king had established his claim to present to cathedral
prebends for as long as the temporalities of the vacant see remained in his hand, regardless of the date of the new bishop's
consecration.[2] Edward I in the Salisbury vacancy of 1288–9
took another step, viewed with distrust by the church. He
appointed to the prebend vacated by the newly appointed
bishop of Salisbury, William de la Corner without first waiting
for that bishop's consecration. In the early fourteenth century
the extension of the king's rights became even more marked.
Edward II presented to benefices in the bishop's gift even when
the bishop was alive and the temporalities had been taken
temporarily into the king's hand merely for political or puni-
tive reasons. Above all the king gradually claimed exemption
from the rules of lapse which limited the rights of advowson of
ordinary patrons. If it was found that the king's right of patronage in regard to some benefice had been neglected at the time
of the vacancy of the see, then the presentation was made
sometimes years after the vacancy had ended and in spite of the

[1] *Ibid., 1318–23*, p. 538.
[2] Miss A. Deeley makes this point and also those mentioned in the remainder of
this paragraph in her article 'Papal Provision and Royal Rights of Patronage in the
Early Fourteenth Century', *Eng. Hist. Review*, XLIII (1928), pp. 497–527.

fact that the benefice had long been filled.[1] Cases of advowson were tried in the royal courts and therein lay the strength of the king's position His claims could be extended simply by the accumulation of judgements in his favour in the lay courts.

It is interesting to notice that in many of these cases, as Miss Deeley discovered, the royal claim was enforced at the expense of a papal providee. Naturally this brought clashes between king and pope. It seems that between 1305 and 1334 'there is . . . not one single instance in which the pope wittingly conferred a benefice which was without doubt in lay patronage',[2] and 'none of the many disputes between king and pope involved the right of *régale* in its simplest form, that is, the right to present to benefices when a bishopric was actually vacant'.[3] What then was the cause of this gradual but bold extension of the crown's rights of patronage *sede vacante*?

Miss Deeley suspected that the pressure may have come partly from needy clerks who would make it their business to hunt out or invent some neglected right of royal presentation. This impression is strongly corroborated by a passage from the provincial constitutions of Archbishop Stratford in 1342:

Esurientis avaritiae cultus sic cupide sitim conatur reficere voluntatis, ut abjecto rationis tramite, clerici quidam fas et nefas improbe permiscentes, ecclesiastica beneficia, patronatus archiepiscoporum, (episcoporum) abbatum, et aliarum tam ecclesiasticarum, quam secularium personarum de possessionibus suis plena et inhumaniter ambientes, eaque temporibus longe retroactis figmentis variis praetendentes vacasse; dum temporalium cathedralium vel conventualium ecclesiarum, ratione vacationis earum, vel terrarum aliarum, quarum custodia fuerat penes regem, se ad ipsa praesentari, vel sibi per ipsum conferri procurant, licet post praetensas vacationes hujusmodi, a diversis tantis temporibus possessa fuerint, quod vix aut nulla sit alicujus memoria causae vacationis deductae, quae etiam quandoque falsissima . . .[4]

---

[1] It is interesting to compare the following comment of M. J. Gaudemet, on the exercise of the *régale spirituelle* by the kings of France: 'Le particularité la plus remarquable et aussi la plus profitable à la royauté était la prolongation fictive de la vacance du siège, permettant au roi de pourvoir *sede plena* a un bénéfice qui avait vaqué penadnt la régale et dont il n'avait pas alors disposé ou dont il n'avait pas disposé efficacement'; 'La Collation par le roi de France des bénéfices vacants en régale', *Bibliothèque de l'Ecole des Hautes Etudes*, LI (Paris, 1935), p. 105.

[2] A. Deeley, *ubi supra*, p. 506.   [3] *Ubi supra*, p. 508.   [4] Wilkins, *Concilia*, II, 701.

Obviously competition for benefices had by this time degenerated into a rough scramble. Although Stratford deplored the greed of these prebend-hunting clerks, Miss Deeley describes them as 'needy'. In the fourteenth century there were more royal clerks than there had been in the thirteenth and the resources of royal patronage seemed proportionately less sufficient to their needs. In England as elsewhere there were also more papal clerks drawing on the total reserves of patronage within the country. These facts alone would account for the increased keenness of the competition for benefices.

There is one other factor which may have been partly responsible for this extension by the king of his right of patronage during an episcopal vacancy. Fourteenth-century vacancies were, generally speaking, shorter than thirteenth-century vacancies. This was one of the penalties which the king had to pay for the many conveniences that were offered him by the system of papal provision to bishoprics. Papal provision might mean that the king could secure the appointment of his own candidate, but the long, disputed elections which had left Winchester vacant for six years at a time[1] and Durham for nearly four in the reign of Henry III,[2] were now a thing of the past.[3] Shorter vacancies meant a smaller intake of revenue into the royal treasury; but in an era of fairly frequent parliamentary grants the actual amount of revenue derived from a vacant see did not matter as much as it had done previously. What did still matter very much was that shorter vacancies meant fewer benefices in the king's gift; worst of all fewer prebends, and this was very serious at a time when demand was threatening increasingly to out-run supply.

An answer to this situation had to be found. When vacancies became shorter the royal rights in respect of vacancies must be intensified to the highest possible point in compensation. The king's neglected rights in vacancies now ended were hunted out by needy clerks and pressed remorselessly, and the judgements given in these cases by the royal courts made possible a gradual development of the king's claims. The government thus

[1] 9 June 1238 to 10 Sep. 1244.
[2] 15 Apr. 1237 to 10 Feb. 1241.
[3] Vacancies in Edward II's reign rarely lasted as long as a year.

mitigated the effects of shorter vacancies on the king's rights of patronage by intensifying the rights themselves.

The effort that was made to extend royal rights of patronage *sede vacante* in the fourteenth century was only one part of a wider struggle. This century was a testing time for the very principles of lay patronage; indeed, for the whole secular approach to patronage.

Sir Maurice Powicke has pointed out that according to thorough-going papalists the Englishman's right of patronage was not part of the *jus commune* of the church.[1] This was serious at a time when the popes were boldly extending and elaborating their conception of the *plenitudo potestatis*, and, by general reservations, were marking out ever larger preserves for the scope of papal provision. Perhaps the moment had come again when 'law had to be met by law'. Certainly in the claims put forward in the Parliament of Carlisle in 1307 and again in the Statute of Provisors[2] a watertight secular theory of patronage was worked out which was an impressive counter to the papal theory of its own plenitude of power. The theme was this: according to the Statute of Provisors all patronage in England was in its origin lay patronage. The patronage in the hands of 'prelates and other people of Holy Church' was derivative; it had come to them through the gift of the king or of other 'lords and donors'.[3] As Miss Deeley says, 'In this feudal scheme there was no room for the pope's claims.'[4] But, of course, in practice the king did not and did not wish to eliminate papal provisions in England. The system could be and was very convenient to him, more especially in the matter of appointments to bishoprics. What the king did need was a theory, as comprehensive and as uncompromising in its way as papal theory: and such a theory he worked out. With this theory behind him, and strengthened by threats almost as forbidding

---

[1] F. M. Powicke, *King Henry III and the Lord Edward* (Oxford, 1947), I, 261.

[2] *Statutes of the Realm*, I, 316–8. (Statute of 1351.)

[3] 'And that prelates and other people of Holy Church, which have advowsons of any benefices of the King's gift, or of any of his progenitors, or of other lords and donors to do divine services, and other charges thereof ordained, shall have their collations and presentments freely to the same, in the manner as they were enfeoffed by their donors'; *loc. cit.*, p. 317.

[4] 'Papal Provision', p. 504.

in their own way as papal anathemas, he was in a position to bargain with the pope on something which approached equal terms.

These claims put forward in the Statute of Provisors were, however, simply the culmination of many less spectacular assertions of the secular theory of patronage in England. They were not mere fabrications made for a political purpose, and without solid foundation. They had a long and substantial history. Some additional light may be thrown on that history by the record of the king's conception in the thirteenth and fourteenth centuries of the right of patronage which he exercised *sede vacante*. The patronage which fell to the king in a vacancy was not, of course, lay patronage at all; it was patronage normally in the hands of a prelate, but temporarily in the hands of a layman, the king. The king's rights of patronage by reason of vacancies, therefore, touched on that important branch of patronage which was in the hands of 'men of Holy Church', the branch which was the main concern of the Statute of Provisors. It seems likely, therefore, that the secular approach to this particular type of patronage would leave its traces more markedly on the events of episcopal vacancies than perhaps anywhere else.

The initial and crucial question was this: by what right did the king claim to present *sede vacante* to livings to which the bishop collated *sede plena*? Was this 'spiritual regalia' in fact 'un droit tout ecclésiastique',[1] something quite distinct from the king's regalian right over the temporalities of the see, or was it not? The question was a delicate one. The bishop *sede plena* 'collated' to livings in his gift; he did not merely present a candidate for institution as a lay patron would do. Since the right to institute and the right to present in the case of a benefice in the bishop's gift were vested in a single person, the bishop himself, he committed a single act, the act of collation. The word collation is by normal definition restricted to the conferring of a benefice by the ordinary and it covers the whole

---

[1] P. Viollet, *Histoire des Institutions Politiques et Administratives de la France* (Paris, 1890–1903), ii, 348. Compare, however, the more cautious statement of J. Gaudemet: 'La collation des bénéfices n'était pas toujours tenue pour un droit spirituel'; 'La Collation des Bénéfices Vacants en Régale', p. 2.

appointment in its spiritual as well as in its temporal aspects,
A vacancy of the see obviously called for modifications in this
procedure. The king *sede vacante* could only *present* his nominee
for a living to which the bishop normally *collated*. He would
present him to the person exercising the spiritual functions of the
bishop during the vacancy, the custodian of the spiritualities[1].
Yet it is interesting to notice that royal writs frequently refer
to the king's act of presentation as 'collation'.[2] The king may

[1] This was the system after about the middle of the thirteenth century when the
metropolitan normally appointed a custodian of the spiritualities. It is explained
in detail by Miss Churchill (*Canterbury Administration*, I, 224–5). Before this time it
seems to have been usual for the presentation to a church to be addressed to the
local archdeacon who was presumably acting in the name of the metropolitan.
Examples from seven sees are given below: (Norwich) presentation directed to
archdeacon of Suffolk (*Cal. Pat. R., 1232–47*, p. 157; 24 Aug. 1236); (Winchester)
presentation to archdeacon of Winchester (*ibid.*, p. 224; 17 June 1238); (Coventry
and Lichfield) presentation to archdeacon of Stafford (*ibid.*, p. 312; 14 July 1242);
(Bath) presentation to archdeacon of Bath (*ibid., 1266–72* (Appendix), p. 723; 23
July 1243); (Exeter) presentation to archdeacon of Totnes (*ibid., 1232–47*, p. 448;
21 Jan. 1245); (Chichester) presentation to archdeacon of Lewes (*ibid.*, p. 473;
3 Feb. 1246); (Carlisle) presentation to archdeacon of Carlisle (*ibid.*, p. 488;
26 Sep. 1246).

It is interesting to notice variations at Norwich and Durham. At Norwich in
the vacancy of 1226 presentations are directed to the metropolitan, the archbishop
of Canterbury; see for example *Pat. R., 1225–32*, p. 91; 9 Nov. 1226 (presentation
of Luke the Chaplain) and *ibid.*, p. 91–2; the same date (presentation of John the
Chaplain) and *ibid.*, p. 88; 4 Nov. 1226 (presentation of Simon of Norwich to a
deanery). In the next Norwich vacancy, however, letters of presentation were
directed in the usual way to an archdeacon (see above).

In the case of Durham; in the vacancy of 1226–8 there seems to be a little confusion. A presentation of 29 Mar. 1227 is enrolled as directed to the archbishop
of York but this is a correction from 'W. Archidiacono Dunholmensi', the original
addressee (*ibid.*, p. 115). The next presentation (of 5 July 1227) is directed to the
archdeacon of Durham but 'Eodem modo scribitur archiepiscopo Eboracensi';
ibid., p. 131. Thereafter it is to the archbishop that all letters of presentation are
addressed: those of Luke the chaplain (*ibid.*, p. 176; 25 Jan. 1228); that of Ralph
of Leicester (*ibid.*, p. 195; 15 July 1228). In future Durham vacancies too this
custom of addressing the letters to the archbishop of York persists. See for example
the presentation of Ottobuono (*Cal. Pat. R., 1232–47*, p. 229; 10 Aug. 1238); of
John of London (*ibid.*, p. 239; 21 Nov. 1240); of Aymer de Lusignan (*ibid., 1247–58*,
p. 42; 11 May 1249.)

In the case of cathedral prebends, of course, the king presented his candidate
with a mandate to the dean and chapter to induct.

[2] This happens in the case of presentations to both churches and prebends.
On 28 Mar. 1260 the king ordered the justiciar not to allow the disturbance of
king's clerks who held benefices in the see of Winchester 'de collacione regis tempore vacacionis' (*Close R., 1259–61*, pp. 281–2).

For further references to the king's act of collation see *Cal. Close R., 1288–96*, p. 37
(concerning the prebend of Nassington in the church of Lincoln); *Cal. Pat. R.,*

perhaps have wished to emphasize that the essence of collation was the act of presentation and that in this respect at least his own right *sede vacante* was as full as that of the bishop *sede plena*.

Fortunately, there is evidence which leaves no possible room for doubt that the king considered his right of patronage *sede vacante* to be a direct result of his control over the temporalities of the bishopric. In the fourteenth century it is fairly common to find a presentation being made by the king *sede vacante* 'by reason of the temporalities of the bishopric being in his hand'.[1] This principle goes back to the thirteenth century. In 1289 the king directed the following writ to Oliver Sutton, bishop of Lincoln:

> Inhibition of his attempting anything by pretext of any letters whatsoever directed or hereafter to be directed concerning the prebend of Nassinton in the church of Lincoln, which is of the king's crown and patronage or concerning anything else pertaining to the king by reason of his barony in the said church . . .

The implication is that the prebend of Nassington itself pertained to the king by reason of the fact that the bishop held his bishopric of the king as a barony.[2] This supposition is strengthened by two incidents which occurred in the reign of Henry III. In 1260 the king had cause to protect the rights of John Mansell, his clerk, in two benefices to which the king had presented him *sede vacante*. One was in the diocese of Durham and the other in that of York. In the case of the presentation to the church of Hutton in the see of Durham, Mansell's rights were suddenly jeopardized when the bishop-elect of Durham, Robert Stichill,

---

1281–92, p. 340 (concerning the prebend of Highworth in the church of Salisbury); *Cal. Close R., 1323–27*, p. 129 (concerning the archdeaconry of Canterbury); and a more general claim in *Close R. 1259–61*, p. 322: 'Cum vacantibus archiepiscopatibus episcopatibus abbaciis et prioratibus in custodia nostra existentibus collaciones ecclesiarum durante custodia predicta vacantium ad nos ex antiqua consuetudine . . . pertinuerint, . . .'.

[1] Edward II describes a prebend as being in the king's gift 'by reason of the temporalities of the bishopric of Salisbury having been in the hand of the king's father' (*Cal. Chan. Warrants, 1244–1326*, pp. 302–3). A presentation to the church of Bredon in the see of Worcester is made 'by reason of the temporalities of the bishopric of Worcester being lately in his [the king's] hand' (*ibid.*, pp. 399–400; 7 May 1314). See also *ibid.*, p. 541; 2 Aug. 1323 and *ibid.*, p. 218.

[2] *Cal. Close R., 1288–96*, p. 37.

whose appointment had been confirmed by the archbishop of York, had presented a candidate of his own to the church to which the king had presented Mansell.[1] Stichill apparently believed:

collacionem dicte ecclesie pretextu confirmacionis sue ante optentam a nobis (i.e. the king) restitucionem temporalium ad se devolvi.

This confusion of thought was promptly punished by a with-holding of the temporalities of the see, until the bishop had admitted the king's right in this matter of the church of Hutton.[2] In short, the king's claim to episcopal patronage in any vacancy was co-extensive in duration with his claim to the custody of the temporalities. In fact the claim to patronage was as it were an appendage to the claim to the temporalities.

This notion is brought out more unequivocally in the second of the disputes of 1260. King Henry III was in this case defend-ing John Mansell's right to the prebend of Fenton in the church of York to which the king had similarly presented him during a vacancy of the see. In a letter to Alexander IV the king ex-plains that the royal right of collation of prebends and bene-fices of churches in the vacancy of a cathedral church lasts from the beginning of the vacancy to the time when the succeeding bishop or bishop-elect receives from the king's hand the tem-poralities of the see:

quibus sunt hujusmodi prebendarum et beneficiorum advocaciones annexe.[3]

The words are carefully chosen. In the first reference to his right the king uses the word 'collation', but when he is stressing

[1] The whole story is told in an enrolment on the Close Rolls (*Close R., 1259–61*, pp. 322–3).
[2] The king proceeded with a nice caution even after the bishop-elect had yielded the point. The keeper of the temporalities was ordered first to give seisin of the church of Hutton to John Mansell, and *then* to give Stichill seisin of the bishopric (*ibid.*, p. 323).
[3] *Ibid.*, pp. 261–2; 16 Jan. 1260:
'Cum ad nos et progenitores nostros temporibus retroactis, dum cathedrales ecclesias regni nostri vacare contingeret, collacio prebendarum et beneficiorum ecclesiarum ipsarum de plano pertinuerit maxime ad tempore quo cathedrales ecslesie supradicte vacare ceperunt usque ad tempora quibus succedentes episcopi aut electi temporalia quibus sunt hujusmodi prebendarum et beneficiorum ad-vocaciones annexe de nostra manu reciperent, . . .'

the fact that the right of presentation is annexed to the temporalities he uses the word *advocacio*, advowson, a word with
wholly secular implications. Advowson was the term normally
used of a layman's right of patronage. The bishop's right of
collation was in the king's view identical with the layman's
right of advowson as far as the actual presentation to the living
was concerned. The right of institution was something quite
distinct, an attribute of the bishop's character as ecclesiastical
ordinary. *Sede vacante*, therefore, the right of presentation, as an
integral part of the temporal rights pertaining to the bishop's
barony, went to the king; the right of institution went to the
keeper of the spiritualities.

Historically there was much to be said for the king's argument as far as the bishop's right of presentation to churches
on his own manors was concerned, and this point had been
clearly and logically worked out in a very interesting letter of
1258:

In the right of patronage and in presentations to ecclesiastical
benefices in England and in the church of England, certain special
customs are observed, amongst which it is claimed that every place,
to wit, any manor with its appurtenances and liberties to whatsoever
lay or clerical person or women, or ecclesiastical or secular persons,
it is assigned in any way whether for a term or at farm, whether for
maintenance or in dowry, (*pro dotaliciis*) or in any other way—the
right of presenting to a church situated in such a manor by such an
assignment always passes with the manor, unless it is especially reserved or excepted in the assignment. Also in the manors of bishops,
when they have the right of patronage and the right of instituting,
the right of patronage always passes with the said manors, according
to the said custom, whereby in void bishoprics and abbeys, the king,
as also his magnates to whom the wardship of the manors belongs in
time of voidance, obtain the right of presenting to churches situated
in the said manors, while the right of instituting remains to the
metropolitan or others to whom the spiritual right devolves. For
although bishops in their dioceses, and even abbots having ponti-
fical right, confer the churches of their manors, because in those
manors the right of patronage and the right of instituting go together, nevertheless they have the right of patronage by reason of
their manors or their baronies, which if either they be of themselves
thrust out (*evincantur*) of these, or if the manors are assigned to others

with their appurtenances as aforesaid, the right of presenting passes with the said manors, the right of instituting thenceforward only remaining with them by reason of their pastoral office.[1]

The layman did not regard the bishop's 'collation' of a benefice as being truly a single act. A collation was the result of the amalgamation of two quite distinct functions, the one spiritual, the other temporal. It was only accidentally that these two functions were in the case of a bishop united in one person. They remained essentially separable. This was the assumption made by the king in presenting *sede vacante* to the churches in the episcopal gift, by reason of the barony being in the king's hand.

However, in respect of cathedral prebends there was much less justification for such an assumption. Here the bishop's right of collation was more distinctly a part of his right as a prelate. It was a part of his connection, which was after all a 'spiritual' connection, with his cathedral church. It could hardly be considered in origin a part of his barony.[2] But this was a distinction which the king was no doubt at pains to ignore. His hold on cathedral prebends, the most useful form of patronage for his clerks, must be a sure one. The king, therefore, speaks of the advowson of prebends, as well as of churches, being 'annexed to the temporalities',[3] and as belonging to the bishop 'by reason of his barony'.[4] Obviously the king's position had some very weak points, but there was an answer, indeed, perhaps only one possible answer. Ultimately, so the layman argued, even the wealth which attached to cathedral prebends had been given to the church either by the king or by some other 'lord or donor'. *All* patronage was in origin lay patronage. And the king, as Advowee Paramount, the patron of bishoprics, was the natural

---

[1] *Cal. Pat. R., 1247–58*, pp. 619–20.

[2] The theory that the right of presentation *sede vacante* to cathedral prebends and the control over the temporalities of the vacant see were coterminous was only being worked out in the thirteenth century. In 1234 the king disputed with the new bishop of Hereford, Ralph Maidstone, about a prebend in the cathedral church which had fallen vacant on the eve of the bishop's confirmation. The new bishop collated to it the next day, whereas the king considered that the right belonged to the crown because the actual vacancy of the prebend had occurred before the confirmation. It is interesting that this should have been the argument which the king used, for this was a week before the restoration of the temporalities, a fact which in the fourteenth century would have been the only argument which the crown considered necessary. (Deeley, 'Papal Provisions', p. 508.)

[3] See above, p. 190.   [4] See above, p. 189.

defender of the ultimate controlling rights of the laity over all patronage whether it had been granted to ecclesiastics or not. That was the answer of the Statute of Provisors, and it was as nearly watertight an answer as could be achieved.

It is only in the light of this development, this gradual definition of the lay approach to problems of patronage, that the king's struggle for the patronage of vicarages *sede vacante* can be fully understood. Presentations to vicarages lay in those precious borderlands between *temporalia* and *spiritualia* over which the church and crown did battle. In the eyes of the church the patronage of vicarages was a matter for the ecclesiastical courts. The claim is clearly stated in the list of complaints against the crown which is recorded in Winchelsey's register, and which has already been cited in other connections:

Item licet patronatus vicariarum que non ad laicum feodum nec ad alias laicas personas sed ad rectores ecclesiarum pertinent tamquam mere spirituale ad forum ecclesiasticum debeat pertinere, curia tamen regia super patronatu hujusmodi vicariarum cognicionem usurpans jurisdiccionem ecclesiasticam super hoc impetit minus juste.[1]

Since this was the attitude of the church it is not surprising to find that when provision was made for a vicarage to which it was intended that the bishop should collate *sede plena*, it was sometimes explicitly stated that during a vacancy of the see presentation to the vicarage should be in the hands of the dean and chapter. Thus in 1236 in the see of London it was arranged that *sede vacante* the dean and chapter of St. Paul's should present to the vicarages of the churches Gillston, Northolt and Rickling.[2] But the crown took a different view of vicarages. Both Edward I and Edward II presented to the vicarage of Rickling in vacancies of the see of London.[3] Moreover although

---

[1] *Reg. R. Winchelsey*, p. 1026.

[2] *Early Charters of the Cathedral Church of St. Paul, London*, ed. M. Gibbs (Camden Society Third Series, LVIII, 1939), pp. 63–4.

A similar arrangement was made concerning the vicarage of Westham in the see of Chichester; *The Chartulary of the High Church of Chichester*, ed. W. D. Peckham (Sussex Record Society, XLVI, 1942–3), p. 53.

[3] Edward I, in the vacancy of 1303–4, first presented Henry de Bray (*Cal. Pat. R., 1301–07*, p. 226; 19 May 1304) but on 4 June 1304 he presented Richard de Madingley, a chaplain (*ibid.*, p. 230). Edward II presented Nicholas de Eyworth (*ibid., 1313–17*, pp. 606–7; 15 Jan. 1317).

O

none of these churches is mentioned in the London vacancies of Henry III's reign, Henry did on occasion present to vicarages *sede vacante*.[1]

However, it may well have been that royal pressure on vicarages became more intensive in the late thirteenth and the early fourteenth centuries than it had been previously. In 1284 there was an inquisition concerning presentations to vicarages in the see of Durham during vacancies to which the following return was made:

> During voidances of the bishopric of Durham all collations of vicarages in county Northumberland belong and have been wont to belong from time beyond memory, to the archbishop of York: as to whom collations of vicarages in the liberty of Durham belong the jurors are ignorant because they have no lands in the liberty; but well know that Sir Godfrey, archbishop of York conferred the vicarage of Herteburne, county Northumberland, on his chaplain, by name Gerbald; on whom he conferred the vicarage of Kellaune they are ignorant because it is within the liberty of Durham.[2]

About the vicarage of Hartburn the jurors were quite sure, the archbishop of York had conferred it *sede vacante*; in short it was a spirituality. But this was in 1284. In 1311 Edward II conferred the vicarage of Hartburn on his clerk, Hugh de Sapy by reason of the voidance of the see.[3]

During the same Durham vacancy of 1311 there was trouble about the vicarage of the church of Norton. The king had presented Hugh de Sapy to this vicarage too on 17 March 1311,[4] but four days later he presented Bernard Kirkby.[5] The archbishop of York, keeper of the spiritualities of Durham *sede vacante* contested the king's right, pleading not only that the king's writ did not run between Tyne and Tees, and that,

---

[1] For example he presented to the vicarage of Bexhill in the Chichester vacancy of 1244–46 (*ibid.*, *1232–47*, p. 473); and to the vicarage of Leominster in the same see in the next vacancy (*ibid.*, *1247–58*, p. 191). It should be noted, however, that in the case of the vicarage of the church of Canewdon, the king 'nominated' his candidate; he did not actually present (above, p. 180).

[2] *Cal. Inq. Misc.*, *1219–1307*, p. 382; 28 June 1284.

[3] *Cal. Pat. R.*, *1307–13*, p. 335. This was on 2 Mar. 1311. On 15 Apr. 1312 the king conferred this same vicarage on Geoffrey de Edenham (*ibid.*, p. 452), and on 14 Jan. 1313 on Master John de Percy (*ibid.*, p. 520).

[4] *Ibid.*, p. 335.

[5] *Ibid.*, p. 335.

therefore, the case should not be tried in the king's court,[1] but also that the vicarage was 'quoddam mere spirituale'. The king's proctor replied that the previous bishop, Anthony Bek, had conferred the vicarage 'tanquam advocatus'. Then came the uncompromising statement:

> Et dicit quod advocationes, tam vicariarum, quam rectoriarum sunt laicale etc. et non spirituale etc., quarum cognitio spectat ad curiam laicalem etc.[2]

According to the judgement of the court the king recovered the presentation to the vicarage of Norton.[3]

From this last case it may be seen that the king's determination to exercise what he considered to be his rights in a vacancy might bring him into conflict with English prelates. This happened quite frequently[4] and sometimes matters might be made difficult for a man appointed by the king even when the king had been successful in pressing his claim. Thus the king's clerk William de Bevercote was successful in obtaining the prebend of Rampton to which the king had presented him in face

---

[1] See *Reg. R. Kellawe*, II, 841–5, where a full account of the case is given, The king's proctor dismissed this particular plea by asserting that all the bishop's rights derived from the king.

[2] *Ibid.*, p. 844. The archbishop then argues that as the vicarage was merely one portion of a whole church and the church had only one advowee it was evident that the vicarage was a spirituality. But the king's proctor firmly replied: 'quod praedictus archiepiscopus itaque se excusare non potest' (*ibid.*, p. 844). It is interesting also to compare the king's answer to one of the grievances of the clergy in 1285: 'Ad nonum articulum, concedit rex quod ad ecclesiam pertineat cognicio de presentacionibus ad vicarias, ad quas non presentant laici patroni, set si agatur causa presentacione laici patroni rex wlt habere cognicionem' (cited by H. G. Richardson and G. Sayles, 'The Clergy in the Easter Parliament, 1285', *Eng. Hist. Review*, LII (1937), p. 234).

[3] The writ stating this is given, *Reg. R. Kellawe*, II, 841–2.

[4] In addition to the examples given below, see also *Cal. Chan. Warrants, 1244–1326*, pp. 302–3; 1 Nov. 1309:
'The king formerly granted to his clerk Master Thomas de Logorre the prebend which Master Matthew Caruche had in the church of Salisbury, vacant by his death, and in the king's gift by reason of the temporalities of the bishopric of Salisbury having been in the hand of the king's father, and many times commanded S. bishop of Salisbury to receive the said clerk to the said prebend and assign him a stall in the choir and a place in the chapter, but the bishop has done nothing. Mandate to appoint one of the king's clerks whom Thomas will name to put him in possession and assign him a stall in the choir and a place in the chapter in default of the bishop. Mandate also, when Thomas has resigned the prebend which he has in the church of Hastingges, to grant it to the king's clerk Thomas de Maurdyn.'

of opposition from the archbishop of York. But Bevercote found that 'after such judgement' and 'before he took possession'—in fact, at a very significant moment—'certain evil doers entered the close of the prebend, felled the trees growing therein, broke the houses of the prebend and carried away his timber and trees'.[1] However, perhaps in the end, it was better to be on the side of the crown. So at any rate thought John de Melton who had been appointed by the king to the church of Great Carleton in the bishopric of Lincoln 'by reason of the temporalities of the bishopric being in [the king's] hand' on finding that the bishop of Lincoln refused to admit him on the king's presentation, although he 'would have given it to him by his own [i.e. the bishop's] collation'.[2] Melton decided to refuse this offer and prayed the king 'to command the council to make ordinance for the despatch of the business and the maintenance of the king's right'. Certainly when a matter of patronage *sede vacante* became an issue between the king and the chapter of a cathedral church, it was of great assistance to the king that he had the keepers of the temporalities within the see ready to do whatever the chapter might be reluctant to do. The king's threat to the chapter of York in 1256, that if they did not admit John Mansell to the treasurership, the keepers of the temporalities would do so instead, has already been noticed.[3] In a Salisbury vacancy in 1288–9, when Edward I presented his kinsman, Peter of Savoy to the prebend just vacated by William de la Corner, the bishop-elect, who was as yet unconsecrated, the king promised that this should not be drawn into a precedent.[4] Meanwhile he had evaded the hostility of the chapter by ordering Malcolm de Harley, keeper of the temporalities to induct Peter into the prebend.[5]

Similarly, when disputes with the pope occurred over matters of vacancy patronage, the king usually took a firm line;[6] but

[1] *Cal. Pat. R., 1313–17*, p. 495; 1 May 1316.

[2] *Cal. Chan. Warrants, 1244–1326*, p. 541; 2 Aug. 1323.

[3] *Close R., 1254–56*, pp. 387–8; 9 Jan. 1256 and *Cal. Pat. R., 1247–58*, p. 458; 22 Jan. 1256. See above, p. 92.

[4] *Ibid., 1281–92*, p. 340; 4 Jan. 1290.   [5] *Ibid.*, p. 313; 15 Feb. 1289.

[6] See for example *Close R., 1242–47*, pp. 478–9; 26 Aug. 1246, or again *Cal. Close R., 1318–23*, p. 510; 1 Dec. 1321:

'To William Ayremynne, clerk. Inhibition of his going outside the realm to answer any citation concerning the prebend of Leighton Bussard, in St. Mary's

there were times when he trod rather more delicately. The following chancery warrant seems to record one of these occasions:

The king sends in a writing (escrouette) the names of the cardinals and others who have sent letters for the church of Monketon, which the king gave to his clerk John de Benstede when the archbishopric of Canterbury was last vacant, and has ordained his answer in a note which he sends in French. Mandate to translate it into Latin as amicably and courteously as possible, write and seal the letters and give them to the bearer, keeping the matter secret to himself and a sure assistant.[1]

This was in 1299. A year later Edward I seems deliberately to have subordinated his interest in a contest over vacancy patronage in his desire for good relationship with the papacy. The king had presented John Bush to a chapel and prebend of York on 30 April 1300.[2] There seems to have been trouble about this presentation,[3] and on 15 May it would appear that the king was again referring to this matter when he wrote:

It seems best to suffer the interference of the pope with the chapel and the prebend of the archbishop because of the business which the king has with the pope; but the king wishes the chancellor to make protestation for him that this shall not be afterwards to the prejudice of himself or his heirs, or the blemish of the estate of the crown.[4]

However, John Bush's claim to the chapel and prebend was

church, Lincoln, or of his sending any attorney (responsalem) to answer outside the realm, the king having conferred the said prebend upon him which pertained to the king's gift by reason of the voidance of the bishopric of Lincoln.'
See also a similar prohibition to the archbishop of Canterbury against acting on any mandate sent him which might disturb the right of Master John de Bruyton to the archdeaconry of Canterbury which the king had conferred on him sede vacante (Cal. Close R., 1323–27, p. 129; 19 Aug. 1323).

[1] Cal. Chan. Warrants, 1244–1326, p. 100.
[2] 'Grant to Master John Bouhs of London, king's clerk, of the chapel or sacristy of St. Mary and the Holy Angels, York, in the king's gift by reason of the voidance of the archbishopric of York. The like to the same of the prebend of Styvelyngton in the church of St. Peter, York, in the king's gift for the like reason' (Cal. Pat. R., 1292–1301, p. 512).
[3] It is worth noting that the 30 Apr., the date of the above writ, was also the date of the restitution of the temporalities of the see to the new archbishop, Thomas Corbridge.
[4] Cal. Chan. Warrants, 1244–1326, p. 109.

reasserted four years later. The king's tactical withdrawal did not prove permanent.[1]

On the periphery of the king's right of ecclesiastical patronage *sede vacante* was the right which occasionally came to him through the bishop's privileges of presenting to certain secular offices within the convent of a cathedral church *sede plena*. This custom seems to have been utilized by the king chiefly in the see of Winchester, but in 1271 there was a small spate of presentations of a similar kind in the vacancy of the archbishopric of Canterbury. The first of these appointments was made on 1 January 1271 'to the keeping of the little gate of the priory of the Holy Trinity, Canterbury'.[2] The second came eight days later in a grant for life to Ralph le Avener, king's serjeant, 'of the keeping of the great gate of the priory of Christ Church Canterbury',[3] and on 4 April in the same year Robert de Rogate, king's serjeant, was granted the stewardship of the priory of Christ Church.[4] The monks of Christ Church took exception to this last appointment on the ground that they had never been certified of the death of Gerard de Castello whom the late Archbishop Boniface had collated to this office for life.[5] They eventually informed the king that Gerard was still alive though abroad, but it was agreed that Rogate should be placed in full possession if Gerard did not come to England within an agreed time and appear personally to prove his case.[6] This succession of appointments at Canterbury within so short a space of time does raise the suspicion that someone may have been looking hard for vacant offices, whether the king or the notorious Richard de Clifford, the keeper in this vacancy,[7] or someone else, we do not know.

At Winchester in the vacancy of 1238–44 the king conferred a number of offices in connection with the priory of St. Swithin's, but in this case they were obedientiary offices.[8] In 1251, in the

[1] By an order of 5 May 1304 the treasurer and some of the king's council were to be summoned to consider 'the best way possible to aid the said John to recover the chapel and prebend, so that the king's right be saved' (*ibid.*, p. 216).

[2] *Cal. Pat. R., 1266–72*, p. 503.

[3] *Ibid.*, p. 503.

[4] *Ibid.*, p. 528.

[5] *Ibid.*, p. 532; 21 Apr. 1271.

[6] *Close R., 1268–72*, pp. 415–6; 10 May 1271.

[7] See above, pp. 106–7.   [8] *Close R., 1237–42*, p. 158; 21 Nov. 1239.

next vacancy, the king appointed his serjeant Alan Burnell to the stewardship of the priory.[1] In 1261 and 1262 there were at least eighteen presentations made by the king to secular offices connected with the priory, almost all being made specifically to the king's own servants.[2] In the following vacancy, of 1268, the office of ushership of the chamber of the prior of St. Swithin's was granted for life to John de Sowy, king's serjeant, 'by reason of the voidance of the bishopric'.[3] Perhaps the spate of appointments in the vacancy of 1260–2 was merely the result of the stormy history of the priory at this time, but even in the normal course of a Winchester vacancy it was evidently usual for at least a small measure of patronage to come to the king from this source.

From this survey of the various kinds of patronage which came into the king's gift as a result of an episcopal vacancy, and the ground on which the king defended his rights, it might be well now to consider the significance of the title of this chapter which groups together patronage and feudal perquisites. The use which the king made of his rights of patronage during a vacancy would in itself justify his linking of advowsons of churches with such feudal perquisites as wardships and escheats. These were some of the various means by which he provided incomes for his servants, clerical in the one case, lay in the other. But there was a more substantial link between these kinds of emoluments than the way in which they were utilized. From the king's point of view advowsons of churches *were* feudal perquisites; they were in every way an integral part of the temporalities of the see. It may be argued that the claim to present to prebends, one of the most highly valued of all the king's *sede vacante* rights, cannot possibly be included in this category. But what is significant is that the king strove hard to force the claim into this category, that he classed it with the claim to

[1] *Cal. Pat. R., 1247–58*, p. 85; 17 Jan. 1251. The grant was for life. The office was again granted to him for life in 1260 (*ibid., 1258–66*, p. 133; 28 Dec. 1260).

[2] *Ibid.*, pp. 134–43 *passim*, and p. 215 and p. 217; *Close R., 1259–61*, pp. 335–6 and pp. 336–7; and *ibid., 1261–64*, p. 17. The last appointment was conditional on the post being vacant. It may be noted that the king also made appointments of monks to certain obedientiary offices (*Cal. Pat. R., 1258–66*, p. 159). There was also a presentation of the king's marshal to the marshalship of the bishopric (*Close R., 1259–61*, p. 424).

[3] *Cal. Pat. R., 1266–72*, p. 219.

advowsons of churches as annexed to the temporalities and that he would not allow a bishop to collate to a prebend until he had done fealty for the temporalities. In a study of episcopal vacancies from the point of view of the king's government this chapter heading is self-determined.

CHAPTER VII

The Nature and Significance
of Regalian Right

REGALIAN right was useful to the king. It was a source of material wealth for himself and for those of his servants whom he chose to favour. The various ways in which the emoluments of vacant bishoprics were used by the king have already been explained. But this access of wealth in itself does not represent the whole significance of the *jus regale*. It now remains to determine the character of the right itself.

In the first place, regalian right in England, unlike France for example, was peculiarly royal. The see of Rochester alone among English bishoprics provides an apparent exception to the general statement.[1]

In November 1214 King John granted the patronage of this bishopric to the archbishop of Canterbury.[2] The underlying

---

[1] The question of the English king's regalian right over the Welsh sees is a matter for separate consideration for that is essentially a part of the constitutional problems peculiar to the Welsh March.

[2] *Rot. Litt. Pat.*, *1201–16*, p. 124a; 22 Nov. 1214. A confirmation of the grant which is much more detailed than the Patent Roll entry is to be found in Wharton, *Anglia Sacra*, I, 386–7:

'. . . Sciatis nos . . . de communi consilio comitum baronum et aliorum fidelium nostrorum, reddidisse et concessisse Deo et ecclesiae Christ Cant.' et venerabili patri nostro Stephano archiepiscopo totius Angliae primati et S.R.E. cardinali patronatum ecclesiae episcopalis Roffensis cum omnibus pertinentiis, dignitatibus, libertatibus et liberis consuetudinibus suis: Ita quod vacante illa sede episcopali, custodiam et ordinationem illius ecclesiae idem archiepiscopus et successores sui habeant libere et pacifice in perpetuum ut patroni. Ita quod in ordinatione illius ecclesiae de episcopo et episcopi electione nec ante nec post electionem episcopi regius requiretur assensus; sed totum ad archiepiscopum quicunque fuerit pertinebit. Episcopus autem vel electus loci illius temporalia quae prius vocabantur regalia, de manu praedicti archiepiscopi et successorum suorum plenarie recipiet; et fidelitatem ei faciet de feodis pertinentibus ad ecclesiam illam episcopalem tanquam patrono ejusdem episcopatus servitia autem, quae nobis inde et haeredibus nostris debentur, episcopus qui pro tempore ibi fuerit faciet praedicto archiepiscopo et successoribus suis in perpetuum tanquam dominis et patronis; et ipse archiepiscopus et successores sui eadem servitia per manus suas nobis et successoribus

assumptions of the charter confirming this privilege are thoroughly feudal. The bishops of Rochester were to perform the services attaching to the temporalities of their see to the archbishops of Canterbury as their 'lords and patrons', and the archbishops were in turn to perform these same services to the king and his successors. In short, the bishop of Rochester was in the position of sub-tenant in the feudal hierarchy.[1] It is also implied by the wording of the charter that although the king 'restored and conceded' the patronage of the see of Rochester to the archbishop, he did not thereby acknowledge that the crown had no rights at all over Rochester. Rather, it implied that the crown had a right, but was willing in this case to yield it. The king was deliberately granting to the archbishop something which it was fully in his power to give. This is clear from the reference to the services from the bishopric 'which are owing to us and our heirs', and also from the very revealing statement that the future bishops-elect of Rochester would receive from the archbishop of Canterbury the temporalities of the see of Rochester 'which were formerly called *regalia*'. The wording is carefully chosen. Not only did John make it clear that the *jus regale* was his alone in origin, he also implied that the right of patronage which he conceded to the archbishop, although it was in fact identical in every practical detail with the right which the king claimed formerly, was not, nevertheless, 'regalian right'. The temporalities of Rochester could no longer be called *regalia*. In fact the archbishops of Canterbury became simply private patrons of the see of Rochester, in much the same way as secular lords sometimes held the patronage of abbeys. Regalian right remained a royal right. The distinction was not accidental, for exactly the same point was made when the patronage of the abbey of Glastonbury was conferred upon the bishops of Bath and Wells. Henry III granted:

to Jocelin bishop of Bath and his successors in frankalmoin the patronage of the abbey of Glastonbury, the abbot receiving at their

---

nostris facient. Faciet quoque episcopus Roffensis nobis et haeredibus nostris fidelitatem tanquam principi, sed non propter feodum . . .'

[1] This position had in fact obtained since the late eleventh century. See H. M. Chew, *op. cit.*, p. 7.

hands the temporalities which would be called *regalia* if the patronage belonged to the king.[1]

In short the position of the see of Rochester was satisfactorily rationalized according to feudal principles of lordship and patronage by John's charter of November 1214.[2]

This fact that regalian right was virtually a royal monopoly is yet another tribute to the strength of Norman and Angevin kingship in the compact realm of England. In France, by way of contrast, where the monarchy stood in greater need of a widespread regalian right in its struggle to extend its authority over too powerful magnates, there were large areas in which the king had had to relinquish this right and was not able to exercise it.[3] In England, on the other hand, although the crown did not need regalian right to strengthen its position *vis à vis* its barons, the *jus regale* increased the royal authority in more subtle ways. In the case of any lay barony held in chief of the king, there was always the chance of its reversion temporarily or permanently into the hands of the crown, through the king's feudal rights of wardship and escheat. In the case of a bishopric there could, of course, be no permanent reversion of the fief to the crown but, on the other hand, the bishop's barony was subject to a fairly regular temporary reversion into the king's custody. No bishopric over which the king exercised regalian right could elude his grasp for longer than the maximum number of years that a single pontificate could last. During these periods of temporary royal custody the tenants of a bishopric were in a similar position in relation to the crown as the tenants of the royal demesne. Their contact with royal administration was peculiarly direct. Moreover in some sees,

[1] This extract is taken from an *inspeximus* of the charter, made 2 Aug. 1242; *Calendar of the Manuscripts of the Dean and Chapter of Wells* (Hist. Manuscripts Commission, London, 1907), I, 309–10.

[2] It has already been mentioned that before the end of the thirteenth century the bishops of Rochester had come to hold a small group of manors in chief from the crown, and over those manors the king exercised rights of custody *sede vacante* (above, p. 62, n. 1.

[3] An example of the political importance of regalian right to the French king in those cases where he did possess it is to be found in 1143 in the struggle of Louis VII against Theobald, count of Champagne. The king's control over the bishopric of Chalons, then vacant, enabled him to introduce his troops into the heart of the Champagne region (Luchaire, *Institutions Monarchiques*, II, 61–2).

such as Durham and Ely, as a result of the bishop's high jurisdictional powers, the tenants were practically shut off from any
contact with the king's government *sede plena*. In these cases the
periodic contact with the crown as a result of a vacancy was
perhaps especially important.

This raises a further point. It was essential for the authority
of the crown that exceptional privileges of justice held by
powerful barons should never be allowed to get out of hand.
They must be fitted into a scheme by which all justice in its
origin should seem to have emanated from the king. Here regalian right was invaluable. The periodic reversion of such rights
to the crown *sede vacante* kept them within the circumference of
royal control. The bishops of Ely, for example, enjoyed jurisdictional rights in the Isle of Ely that fell little short of those of a
palatinate. Consequently it was only when the see was in the
king's hand that royal justices would sit in the Isle,[1] and the
king did not neglect to send his justices into the bishopric on
these occasions of vacancy.[2] Similarly in the palatinate of
Durham the royal justices did not normally penetrate.[3] But they
did, at least sometimes, during a vacancy. Hugh Bolbeck,
William of York, and the invaluable Stephen de Lucy were
appointed justices in eyre in this bishopric in 1228.[4] In 1237
justices were appointed, though instructed at one point not to
proceed.[5] In the vacancies of 1274 and 1283 the keepers are

---

[1] Miller, *Abbey and Bishopric of Ely*, p. 233.

[2] For example in the vacancy of 1229 the local sheriffs were ordered to allow
the keepers of the bishopric to collect amercements of the men of the bishopric,
levied in the course of an eyre (Fine R. 28, m.10; 12 Feb. 1229, and a further reference to the same matter, *ibid.*, m.8; 7 Apr.).

In the vacancy of 1256–8 Robert Walerand accounted for amercements of the
bishop's men in Norfolk on the occasion of an eyre:
'Robertus Walerand custos espiscopatus Elyensis reddit compotum de iiij xij li.
xvj s. x d. de misericordiis hominum et villarum episcopi Elyensis in comitatu
Norf' quorum nominibus proponitur littera t. . . . in rotulo de eodem itinere'
(Pipe R. 101, m.3, Norfolk).

Three days after the death of Bishop Hugh of Balsham in June 1286 four justices
were appointed to hold an eyre in the Isle of Ely (*Cal. Pat. R., 1281–92*, p. 249;
18 June 1286); and in the account for the issues of the bishopric in the vacancy of
1298–9 there is a detailed list of the *expense itineris* on that occasion also (Pipe R.
144, m.30d).

[3] G. T. Lapsley, *The County Palatine of Durham, etc.* (Cambridge, 1924), pp. 209–11).

[4] *Close R., 1227–31*, p. 34.

[5] 'Rex Rogero Bertram et sociis suis justiciariis in episcopatu Dunholm', salutem.

known to have held pleas of the crown in the district between Tyne and Tees, the region within which the king's writ did not normally run.[1] Anthony Bek was ordered in 1304 to account at the exchequer for amercements made before the justices of *oyer* and *terminer* in the bishopric while it was in the king's hand,[2] and in the vacancy between Bek and Kellawe (1311) the king was again about to hold an eyre within the see, but the tenants of the bishopric persuaded their bishop-elect to buy off the king's intention for the sum of 1,000 marks.[3] No doubt the king's motives were partly financial, but it seems likely that the question of royal authority was present in some measure too. Lapsley has remarked:

> The whole judicial system of the palatinate was overshadowed by the ultimate supremacy of the crown. This made itself little felt up to and even during the brilliant pontificate of Anthony Bek (1283–1310). After that time, however, the crown exerted its authority in various ways.[4]

Lapsley suggests that Bek's pontificate had, perhaps, been a little too brilliant from the king's point of view. It is interesting therefore to notice that it was in the vacancy of 1311, which followed Bek's pontificate, that the archbishop of York in a dispute with the king over a matter of patronage *sede vacante*

Mandamus vobis quod ad assisas capiendas vel alia placita ejusdem episcopatus placitanda, ad que vos justiciarios constitueramus, non procedatis donec aliud inde preceperimus. . . .' (*ibid.*, *1234–37*, p. 543; 2 Aug. 1237).

[1] Pipe R. 118, m.18d. The keepers accounted for £408.8.11½ 'de placitis et perquisitis curiarum catallis fugitivorum et dampnatorum quia iidem Johannes et Galfridus [the keepers of the temporalities] tenuerunt placita de corona inter tinam et teisam.' See also Pipe R. 127, m.2d where there is a similar entry on Malcolm de Harley's account for the vacancy of 1283.

[2] *Cal. Fine R.*, *1272–1307*, p. 497. The bishopric had in this case been in the king's hand 'for certain causes', not through vacancy.

[3] Iterum cum electus confirmatus esset, accepturus temporalia a rege, et rex disposuerat mittere justiciarios suos itinerantes in episcopatum, homines episcopatus, conjecturantes vexationes et jacturas ex hoc eis proventuras, rogabant electum ut redemptionem faceret, et ipsa eis (ita) retribuerent quicquid circa hoc effunderet. Electus vero condescendens eis redemptionem fecit datis mille marcis, sed redemptione facta homines episcopatus denarios retribuere noluerunt.' (Robert Graystane in *Hist. Dunelm. Script. Tres*, ed. J. Raine, p. 93).

In 1345 the commonalty of Durham paid 600 marks fine 'for the remission of the eyre of that bishopric for this turn' (*Cal. Fine R.*, *1337–47*, p. 422).

[4] *County Palatine of Durham*, p. 210.

brought forward the point that the king's writ did not run between Tyne and Tees.[1] The king's proctor refuted this plea by the reply that all the bishop of Durham's jurisdictional powers came ultimately from the crown. The establishment of that point was of considerable importance to the king, and while he exercised regalian right, it would have been very difficult to gainsay it. The periodic reversion of the bishopric into the king's hand was a visible and outward sign of the fact that a bishop's barony and all his temporal rights derived from the king alone.

The question of royal authority in respect of regalian right had another, perhaps an even more important aspect. Not only did it strengthen the hold of the crown over the bishops as barons, but it also strengthened the crown's authority in respect of the church itself. Regalian right was a sign of the king's feudal overlordship over the episcopate by reason of their baronies. But that was not all. The king never narrowed his authority over the episcopate to feudal overlordship alone. The king was overlord, but he was also 'Advowee Paramount' of the church in England. This is partly reflected in a matter which has already been touched upon, the king's right of patronage in a cathedral church *sede vacante*. The king did in fact take over *more* than the temporalities of a vacant see, and there are moments when this fact stands out quite clearly. Mr. Lunt has pointed out, as we have seen, that in the writs for the restitution of the temporalities to a bishop-elect, after about 1260 the single word *temporalia* is almost invariably used.[2] Shortly before and shortly after this date, however, there are several interesting examples of a different phrasing. In these cases it is not simply 'the temporalities of the bishopric' which are restored but 'the bishopric *with* the temporalities'. This phrasing is to be found in the case of Ely in 1254,[3] St. David's in 1256,[4]

[1] The question at issue was the presentation to the vicarage of the church of Norton (see above, pp. 194–5); *Reg. R. Kellawe*, II, 841–5.

[2] *Valuation of Norwich*, p. 74, n. 2.

[3] *Cal. Pat. R., 1247–58*, p. 388: '. . . the king of his special grace wills that the said William receive all the [arrears] of the issues of the said bishopric and of the temporalities belonging to it [since its voidance]'.

[4] Fine R. 53, m.12; 18 May 1256: 'Et mandatum est Willelmo de Axem' et Galfrido de North' custodibus predicti episcopatus quod eidem episcopo de predicto episcopatu una cum omnibus temporalibus et possessionibus ad eundem episcopatum pertinentibus plenam seisinam habere faciant.'

Exeter in 1258,[1] Durham in 1261[2] and Bath in 1267.[3] The implication of these writs undoubtedly seems to be that at this stage the government was doubtful whether the single word *temporalia* fully covered the extent of royal rights during a vacancy of the see. Later, when it had been made quite clear that the king's power to confer prebends in a vacant cathedral church was in the king's view 'annexed to the temporalities',[4] then the simpler term was presumably considered sufficient.

The king was bound to rest his claim to authority over the episcopate on something more than *mere* secular rights of lordship. He was lord of their baronies, it was true, but he was more than this. He was patron of their bishoprics. This right of patronage included of course, the power to grant the licence to elect and to assent to the election to a vacant see. With these two privileges, combined with his right to take in hand the temporalities of a vacant see and to present to vacant prebends in the cathedral church the king's position was a strong one. With this authority, the king could and did on occasion wear down the resistance of a chapter reluctant to elect the royal candidate by oppressive treatment of the vacant see.[5] Such measures, however, were rarely necessary in the case of secular cathedrals, and it seems reasonable to infer that the difference in attitude between the secular and monastic chapters was mainly due to the type of men who composed them. The king's presentations to prebends *sede vacante* could hardly fail to affect the general tone of the secular chapters and to incline them to be more accommodating to the king's wishes.[6] As Sir Maurice Powicke has said, writing of the thirteenth century: 'The king was the greatest danger to a free episcopate.'[7]

When papal provisions first threatened to weaken the king's

---

[1] Fine R. 55, m.11; 1 Jan. 1258: 'Rex commisit Willelmo de Axem'. episcopatum Exoniensem vacantem cum omnibus temporalibus et possessionibus ad eundem episcopatum spectantibus custodiendum.'

[2] *Cal. Pat. R., 1258–66*, p. 139.

[3] *Ibid., 1266–72*, p. 44.

[4] See above, p. 190.

[5] See above, pp. 92–4.

[6] Quite frequently the bishops were pressed by the king *sede plena*, to appoint royal candidates to vacant prebends (see K. Edwards, *English Secular Cathedrals*, p. 121).

[7] Powicke, *Henry III and the Lord Edward*, i, 266.

influence over the election of bishops, Edward I skilfully brought his twin rôles of lord and patron before the pope's notice. In 1272 the pope had preferred Robert Kilwardby to the arch-bishopric of Canterbury. The king gave this warning to the papacy:

. . . it seems to the king and his council that prejudice would be done to him and to the church of Canterbury *whereof he is patron and defender*, in this behalf, especially if the matter were drawn into an example in other churches of England if the pope should assume to himself the power of providing for that church, . . .[1]

Then comes the threat—that the king shall not consider himself in future bound to restore the temporalities of any cathedral church thus provided to.

The papacy, however, had still more deadly weapons in the background. With the pontificate of Boniface VIII came the beginning of papal reservations of intercalary fruits from bishop-rics, that is, of the whole revenues of a bishopric during the period of vacancy.[2] Such reservations were not made in England at least before 1327,[3] but already in Edward I's reign there were occasional disturbing references to the temporalities in papal bulls of provision to English sees. They met with firm suppressive treatment from the English government. Thus in October 1299 John Salmon, bishop-elect of Norwich had to assure the king that such a reference was none of his procuring, and 'to supplicate the king to restore the said temporalities of his grace and mere liberality as king'.[4] After the papal provision of Walter Gainsborough to Worcester in October 1302, the new bishop had to make fine with the king for 1,000 marks, 'for his trespass in admitting an apostolic bull containing that the pope has committed to the said bishop the administration of the temporalities'.[5]

The king was here faced with a challenge to his rights of patronage at the highest level of all, his patronage over the

---

[1] *Cal. Close R., 1272–79*, p. 39. The italics are mine.

[2] W. E. Lunt, *Financial Relations of the Papacy with England*, pp. 502–3.

[3] *Ibid.*, p. 503.

[4] *Cal. Pat. R., 1292–1301*, p. 442.

[5] *Cal. Fine R., 1272–1307*, p. 449. The date given is 4 Feb. 1302, but this must be in error. The date of restitution according to the Patent Rolls is 4 Feb. 1303 (*Cal. Pat. R., 1301–07*, p. 110).

episcopal churches themselves. As in the other matter of patronage of cathedral prebends, so in this case too there was a necessity that the pope's claims should be met by a claim equally compact, watertight and uncompromising; a claim which could be used as a weapon. That claim was worked out; and it found clear expression in a statement found in the Worcester *Registrum Sede Vacante* on the occasion of the vacancy of 1307-8:

Be it remembered that before the time of King John, all his ancestors kings of England—since the time that Christianity was established in England and the bishoprics ordained—freely conferred bishoprics without any contradiction, as freely as kings give prebends in their free chapels at the present time. King John in his time gave to the cathedral churches, which now are, free election, which grant was confirmed by Pope Innocent; but that king always saved to himself and his successors, kings of England, the vacancies, and retained also to him and them the patronages of the bishoprics and the gift of all things during those vacancies, which appears clear, because he gives the prebends and the churches in the time of vacancy, like the bishops, when the see is filled. On the other hand when a bishop dies, the chapter asks the king for a *congé d'élire*, and when the election is made then they ought to present the person chosen to the king, and with him it lies to accept or retain him or not, . . . [But] he has never relinquished anything which concerns his temporality and the right of his crown, wherefore it seems that the pope cannot confer bishoprics in England nor make reservation of them, as the matter concerns lay patronage . . .[1]

This remarkable and unhistorical statement met the king's needs. The church might indeed deny that all English kings before John had 'freely conferred bishoprics, as freely as kings give prebends in their free chapels at the present time'. But the statement had a sufficient element of truth to give it the necessary usefulness. The theory was repeated frequently in the fourteenth century, and it was bolstered up by threats in the Statutes of Provisors especially.[2] It is sometimes difficult to

[1] *Reg. Worcs. Sede Vacante*, p. 106. The French original is printed, ibid., pp. 104-5.
[2] *Statutes of the Realm*, I, 316-8 and II, 68-74.
'And if the king send by letter or in any other manner to the court of Rome, at the entreaty of any person, or if any other send or sue to the same court, whereby any thing is done contrary to this statute touching any archbishopric, bishopric dignity or other benefice of Holy Church within the said realm, if he that maketh such motion or suit be a prelate of Holy Church, he shall pay to the king the value of his temporalities of one year . . .'; Statute of Provisors, 1390.

P

to be certain how far the initiative in these measures lay with the king and how far with the magnates and commons. Certainly the king found the power of papal provision to bishoprics useful to himself when it was employed to promote his own candidates, and it is perhaps significant that parliament in 1393 agreed that the king might take the whole matter of the Statute of Provisors into his own hands, 'giving him power to modify the statute and to make ordinance respecting it'.[1] This was a fitting solution. Primarily these statutes against papal provisions were his weapon, the counter with which he could play his diplomatic game with the papacy. It was perhaps only as a counter that they were taken seriously by either side. But that counter was invaluable to the king. Its most solid historical basis was the reservation which John had made when he granted free election to the English churches, the reservation of the king's rights to grant the licence to elect, to assent to the election, and to have custody of the vacancies. John had reserved to himself and his successors all that was needful, their position as lords and patrons of the English bishoprics. That fundamental relationship between crown and episcopate, which was the corner stone of the relationship between church and state in England, was capable of modification and adaptation. Indeed, it had been most freely adapted by the end of the fourteenth century. But it was a relationship securely built on a strong secular foundation. Regalian right was a part of that foundation, a substantial part.

[1] W. T. Waugh, 'The Great Statute of Praemunire', *Eng. Hist. Review*, xxxvii (1922) p. 182.

Appendix A

Table of Enrolled Accounts of Episcopal Vacancies to the Year 1307

In the following table column (5) (net receipts) gives a notional figure of the extent to which the king actually profited from each vacancy listed. To obtain a notional figure for the gross income which a bishop might perhaps expect to receive from his bishopric during a period such as that covered by the relevant vacancy account one should subtract the figure in column (3) from that in column (2). This would give the gross receipts *minus* tallage, aid or recognitions, which were extraordinary payments

The methods of calculating the expenses column (4) have been the most difficult to standardize. In the late thirteenth-century accounts, the day-to-day expenses incurred in the administration of the bishopric are usually conveniently grouped together and separated from other outpayments which often concern the king's business but which would not have been made by a bishop *sede plena*. It seemed most natural to follow this distinction in analysing the earlier accounts too and the expenses column therefore represents as far as possible only those payments which were made in the ordinary running of the bishopric and excludes outpayments of a more peculiarly 'royal' character, such as expenses incurred by the king in the business of an episcopal election for example, or in repairs on a royal castle.

The figures for the vacancies of Henry II's reign need to be regarded with very great caution. In some cases the whole issues of the bishopric were farmed for a fixed sum, which partly explains the slightness of the expenses in some of these accounts. In other cases the issues of the manors were farmed but other receipts in the account were not. In view of the variety of procedure no indication has been given in this table of the use of the word *firma* in the original account, but where the vacancy lasts for several years it will usually be obvious if the method of farming has been adopted. The practice of farming dies out early in the thirteenth century.

Payments of scutage also figure frequently among the receipts on the twelfth-century accounts but have not been included in the receipts given in this table. Similarly the levy of an aid on the knights of the vacant bishoprics for the marriage of Henry II's daughter in 1168 has not been included, although payments made in this year by the non-military tenants of vacant bishoprics have been noted in column (3). Otherwise the total gross receipts represent all sums accounted for by the keeper of the bishopric for the period covered by the account, but excluding any arrears from previous accounts.

Further, in the case of the twelfth-century accounts, those which cover only fractions of a year have not usually been included in the table. Also, owing to the dearth of accounts or their incompleteness no mention has been made of the bishoprics of Bangor, St. Asaph, Llandaff and Rochester. Moreover in a few of the early accounts there are traditional small payments of besants which are given separate mention in the Pipe Roll accounts but they have been omitted from the calculations in the table below.

BATH AND WELLS

Period	Gross Receipts			Tallage, Aid or Recognitions			Expenses			Net Receipts		
	£	s.	d.	£	s.	d.	£	s.	d.	£	s.	d.
HENRY II Aug. 1166 to Mich. 1166										25	0	0
Mich. 1166 to Mich. 1167 P.R. 13 Henry II, p. 202	438	11	8				3	15	0	434	16	8
Mich. 1167 to Mich. 1168 P.R. 14 Henry II, p. 168	533	5	8	100	0	0[1]	6	5	0	527	0	8
Mich. 1168 to Mich. 1169 P.R. 15 Henry II, pp. 23–4	433	5	8				3	5	0	430	0	8
Mich. 1169 to Mich. 1170 P.R. 16 Henry II pp. 64–5	433	5	8				13	15	0	419	10	8

[1] 'assisa facta super dominia episcopatus ad maritandam Matildam.'

BATH AND WELLS (*continued*)

Period	Gross Receipts £ s. d.	Tallage, Aid or Recognitions £ s. d.	Expenses £ s. d.	Net Receipts £ s. d.
NRY II (*continued*)				
ch. 1170 to ch. 1171 R. *17 Henry II*, » 23–4	433 5 8		11 12 0	421 12 10
ch. 1171 to ch. 1172 R. *18 Henry II*, » 128–9	433 5 8		8 19 8	424 6 0
HN ch. 1211 to ch. 1212[1] R. *14 John, 1212*, 8	640 6 9		186 7 4½	453 19 4½
ch. 1212 to May 1213[1] R. 60, m.7d	313 5 0		69 2 9½	244 2 2½
NRY III Nov. 1242 to May 1244 R. 91, m.14d	1,312 7 4½	192 6 8 (tallage)	384 13 3	927 14 1½
Apr. 1264 to Sep. 1264[2] R. 108, m. 15	244 18 6	[3]	6 2 8½	238 15 9½
Dec. 1266 to Mar. 1267 R. 111, m.28	99 0 2½[4]	51 6 8 (recognitions)	10 0 2½	89 0 0
WARD I Dec. 1274 to Feb. 1275 R. 118, m.18d	202 13 0½	55 5 5½ (recognitions)	31 16 2½	170 16 10
Oct. 1292 to Mar. 1293 R. 139, m.5	422 4 4½	62 1 4 (recognitions)	42 1 9¼	380 2 7¼
June 1302 to Sep. 1302 R. 150, m. 32 P.R. 151, 7d	623 15 10¼	41 0 0 (recognitions)	66 14 4¾	557 1 5½

Both these accounts are interdict accounts, *sede plena*.
Some manors are specifically excepted from the account.
Recognitions were paid but not classed separately.   [4] *Rectius* £98.10.2½.

APPENDIX A

CANTERBURY

Period	Gross Receipts			Tallage, Aid or Recognitions			Expenses			Net Receipts		
	£	s.	d.	£	s.	d.	£	s.	d.	£	s.	d.
HENRY II Mich. 1164 to Mich. 1165 *P.R. 11 Henry II,* pp. 108–9	1,562	15	5½				215	3	1	1,347	12	4
Mich. 1165 to Mich. 1166 *P.R. 12 Henry II,* pp. 114–15	1,562	15	5½				185	17	1½	1,376	18	4
Mich. 1166 to Mich. 1167 *P.R. 13 Henry II,* pp. 201–2	1,562	15	5				315	17	3	1,246	18	2
Mich. 1167 to Mich. 1168 *P.R. 14 Henry II,* pp. 153–6	1,785	12	1½	222	16	8 (aid)[1]	188	16	11½	1,596	15	2
Mich. 1168 to Mich. 1169 *P.R. 15 Henry II,* pp. 165–6	1,562	15	5				183	5	8	1,379	9	9
Mich 1169 to Mich. 1170 *P.R. 16 Henry II,* p. 161	1,562	15	5				183	15	8	1,378	19	9
Mich. 1171 to Mich. 1172 *P.R. 18 Henry II,* pp. 139–40	1,560	15	5				186	3	0	1,374	12	5
JOHN 24 June 1205 to Mich. 1206 *P.R. 8 John,* pp. 54–5	5,169	19	5[2]	1,065	2	3 (tallage)	829	4	2½	4,340	15	5
25 Mar. 1211 to Mich. 1211[3] *P.R. 13 John,* pp. 244, 101, 112	1,105	17	5				183	8	5½	922	8	1

[1] This is the aid levied on the demesnes only and does not include the £56.10.0 which w[as] levied on the knights, which was an exaction of a purely feudal nature.

[2] This sum however includes the curious item of 1,000 marks received by the keepers '[de] thesauro per manum thesaurarii'.

[3] This is a *sede plena* accou[nt]

CANTERBURY (*continued*)

Period	Gross Receipts			Tallage, Aid or Recognitions			Expenses			Net Receipts		
	£	s.	d.	£	s.	d.	£	s.	d.	£	s.	d.
HN (*continued*) ich. 1211 to June 1212[1] R. *14 John, 1212,* 40	1,152	15	9½[2]	184 2 5 (tallage)			314	11	10½	838	3	11
NRY III July 1228 to Mar. 1229 R. *73, m.1*	1,838	0	1½	666 13 4 (tallage)			452	1	7¾	1,385	18	5¾
Sep. 1231 to Aug. 1232[3] R. *76, m.5d*	2,239	6	7½	317 4 8 (tallage)			803	5	8½	1,436	0	11
Aug. 1270 to Dec. 1272 R. *119, m.21* d 21d	7,541	7	11½	294 19 0 (tallage)			2,501	1	3¼	5,040	6	8¼
WARD I June 1278 to May 1279 R. *124, m.23d.*	4,125	16	11½	254 3 4 (tallage)			941	3	0½	3,184	13	11
Dec. 1292 to Feb. 1295 R. *141, mm.* d–29d and R. *142, m.5d*	16,964	17	2¼[4]	259 4 1½ (recognitions)			6,828	9	8½	10,136	7	5¾

CARLISLE

Period	Gross Receipts			Tallage, Aid or Recognitions			Expenses			Net Receipts		
NRY II Nov. 1186 to ich. 1188 R. *34 Henry II,* 7	52	19	6							52	19	6
NRY III June 1246 to Dec. 1246 R. *97, m.9d.*	51	14	3½				27	18	4	23	15	11½

[1] A *sede plena* account.   [2] *Rectius* £1,127.10.6.

[3] The figures given here exclude the manors of Harrow and Hayes for which the period of count is different.

[4] These figures cover large sums (over £2,000) on the credit side for the value of stock ught from the late archbishop's executors and payment for it among the expenses.

CARLISLE (continued)

Period	Gross Receipts £ s. d.	Tallage, Aid or Recognitions £ s. d.	Expenses £ s. d.	Net Receipts £ s. d.
EDWARD I 3 Oct. 1278 to 10 July 1280 P.R. 128, m.34d	425 2 10¾	6 0 0 (recognitions)	13 2 2	412 0 8¾
28 Feb. 1292 to 18 June 1292 P.R. 142, m.29d	43 14 9¾	6 1 8 (recognitions)	2 0 11½	41 13 10½

CHICHESTER

Period	Gross Receipts £ s. d.	Tallage, Aid or Recognitions £ s. d.	Expenses £ s. d.	Net Receipts £ s. d.
HENRY II Mich. 1170 to Mich. 1171 P.R. 17 Henry II, pp. 134–6	246 18 3		12 13 8	234 4 7
Mich. 1171 to Mich. 1172 P.R. 18 Henry II, pp. 132–3	253 2 6		3 13 8	249 8 10
JOHN Mich. 1209 to Mich. 1210 P.R. 12 John, pp. 4–5	306 0 4	38 4 8 (tallage)	34 0 8½	271 19 7
Mich. 1210 to Mich. 1212 P.R. 14 John, 1212, pp. 8–9	591 9 6½		95 10 4½	495 19 2
HENRY III 9 Feb. 1244 to 21 July 1246 P.R. 90, m.9	1,331 1 8	63 11 0 (tallage)	274 11 6	1,056 10 2
25 May 1262 to 20 June 1262 P.R. 112, m.1d	75 6 3	30 13 4[1]	5 19 11½	69 6 3
EDWARD I 25 Oct. 1287 to 24 June 1288 C.R. 81, m.17d	805 15 6½[2]	66 6 8 (tallage)	166 15 9¼	638 19 9

[1] 'de fine custumariorum . . . pro tallagio'.
[2] Rectius £805.14.8½.

CHICHESTER (continued)

Period	Gross Receipts £ s. d.	Tallage, Aid or Recognitions £ s. d.	Expenses £ s. d.	Net Receipts £ s. d.
WARD I (continued) Feb. 1305 to July 1305 R. 152B, m.8	565 7 10½	63 13 4 (tallage)	194 16 5½	370 11 5

DURHAM

Period	Gross Receipts £ s. d.	Tallage, Aid or Recognitions £ s. d.	Expenses £ s. d.	Net Receipts £ s. d.
NRY I ich. 1128 to ich. 1130 R. 31 Henry I, 130–3	1,340 6 10	58 6 8 (donum) 46 5 4 (from thanes etc.)	46 6 9	1,294 0 1
CHARD I Feb. 1195 to b. 1196[1] R. 8 Richard I, 253–61	4,581 10 0½	341 4 2 (tallage) 46 9 4 (aid of churches)[2] 611 16 8 (fines of clergy)[2] 677 13 4 (fines of servants of bishop)[2] 21 6 8 (donum of a priest)[2]	437 19 2½	4,143 10 10
HN June 1208 to Nov. 1211 R. 13 John, 35–41	13,575 5 5½[3]	1,154 1 8 (tallage) 205 15 8 (2nd tallage) 735 9 5 (fines of clergy)	1,521 4 3	12,054 1 2½

[1] The dating of this account presents difficulties. The account is divided into two parts: (a) the count of Gilbert Fitz Renfrew and Richard Brewer 'de tribus partibus anni dum fuit in manu gis', and (b) that of Hugh Bardolf from the second Sunday in Lent to the following Easter. Since Bardolf is elsewhere stated to have been the first keeper in this vacancy (see Hist. Dun- n Script. Tres. p. 16), this probably means 26 Feb. 1195 to 2 Apr. 1195 (although the death of ugh le Puiset according to Roger of Howden was 3 Mar. 1195). The bishopric seems to ve been in the king's hand for a year (William of Newburgh, p. 441), which would bring to Feb. 1196 as the closing date of the account.

[2] These items are difficult to place in any column, but seem best separated from the regular ues.

[3] The final summa summarum on the account is £16,787.14.10½ but this includes arrears from a evious account and fines and scutages which cannot properly be considered as 'vacancy issues'.

DURHAM (*continued*)

Period	Gross Receipts	Tallage, Aid or Recognitions	Expenses	Net Receipts
	£ s. d.	£ s. d.	£ s. d.	£ s. d.
JOHN (*continued*) 11 Nov. 1211 to 11 Nov. 1212 *P.R. 14 John, 1212,* pp. 46–50	2,803 0 0½		992 7 11½[1]	1,810 2 1
HENRY III 12 Sep. 1226 to 12 Aug. 1228 P.R. 73, m.1	6,408 10 3	351 13 7½ (aid) 42 6 8 (aid of burgesses) 405 5 6 (tallage)	546 11 10	5,861 18 5
19 Apr. 1237 to 2 Feb. 1239[2] P.R. 84, m.2	6,861 15 10½	336 7 4 (common aid)	1,043 14 6½	5,818 1 4
2 Feb. 1239 to 24 June 1240[2] P.R. 84, m.2	4,366 18 5		653 1 0	3,713 17 5
24 June 1240 to 10 Feb. 1241[2] P.R. 85, m.6d	2,524 8 5½[3]		349 11 5½	2,174 17 0
10 Feb. 1249 to 20 Oct. 1249 P.R. 94, m.18	2,617 17 2	315 17 2 (common aid)	291 6 8	2,326 10 6
EDWARD I 20 Aug. 1274 to 12 Nov. 1274 P.R. 118, m. 18	2,668 19 10½[4]	626 7 8½ (tallage)	99 9 10½	2,569 10 0
13 June 1283 to 4 Sep. 1283 P.R. 127, m.2d	2,620 7 9¾	693 19 1¼ (tallage)	79 9 9½	2,540 18 6

[1] Much of this was spent on the provisioning and fortifying of the castles of the bishopric.
[2] All three accounts for this vacancy exclude the manors of Wearmouth and Ryhope.
[3] *Rectius* £2,534.8.5½.
[4] *Rectius* £2,669.0.0½.

ELY

Period	Gross Receipts	Tallage, Aid or Recognitions	Expenses	Net Receipts
	£ s. d.	£ s. d.	£ s. d.	£ s. d.
HENRY II				
Mich. 1169 to Mich. 1170 P.R. 16 Henry II, p. 95–6	888 0 10		93 14 7	794 6 3
Mich. 1170 to Mich. 1171 P.R. 17 Henry II, p. 115–17	935 3 6		42 17 6	892 6 0
Mich. 1171 to Mich. 1172 P.R. 18 Henry II, p. 115–17	941 19 (		49 6 0	892 13 6
HENRY III Foreign R. 1, m.3d[1]	623 16 11		32 19 3½	590 17 7½
2 Dec. 1228 to 6 May 1229 P.R. 72, m.10d	744 0 9½	450 15 10 (tallage)	65 2 2	678 18 7½
2 Aug. 1254 to 5 Dec. 1254 P.R. 101, m.4	767 5 5½	189 0 2 (tallage)	54 6 6	712 18 11½
9 Oct. 1256 to 5 Jan. 1258 P.R. 101, m.4 and 4d. and m.6	3,707 18 3½[2]	249 17 4 (aid and tallage)[3]	546 2 8½	3,161 15 7[4]
EDWARD I 6 June 1286 to Sep. 1286 P.R. 144, m.34 and 34d	1,055 10 1¾	245 10 0 (recognitions)	75 14 8½	979 15 5¼

[1] The account is for three parts of the third year of the reign (1218–19) and the assized rents for the terms of St. John the Baptist, Michaelmas and St. Andrew are accounted for.
[2] This includes the £92.16.10 which were the profits from the Norfolk eyre within the bishopric.
[3] 'de auxilio libere tenencium et tallagio villanorum'.
[4] Robert Walerand, the keeper, is left with a debt of £423.11.1, but the cross reference to P.R. 104, m.8d is merely to a restatement of the debt.

ELY (*continued*)

Period	*Gross Receipts* £ s. d.	*Tallage, Aid or Recognitions* £ s. d.	*Expenses* £ s. d.	*Net Receipts* £ s. d.
EDWARD I (*continued*)				
4 Apr. 1290 to 30 May 1290 P.R. 135, m.1	728 14 11¾	248 12 0¾ (aid and recognitions)[1]	59 17 11½	668 17 0¼
28 Mar. 1298 to 13 Oct. 1299 P.R. 144, mm.29–31 and P.R. 147, m.3d	7,983 11 5¾	258 11 1¼ (recognitions)	3,238 8 7¼	4,745 2 10½
20 Mar. 1302 to 18 July 1302 P.R. 150, m.34	1,132 3 0¾	253 0 0½ (recognitions)	368 15 10½	763 7 2¼
18 July 1302 to 4 Feb. 1303 P.R. 150, m.34 and 34d.	3,179 12 2½[2]		1,224 10 2	1,955 2 0½

EXETER

Period	*Gross Receipts* £ s. d.	*Tallage, Aid or Recognitions* £ s. d.	*Expenses* £ s. d.	*Net Receipts* £ s. d.
HENRY II				
P.R. 32 Henry II, p. 157[3]	270 18 0		19 18 9	250 19 3
JOHN				
Mich. 1206 to Mich. 1207 *P.R. 9 John*, pp. 221–3	655 8 10½	177 2 11½ (tallage)	109 3 0	546 5 10½
Mich. 1210 to Mich. 1211 *P.R. 13 John*, pp. 272–3	516 9 7½	139 18 4 (tallage)	73 8 1	443 1 6½
P.R. 14 John, 1212,[4] pp. 7–8	157 9 5½		18 15 7	138 13 10½
Mich. 1212 to Dec. 1213[5] P.R. 60, m.7d	591 0 9½[6]		84 9 0½	506 11 9

[1] Aid of freeholders and recognitions of villeins.
[2] *Rectius* £3,180.12.2½.
[3] Three-quarters of the exchequer year ending Michaelmas 1186.
[4] Half of the year ending Michaelmas 1212.
[5] The account is for the whole of the fifteenth year of the reign and 'quarta parte anni xvj'
[6] *Rectius* £591.19.1.

EXETER (continued)

Period	Gross Receipts £ s. d.	Tallage, Aid or Recognitions £ s. d.	Expenses £ s. d.	Net Receipts £ s. d.
ɛNRY III				
ich. 1223 to				
ich. 1224	187 11 7½	79 8 8	1 19 0	185 12 7½
R. 69, m.3d		(tallage		
d Foreign R. 1,		and aid)[1]		
3d				
Dec. 1244 to				
Apr. 1245	179 14 9	45 5 0	20 7 10	159 6 11
R. 91, m.14d		(tallage)[2]		
ɔWARD I				
Aug. 1280 to				
Oct. 1280[3]	331 5 1½	127 6 0½		331 5 1½
R. 134, m.1d		(recognitions		
d P.R. 139, m.21		and aid)		

HEREFORD

Period	Gross Receipts £ s. d.	Tallage, Aid or Recognitions £ s. d.	Expenses £ s. d.	Net Receipts £ s. d.
NRY II				
ch. 1168 to				
ch. 1169	341 11 8	40 0 0[4]	34 2 9	307 8 11
R. 15 Henry II,				
, 142–3				
ch. 1169 to				
ch. 1170	311 6 0		31 13 0	279 13 0
R. 16 Henry II,				
59–60				
ch. 1170 to				
ch. 1171	300 9 4		31 13 0	268 16 4
R. 17 Henry II,				
98				
ch. 1171 to				
ch. 1172	301 9 4		35 1 0	266 8 4
R. 18 Henry II,				
3–4				

The payment is styled tallage on P.R. 69, m.3d but it is called an aid in the case of the
ɪors of Chidham and Farringdon (Foreign R. 1, m.3d).
It seems possible that no tallage was levied on the Cornish manors on this occasion.
This account does not include the manors of Chidham, Horsley, Tyting and Thorney
ch are said to be accounted for separately on P.R. 145. The reference on P.R. 145, m.8
ʋever merely restates the responsibility of Nicholas le Gras for these manors.
'de auxilio dominicorum episcopatus ad maritandam filiam Regis'.

HEREFORD (continued)

Period	Gross Receipts £ s. d.	Tallage, Aid or Recognitions £ s. d.	Expenses £ s. d.	Net Receipts £ s. d
HENRY III 24 Aug. 1234 to 2 Oct. 1234 P.R. 80, m.2d	124 7 3½		7 0 5½	117 6 10
10 Dec. 1268 to 21 Apr. 1269 P.R. 119, m.21	265 1 2½	21 2 0 (tallage)	22 0 11½	243 0
EDWARD I 11 May 1275 to 27 June 1275 P.R. 120, m.22	258 2 0½	42 19 3 (tallage)	16 19 2	241 2 10
24 Aug. 1282 to 8 Jan. 1283 P.R. 128, m.34d	361 2 5½	30 0 6 (tallage)	20 0 0	341 2

LICHFIELD

Period	Gross Receipts £ s. d.	Tallage, Aid or Recognitions £ s. d.	Expenses £ s. d.	Net Receipts £ s. d
HENRY II P.R. 29 Henry II, pp. 152–3[1]	123 15 1		7 6 11	116 8
HENRY III 27 Dec. 1238 to 1 Jan. 1240 P.R. 84, m.2	32 18 11[2]		4 3	32 14
P.R. 85, m.3	434 9 9[3]	82 5 4[4] (aid and tallage)	65 10 4	368 19
21 Dec. 1241 to 6 May 1242 P.R. 95, m.6d and P.R. 97, m.12	88 14 0		25 17 5½	62 16
EDWARD I 22 Dec. 1295 to 4 June 1296 P.R. 146, m.55d.	24 15 0[5]	Recognitions[6]	[7]	

[1] Three-quarters of the exchequer year ending Michaelmas 1183.
[2] Lands within county of Chester. [3] Lands outside county of Chester.
[4] 'de auxilio militum et libere tenentium rusticorum et tallagio burgorum et rusticorum'.
[5] Lands within the county of Chester only.
[6] Recognitions are classed with fines and perquisites.
[7] Expenses are not classed separately.

LINCOLN

Period	Gross Receipts			Tallage, Aid or Recognitions			Expenses			Net Receipts		
	£	s.	d.	£	s.	d.	£	s.	d.	£	s.	d.
HENRY II												
Mich. 1167 to Mich. 1168 *P.R. 14 Henry II,* p. 76–8	1,058	9	8½				148	5	3½	910	4	5
Mich. 1168 to Mich. 1169 *P.R. 15 Henry II,* p. 44–6	1,152	4	7½	140 (aid)[1]	0	0	173	16	9½	978	7	10
Mich. 1169 to Mich. 1170 *P.R. 16 Henry II,* p. 151–3	1,007	6	11				165	8	11	841	18	0
Mich. 1170 to Mich. 1171 *P.R. 17 Henry II,* p. 111–12	1,005	15	5				164	13	3	841	2	2
Mich. 1171 to Mich. 1172 *P.R. 18 Henry II,* p. 95–8	1,009	10	5				174	3	9	835	6	8
Mich. 1181 to Mich. 1182 *P.R. 28 Henry II,* p. 59–60	1,468	6	2				244	2	3	1,224	3	11
JOHN												
Mich. 1200 to Mich. 1201 *P.R. 3 John,* p. 192–4 and p. 173	1,481	3	6½	522 (tallage)	5	2	253	18	9½	1,227	4	9
Mich. 1201 to Mich. 1202 *P.R. 4 John,* p. 277–9	1,760	5	0½				338	5	8	1,421	19	4½

[1] 'ad maritandam filiam Regis'. It is clear from other entries that this payment comes from
the men of the demesnes and not from the knights.

LINCOLN (continued)

Period	Gross Receipts £ s. d.	Tallage, Aid or Recognitions £ s. d.	Expenses £ s. d.	Net Receipts £ s. d.
JOHN (continued) Easter 1206 to Mich. 1207[1] P.R. 9 John, pp. 13-14	1,838 6 9	436 0 8 (tallage)	371 13 2½	1,466 13 6½
Mich. 1211 to Mich. 1212[2] P.R. 14 John, 1212, p. 2	1,113 9 7		144 9 7	969 0 0
HENRY III 3 Feb. 1235 to 15 Apr. 1235 P.R. 78, m.16d	435 2 7	286 18 5 (tallage)	45 6 5	389 16 2
11 Oct. 1253 to 1 Apr. 1254 P.R. 101, m.4	899 16 2½	352 17 5 (aid, tallage and recognitions)[3]	336 15 3½	563 0 11
16 Aug. 1258 to 17 Oct. 1258 P.R. 104, m.2	312 17 2½	27 2 4[4] (tallage and recognitions)	16 14 10½	296 2 4
EDWARD I 18 Dec. 1279 to 28 Feb. 1280 P.R. 125, m.3d	277 16 2	111 8 8 (aid and tallage)[5]	14 19 9	262 16 5
16 Nov. 1299 to 18 Mar. 1300 P.R. 150, m.36 and 36d	643 7 4	Recognitions[6]	81 15 8½	561 11 7

[1] This account excludes the issues of the manor of Newark for the first half year and those of the manor of Banbury for the whole period.

[2] A *sede plena* account.

[3] 'de auxilio libere tenencium et tallagio villanorum et recognitionibus quorundam'.

[4] 'de tallagio custumariorum et recognicionibus quorundam'. This seems a surprisingly small sum.

[5] 'de auxilio libere tenencium et tallagio custumariorum'.

[6] The recognitions are in some instances grouped with perquisites and the exact amount is therefore not ascertainable.

LONDON

Period	Gross Receipts £ s. d.	Tallage, Aid or Recognitions £ s. d.	Expenses £ s. d.	Net Receipts £ s. d.
HENRY II				
R. *33 Henry II,* 29[1]	259 11 2		52 0 3	207 10 11
ich. 1187 to ich. 1188 R. *34 Henry II,* ». 11–12	427 4 8½		98 3 1	329 1 7½
JOHN				
June 1211 to Jan. 1213[2] R. *14 John, 1212,* ». 9–10, and R. 60, m.1	942 19 3		97 5 6½	845 13 8½
HENRY III				
Nov. 1228 to Apr. 1229 R. 72, m.10d and R. 73, m.13	197 14 9	93 0 0 (tallage)	16 16 7½	180 18 1½
ich. 1241 to ich. 1242 R. 87, m.3 (a)	286 17 10½		28 13 4	258 4 6½
(b)	292 11 8		118 10 6[3]	174 1 2
ich. 1242 to Mar. 1244 R. 87, m.3	1,390 15 6½		319 19 9½	1,070 15 9
July 1262 to Jan. 1263 R. 108, m.15d d m.12d	420 14 1½	28 7 10 (aid)	16 12 3½	404 1 10
EDWARD I				
Sep. 1273 to Mar. 1274 R. 117, m.7d	417 2 2	16 3 8 (aid and recognitions)	90 14 0	326 8 2
Dec. 1303 to June 1304 R. 149, m.37	798 3 1¾	30 12 4 (recognitions)	291 3 10½	506 19 3¼

[1] Three parts of the exchequer year ending Michaelmas 1187.
[2] A *sede plena* account.
[3] This figure includes harvest expenses.

Q

APPENDIX A

NORWICH

Period	Gross Receipts £ s. d.	Tallage, Aid or Recognitions £ s. d.	Expenses £ s. d.	Net Receipts £ s.
HENRY III 13 Dec. 1218 to 17 Mar. 1219 P.R. 63, m.4 and 4d	118 16 6			118 16
21 Aug. 1236 to 26 Mar. 1237 P.R. 81, m.13	478 13 6	131 8 4[1] (aid)	360 0 2[2]	118 13
20 May 1257 to 11 Aug. 1257 P.R. 101, m.4	306 3 3½	64 0 0 (aid)	18 17 11½	287 5
EDWARD I 19 Jan. 1278 to 16 Mar. 1278 C.R. 74, m.2	201 13 3	109 6 8 (tallage)	21 0 8	180 12
14 Oct. 1288 to 17 Feb. 1289 P.R. 133, m.20d.	596 12 6¾	30 6 8[3] (recognitions)	86 18 8½	509 13 1
3 Oct. 1299 to 19 Oct. 1299 P.R. 149, m.29d.	160 5 7	78 7 0 (recognitions)		

ST. DAVID'S

Period	Gross Receipts £ s. d.	Tallage, Aid or Recognitions £ s. d.	Expenses £ s. d.	Net Receipts £ s.
HENRY III 1 Apr. 1247 to 26 Sep. 1247 C.R. 45, m.20d	66 12 10			66 12 1
EDWARD I 1 Apr. 1280 to 10 June 1280 P.R. 124, m.24	87 8 1½		16 15 0	70 13

[1] This includes the payment of £100 by the men of King's Lynn, which is recorded on t. wardrobe account, P.R. 82, m.13.

[2] Large purchases of stock and grain were made for which the next keeper, Jeremiah Caxton was to account, but there seems to be no record of an account at the exchequer Caxton although he paid money from the issues of this bishopric into the wardrobe (P.R. 8 m.13).

[3] This is from the Suffolk manors only. Henry de Bray is said to answer for those from t Norfolk manors, but there is merely a statement of his debt.

[4] The expenses are grouped with other items.

ST. DAVID'S (continued)

Period	Gross Receipts £ s. d.	Tallage, Aid or Recognitions £ s. d.	Expenses £ s. d.	Net Receipts £ s. d.
DWARD I (continued)				
2 Apr. 1293 to				
Oct. 1293	195 1 0		23 1 5	171 19 7
.R. 139, m.3d				
1 May 1296 to				
4 Jan. 1297	235 14 10¼	Recognitions[1]	22 18 3¼	212 16 7
.R. 143, m.25d				

SALISBURY

Period	Gross Receipts £ s. d.	Tallage, Aid or Recognitions £ s. d.	Expenses £ s. d.	Net Receipts £ s. d.
ENRY II				
lich. 1185 to				
lich. 1186	453 7 1		69 10 0	383 17 1
.R. 32 Henry II,				
p. 166–7				
lich. 1186 to				
lich. 1187	513 3 11	62 0 2[2] (tallage)	72 19 6	440 4 5
.R. 33 Henry II p. 187–8				
lich. 1187 to				
lich. 1188	480 0 8		72 2 1	407 18 7
.R. 34 Henry II,				
p. 184–5				
OHN				
lich. 1210 to				
lich. 1211[3]	716 15 8½		120 6 5½	596 9 3
.R. 13 John,				
p. 244–5 and p. 110				
lich. 1211 to				
lich. 1212[3]	621 15 9½	70 7 0 (tallage)	139 10 2	482 5 7½
.R. 14 John, 1212,				
p. 40–1				
ENRY III				
o July 1228 to				
8 Feb. 1229	433 3 5	106 7 8 (tallage)	2 0 6	431 2 11
.R. 72, m.10.				
o Nov. 1246 to				
9 Jan. 1247	204 6 1½	50 9 4 (tallage)	51 6 4	152 19 9½
.R. 92, m.16				

[1] Grouped with pleas and perquisites.
[2] The individual items of the tallage are styled *donum*.   [3] Both are *sede plena* accounts.

SALISBURY (continued)

Period	Gross Receipts	Tallage, Aid or Recognitions	Expenses	Net Receipts
	£ s. d.	£ s. d.	£ s. d.	£ s. d.
HENRY III (continued)				
5 Feb. 1256 to 17 Aug. 1256 P.R. 100, m.19	532 19 1½[1]	104 18 2[2] (recognitions and tallage)	25 4 0	507 15 1
15 Dec. 1262 to 6 Apr. 1263 P.R. 112, m.1d and C.R. 51, m.6d	479 16 11	96 5 10[3] (recognitions and tallage)	20 17 0	458 19 11
12 Jan. 1271 to 16 June 1271 P.R. 116, m.2d	449 2 9½	15 18 0[4] (recognitions) 79 6 8 (tallage)[5]	18 5 6½	430 17 3
EDWARD I				
22 Apr. 1284 to 10 Aug. 1284 P.R. 133, m.29	449 19 10½	8 11 10[4] (recognitions) 75 9 4 (tallage)[5]	21 1 3	428 18 7
25 Sep. 1286 to 25 Mar. 1287 P.R. 133, m.28d.	1,405 13 4½	99 5 0[6] (recognitions)	295 19 9¾	1,109 13 6½
12 Oct. 1291 to 24 Dec. 1291 P.R. 137, m.26d and P.R. 138, m.22d	843 3 11¾	15 6 4[8] (recognitions) 87 9 4[9] (tallage)	193 16 4½	649 7 7
18 May 1297 to 7 Aug. 1297 P.R. 143, m.25d	380 12 3¾	15 6 2[8] (recognitions) 87 16 0 (tallage)[9]	32 15 1¼	347 17 2

[1] This excludes the sum of £184.4.8 which was the value of the summer corn and hay an which was separately accounted for (P.R. 100, mm.19, 11d and 13d). Of this only £28.11. found its way to the royal treasury. A further £89 was paid to the executors of the late bishop

[2] 'de recognicionibus libere tenentium et tallagio villanorum'.

[3] 'de recognicionibus liberorum hominum et tallagio custumariorum'.

[4] 'de recognicionibus liberorum hominum'.

[5] 'de tallagio villanorum'.

[6] 'de recognicionibus villanorum . . . una cum recognicionibus quorundam liberorum'.

[7] This high total is partly explained by the inclusion of £663.2.3 for crops sold.

[8] 'de recognicionibus liberorum hominum'.

[9] 'de tallagio villanorum'

WINCHESTER

Period	Gross Receipts			Tallage, Aid or Recognitions			Expenses			Net Receipts		
	£	s.	d.	£	s.	d.	£	s.	d.	£	s.	d.
HENRY II Mich. 1171 to Mich. 1172 P.R. 18 Henry II, . 85-7	1,555	1	6				114	19	1½	1,440	2	4½
RICHARD I Mich. 1188 to Mich. 1189[1] P.R. 1 Richard I, 5	1,117	9	9[2]				126	19	7	990	10	2
JOHN Sep. 1204 to June 1205 P.R. 7 John, . 11-14	3,189	8	2	1,217	19	4[3]	103	11	0½	3,085	17	1½
HENRY III June 1238 to Apr. 1240[4] P.R. 85, m.3	7,018	14	9½	401	3	11½ (tallage)	2,158	16	11	4,859	17	10½
Apr. 1240 to Sep. 1241[4] P.R. 85, m.3 and 3d	6,138	11	11				1,116	13	9	5,021	18	2
Sep. 1241 to Sep. 1243[4] P.R. 87, m.3d and P.R. 88, m.12	6,150	12	0½				1,471	16	8½	4,678	15	4
Sep. 1243 to Sep. 1244[4] P.R. 88, m.12	3,682	7	11[5]				628	0	4½	3,054	7	6½

[1] The account is for three parts of the exchequer year ending Mich. 1189 and the late bishop, Richard of Ilchester died 22 Dec. 1188 (*Handbook*).

[2] This sum includes £300 'de pecunia Ricardi Winton. episcopi'.

[3] This is a complex sum 'de auxiliis et perquisitionibus et minutis exitibus'. Only the 'aids' properly belong to this column.

[4] These four accounts, which all relate to one vacancy, exclude the manors of Taunton and Rimpton. These two manors were accounted for separately and the dates of the accounts do not coincide with those of the main accounts. The net income from the two manors between Christmas 1241 and Christmas 1242 was £492.5.2½ (P.R. 86, m.7), and between Christmas 1242 and Christmas 1243 it was £447.13.9 (P.R. 87, m.3), thus giving a yearly average net income of almost £470.

[5] Of this total, however, £462.10.8 was conceded by the king to the incoming bishop, William Raleigh.

WINCHESTER (continued)

Period	Gross Receipts £ s. d.	Tallage, Aid or Recognitions £ s. d.	Expenses £ s. d.	Net Receipts £ s.
HENRY III (continued) 12 Sep. 1250 to 28 Mar. 1251 P.R. 95, m.6	1,723 1 2½	510 18 6½ (tallage)	615 0 7½	1.108 0
29 Sep. 1258 to 25 Dec. 1260 P.R. 104, m.2 and m.1	12,490 2 4		2,426 0 8½[1]	10,064 1
25 Dec. 1260 to 14 Aug. 1262 P.R. 106, m.21 and 21d	7,776 17 10		1,560 12 6	6,216 5
26 Feb. 1268 to 2 May 1268 C.R. 61 m.6d and m.27d	996 0 0[2]	487 16 10 (aids and recognitions)	220 7 8½	775 12
EDWARD I 10 Feb. 1280 to 11 Aug. 1282 P.R. 128, m.28	15,737 17 2	482 5 4 (recognitions)	4,405 11 6	11,332 5
6 Dec. 1304 to 12 Mar. 1305 P.R. 152B, m.20	1,398 2 3¼	499 17 8 (recognitions)	303 4 1¾	1,094 18

WORCESTER

Period	Gross Receipts £ s. d.	Tallage, Aid or Recognitions £ s. d.	Expenses £ s. d.	Net Receipts £ s.
HENRY II Mich. 1161 to Mich. 1162 P.R. 8 Henry II, p. 61	300 + [3]			300 +
P.R. 32 Henry II, p. 42[4]	288 19 1		17 7 6	271 11
JOHN Mich. 1211 to Mich. 1212[5] P.R. 14 John, 1212, pp. 60–1	399 1 10½	38 18 10 (tallage)	55 1 11	343 19 1

[1] This excludes £666.13.4 which was paid by the king's concession for the maintenance Andrew, prior of Winchester and at the time bishop-elect.

[2] *Rectius* £996.14.9½.   [3] The account is very imperfe

[4] Three terms of the exchequer year ending Mich. 1186.

[5] Bishop Mauger died 1 July 1212.

WORCESTER (*continued*)

Period	Gross Receipts £ s. d.	Tallage, Aid or Recognitions £ s. d.	Expenses £ s. d.	Net Receipts £ s. d.
ЄNRY III Aug. 1236 to Sep. 1236 R. 81, m.15d.	164 12 10½	51 11 0½ (aid)	6 0 0	158 12 10½
Feb. 1266 to July 1266[1] R. 110 m.13	264 15 4½	42 19 4½ (aid)	23 4 3½	241 11 1
May 1268 to May 1268 R. 112, m.2d	66 11 9	31 19 2 (fines and recognitions)	2	
ϽWARD I Jan. 1302 to Feb. 1303 R. 147, mm.24–5	1,320 17 10½	38 7 4 (recognitions)	469 19 2½	850 18 8

YORK

Period	Gross Receipts £ s. d.	Tallage, Aid or Recognitions £ s. d.	Expenses £ s. d.	Net Receipts £ s. d.
ЄNRY II Їich. 1182 to Їich. 1183 R. 29 Henry II, 59	1,791 10 10[3]		40 10 10	1,751 0 0
Їich. 1183 to Їich. 1184 R. 30 Henry II, Ͻ. 39–41	1,469 13 0		51 17 9	1,417 15 3
Їich. 1184 to Їich. 1185 R. 31 Henry II, Ͻ. 78–9	1,498 7 9		48 16 6	1,449 11 3

[1] The date may be 18 June. On the Pipe Roll the account is said to extend 'usque ad xviij ᵉm Julii anno eodem antequam liberarent dictum episcopatum Nicholao Wigorn. electo ᵉr breve regis in quo continetur quod liberarent eidem electo omnes exitus et proventus a ⁻iij die Junii eiusdem anni'. The mandate for the restitution of the temporalities is dated ₃ June 1266. (*Cal. Pat. R. 1258–66*, p. 607.)

[2] The expenses are not grouped separately.

[3] Some arrears are unavoidably included in this sum.

APPENDIX A

YORK (continued)

Period	Gross Receipts			Tallage, Aid or Recognitions			Expenses			Net Receipts	
	£	s.	d.	£	s.	d.	£	s.	d.	£	s.
HENRY II (continued) Mich. 1186 to Mich. 1187[1] P.R. 33 Henry II, pp. 97–8 and pp. 75–6	1,313	16	9	8	0	0[2]	70	16	11	1,242	19 1
Mich. 1187 to Mich. 1188 P.R. 34 Henry II, pp. 9–10	1,281	14	10				87	10		1,194	4
JOHN Mich. 1211 to Mich. 1212[3] P.R. 14 John, 1212, pp. 2–3	1,442	6	4[4]				91	9	3½	1,350	17
HENRY III 4 May 1255 to 4 May 1256 P.R. 101, m.4d	2,344	10	10½	661 8 10 (aids and tallages)			263	14	7	2,080	16
18 Jan. 1265 to 12 Aug. 1265[5] P.R. 109, m.11	893	8	10½				535	16	6	357	12
12 Aug. 1265 to 20 Dec. 1266[5] P.R. 110, m. 13	3,409	5	3	188 2 2 (aid and tallage)			602	15	1	2,806	10
EDWARD I 28 Apr. 1279 to 28 Oct. 1279 C.R. 74, m.7	1,608	5	11½	251 3 4 (tallage)			105	3	7	1,503	2

[1] The account for the year 1185–6 is partly obliterated and has therefore not been includ here.

[2] This is from the lands of the archbishopric in Lincolnshire only.

[3] A *sede plena* account.

[4] This sum includes substantial payments in gifts of clergy in Yorkshire and in the bisho ric of Carlisle and from churches and prebends of the archbishopric in the king's hand. T total of £1242.6.4 on the Pipe Roll is a slip.

[5] This account excludes the issues of the manors of Churchdown and Oddington which we in separate custody.

YORK (*continued*)

Period	Gross Receipts	Tallage, Aid or Recognitions	Expenses	Net Receipts
	£ s. d.	£ s. d.	£ s. d.	£ s. d.
EDWARD I (*continued*)				
15 Sep. 1285 to 16 Apr. 1286 P.R. 133, m. 28	2,061 13 2¾	201 6 2 (tallage)	477 5 10¾	1,584 7 4
16 Aug. 1299 to 30 Apr. 1300 P.R. 150, mm.30–31d		(recognitions)[1]		1,350 14 4½[2]
1 Oct. 1304 to 21 Mar. 1306 P.R. 152B, mm.16–19		(tallage)[3]		3,301 6 6¼[2]

[1] The recognitions are not always given separately and cannot therefore be calculated separately.

[2] There seemed little to be gained by a separate calculation of the gross receipts and the expenses on the whole of these two York accounts. Instead a calculation has been made of the gross receipts and the expenses for the regnal year 1304–5 on the account of 1304–6. The total gross receipts during that year were £1,730.2.2¼; the agricultural expenses amounted to £518.14.10½ (P.R. 152B, mm.16d–17d). The receipts included the tallage.

[3] The tallage is sometimes grouped with other payments. Very occasionally it goes under the name of recognitions.

Appendix B

The Destination of the Issues of Vacant Bishoprics in the Reigns of Henry III and Edward I

THE vacancy accounts included in this table have been arranged in chronological order of their initial dates, in order to bring out the main trends in the destination of the issues. A few accounts have been omitted from the list, those in which the receipts from the bishopric are not treated separately but classed with other sums received by the same accountant. Usually such accounts are only for small sums of money.

In the last column of the table a note has been made of any very substantial payments made elsewhere than into the treasury or the wardrobe.

The figure of net total receipts in column (2) is the same in every case as that given in column (5) of Appendix A, unless otherwise stated.

HENRY III

Bishopric and Period	Net Receipts			In Thesauro			In Garderoba			Large Payments Elsewhere			
	£	s.	d.	£	s.	d.	£	s.	d.		£	s.	d.
ELY													
1218 to 1219 (3 terms only)	590	17	7½	310	10	11½				The bishop (expenses at Rome)	66	13	4
										Hospitallers in Tower of London	136	13	4
NORWICH													
13 Dec. 1218 to 17 Mar. 1219	118	16	6							Abbot of Bury St. Edmunds	118	16	6
EXETER													
29 Sep. 1223 to 29 Sep. 1224	185	12	7½	51	18	1	86	18	2½				

HENRY III (*continued*)

Bishopric and Period	Net Receipts £ s. d.	In Thesauro £ s. d.	In Garderoba £ s. d.	Large Payments Elsewhere £ s. d.
DURHAM 2 Sep. 1226 to 2 Aug. 1228	5,861 18 5	4,732 18 2	746 13 4	
CANTERBURY 7 July 1228 to 1 Mar. 1229	1,475 13 9¾[1]	866 13 4	443 6 8	
SALISBURY 0 July 1228 to 8 Feb. 1229	485 16 0[1]	462 15 0½		
LONDON Nov. 1228 to 7 Apr. 1229	225 2 5½[1]	200 17 8		
ELY 2 Dec. 1228 to 8 Feb. 1229	732 5 3½[1]	732 5 3½		
CANTERBURY 1 Sep. 1231 to Aug. 1232	1,496 7 11½[1]	930 1 3½	180 6 8	
HEREFORD 4 Aug. 1234 to Oct. 1234	117 6 10	104 0 0		
LINCOLN Feb. 1235 to 5 Apr. 1235	389 16 2	383 6 8		
WORCESTER 2 Aug. 1236 to 9 Sep. 1236	158 12 10½		3 0 0	Walter de Burgh 99 0 0[2] Walter Cantilupe (bishop-elect) 55 0 0
NORWICH 1 Aug. 1236 to 6 Mar. 1237	118 13 4		110 0 0	
DURHAM 9 Apr. 1237 to Feb. 1239	5,818 1 4		5,238 1 0	Keepers of thirtieth in Tower of London 333 6 8

[1] These figures differ from those given in the table in Appendix A because it was necessary in the present table to include payments of scutage with the other receipts.

[2] This was for the stocking of the royal demesnes.

HENRY III (continued)

Bishopric and Period	Net Receipts			In Thesauro			In Garderoba			Large Payments Elsewhere		
	£	s.	d.	£	s.	d.	£	s.	d.		£	s. d
WINCHESTER 14 June 1238 to 15 Apr. 1240	4,859	17	10½	388	6	8	3,102	15	10	Works at Winchester 386 6 9 Works at Devizes 124 0 0		
LICHFIELD 27 Dec. 1238 to 1 Jan. 1240	32 368	14 19	8[1] 5[2]				334	3	4	Hugh Pateshull (bishop-elect) 32 14 8		
DURHAM 2 Feb. 1239 to 24 June 1240	3,713	17	5	178	13	4	3,353	6	8			
WINCHESTER 15 Apr. 1240 to 29 Sep. 1241	5,021	18	2	615	0	0	1,635	0	0	Works at Tower of London 200 0 0 Works at Windsor 716 13 4 Works at Winchester 1,177 15 6		
DURHAM 24 June 1240 to 10 Feb. 1241	2,174	17	0	30	0	0	1,342	10	10	King of Scotland 400 0 0		
LONDON 29 Sep. 1241 to (a) 29 Sep. 1242 (b)	258 174	4 1	6½ 2	171	10	3	155	16	8	Expenses of king 87 10		
WINCHESTER 29 Sep. 1241 to 29 Sep. 1243	4,678	15	4	444	17	4	483	0	0	'Camerariis Regis' 1,000 0 0		
LICHFIELD 21 Dec. 1241 to 6 May 1242	62	16	6½				53	0	0			
LONDON 29 Sep. 1242 to 17 Mar. 1244	1,070	15	9	738	6	8	100	0	0			
BATH AND WELLS 27 Nov. 1242 to 10 May 1244	927	14	1½	860	0	0						

[1] Lands within county of Chester.   [2] Lands outside county of Cheste

[3] ' quas Rex debuit ei assignasse'.

[4] There were also considerable outpayments concerned with the expenses of the Gasco campaign.

HENRY III (*continued*)

Bishopric and Period	Net Receipts £ s. d.	In Thesauro £ s. d.	In Garderoba £ s. d.	Large Payments Elsewhere £ s. d.
NCHESTER Sep. 1243 to Sep. 1244	3,054 7 6½	22 0 0	160 0 0	William Raleigh (bishop-elect) 462 10 8 Earl of Cornwall 500 0 0 Works at Windsor 534 6 8 Works at Winchester 626 16 2½ Expenses of queen 133 6 8
ICHESTER 'eb. 1244 to July 1246	1,056 10 2		45 0 0	Works at Windsor 423 6 8
ETER Dec. 1244 to Apr. 1245	159 6 11	154 0 0		
RLISLE June 1246 to Dec. 1246	23 15 11½[1]		28 12 5	
LISBURY Nov. 1246 to Jan. 1247	152 19 9½[2]		153 0 0	
DAVID'S Apr. 1247 to Sep. 1247	66 12 10[3]		66 13 4	
RHAM Feb. 1249 to Oct. 1249	2,326 10 6	25 19 6	253 18 1	Earl of Cornwall 2,020 0 0
NCHESTER Sept. 1250 to Mar. 1251	1,508 0 7[4]		400 0 0	Works at Windsor 166 13 4 Aymer de Valence (bishop-elect) 330 10 11 Works at Winchester 166 13 4 Purchases for king 100 0 0

[1] The keeper has a 'surplus' of £18.3.1½ owing to him at the end of the account.
[2] This account ends 'Et quietus est'—although to be exact the keeper should have had d. 'de superplusagio'. [3] The keeper has 6d. 'de superplusagio'.
[4] This figure necessarily includes a fine of £400, taken from the property of the late bishop payment of his debts to the king.

HENRY III (continued)

Bishopric and Period	Net Receipts £ s. d.	In Thesauro £ s. d.	In Garderoba £ s. d.	Large Payments Elsewhere £ s.
LINCOLN 11 Oct. 1253 to 1 Apr. 1254	770 1 9[1]	519 13 4		
ELY 12 Aug. 1254 to 25 Dec. 1254	712 18 11½			Manneby, Axmouth and Chishull (super-keepers) 709 8
YORK 4 May 1255 to 4 May 1256	2,080 16 3½		1,393 6 8	Queen's wardrobe 100 0 Queen's expenses 300 0 Nicholas, bishop of Durham[3] 133 6
SALISBURY 5 Feb. 1256 to 17 Aug. 1256	507 15 1½		340 0 0	Queen's wardrobe 80 0
ELY 29 Oct. 1256 to 15 Jan. 1258	3,161 15 7	193 15 6½	1,040 0 0[4]	Executors of late bishop 1,333 6
NORWICH 20 May 1257 to 11 Aug. 1257	287 5 4	246 0 0		
LINCOLN 16 Aug. 1258 to 17 Oct. 1258	296 2 4	1 0 0	161 15 8	Purchase for king 133 6
WINCHESTER 29 Sep. 1258 to 25 Dec. 1260	10,064 1 7½	2,529 7 6	1,213 6 8	Count of Savoy 2,000 0 John of Brittany 666 13 Constable of Dover castle 133 6 Buyers of wardrobe 1,680 7 Wine for king 318 6

[1] This figure necessarily includes £207.0.10, the payment of a regular aid by the knights the bishopric for the knighting of the king's eldest son.

[2] See *supra*, p. 154.

[3] Nicholas Farnham had however resigned in 1249.

[4] Robert Walerand's debt of £423.11.1 is merely restated on Pipe R. 104, m.8d.

[5] See *supra*, p. 155, n. 3. This sum appears on both the receipt and the outpayment si of the present account.

HENRY III (*continued*)

Bishopric and Period	Net Receipts £ s. d.	In Thesauro £ s. d.	In Garderoba £ s. d.	Large Payments Elsewhere	£ s. d.
NCHESTER (*continued*)				John Clarel (expenses at Roman curia)	200 0 0
				Andrew (bishop-elect)	666 13 4
NCHESTER Dec. 1260 to Aug. 1262	6,216 5 4	476 13 4	4,430 13 3	John of Brittany	666 13 4
				Wines for king	76 0 0
				Works at Westminster	100 0 0
ICHESTER May 1262 to June 1262	69 6 3½		68 13 4		
NDON July 1262 to Jan. 1263	404 1 10	313 3 5½			
LISBURY Dec. 1262 to Apr. 1263	458 19 11	78 1 11	340 0 0		
TH AND WELLS Apr. 1264 to Sep. 1264	238 15 9½		203 6 8		
RK Jan. 1265 to Aug. 1265	357 12 4½[11]	5 0 0	301 13 4	Wines for king	100 0 0
RK Aug. 1265 to Dec. 1266	2,806 10 2	52 19 1	1,075 3 4	Queen	500 0 0
				Archbishop of York	166 13 4
				H. Ostiensi	100 0 0
				William de Chavenz	300 0 0
				Keeper, for corn delivered to archbishop of York as gift	191 17 4
ORCESTER Feb. 1266 to July 1266	241 11 1			Edmund, king's son	114 10 6½
				Wines for king	120 0 0

[1] The accountant is left with £49.0.11½ 'de superplusagio'.

HENRY III (*continued*)

Bishopric and Period	Net Receipts	In Thesauro	In Garderoba	Large Payments Elsewhere
	£ s. d.	£ s. d.	£ s. d.	£ s.
BATH AND WELLS 27 Dec. 1266 to 4 Mar. 1267	89 0 0			Chancellor 89 0
HEREFORD 10 Dec. 1268 to 21 Apr. 1269	243 0 3	54 6 8	161 6 8	
CANTERBURY 14 Aug. 1270 to 12 Dec. 1272	5,040 6 8¼	1,393 6 8	1,552 3 7	Archbishop of York[1] 1,591 1 : Executors of Archbishop Boniface 73 6 Wines for king 153 6 For proctors at Rome 200 0 For king's jewels mortgaged abroad 250 0

EDWARD I

Bishopric and Period	Net Receipts	In Thesauro	In Garderoba	Large Payments Elsewhere
LONDON 20 Sep. 1273 to 15 Mar. 1274	326 8 2	316 16 4		
DURHAM 20 Aug. 1274 to 12 Nov. 1274	2,569 10 0		912 6 0	Merchants, for loans to king 1,467 0 King of Scotland 175 0
BATH 15 Dec. 1274 to 17 Feb. 1275	170 16 10	7 19 10½	160 0 0	
HEREFORD 11 May 1275 to 27 June 1275	241 2 10½		36 10 0	Constable of Windsor 200 0
NORWICH 19 Jan. 1278 to 16 Mar. 1278	180 12 7			Subconstable of Tower of London 170 0
CANTERBURY 6 June 1278 to 30 May 1279	3,184 13 11	60 6 11	2,485 5 10	King's works in Wales 433 6 Bishop of Bath and Wells (Chancellor) 152 7 1

[1] In connection with sale of corn to archbishop.

EDWARD I (*continued*)

Bishopric and Period	Net Receipts			In Thesauro			In Garderoba			Large Payments Elsewhere		
	£	s.	d.	£	s.	d.	£	s.	d.		£ s.	d.
ORK Apr. 1279 to Oct. 1279	1,503	2	4½	40	0	0	381	8	2	William de Perton (for Rhuddlan castle)	1,042	1	2
NCOLN Dec. 1279 to Feb. 1280	262	16	5	26	13	4	200	0	0			
INCHESTER Feb. 1280 to Aug. 1282	11,332	5	8	1,880	0	0	6,519	4	0	Corn bought to be sent to Chester 515 0 0 / Flint castle 266 13 4 / Flint and Rhuddlan castles 1,583 6 8		
ETER Aug. 1280 to Oct. 1280	331	5	1½	300	0	0						
REFORD Aug. 1282 to Jan. 1283	341	2	5½	110	0	0				Food for king 80 0 0 / Soldiers 160 0 0		
URHAM June 1283 to Sep. 1283	2,540	18	0¼	50	13	7¼	2,490	4	5			
LISBURY Apr. 1284 to Aug. 1284	428	18	7½	364	6	8						
ORK Sep. 1285 to Apr. 1286	1,584	7	4	212	0	8				Caernarvon castle 1,264 13 6		
LISBURY Sep. 1286 to Mar. 1287	1,109	13	6¾	986	1	10						
ICHESTER Oct. 1287 to June 1288	638	19	9¼	597	5	5½						
ORWICH Oct. 1288 to Feb. 1289	509	13	10¼	344	1	8						

R

EDWARD I (*continued*)

Bishopric and Period	Net Receipts £ s. d.	In Thesauro £ s. d.	In Garderoba £ s. d.	Large Payments Elsewhere £ s.
ELY 4 Apr. 1290 to 30 May 1290	668 17 0¼	608 13 0		
SALISBURY 12 Oct. 1291 to 24 Dec. 1291	649 7 7¼	624 1 11		
BATH AND WELLS 25 Oct. 1292 to 19 Mar. 1293	380 2 7¼	372 0 0		
CANTERBURY 9 Dec. 1292 to 4 Feb. 1295	10,136 7 5¾	8,345 4 11½[1]		
ST. DAVID'S 22 Apr. 1293 to 11 Oct. 1293	171 19 7	133 14 0		
ST. DAVID'S 31 May 1296 to 24 Jan. 1297	212 16 7			Bishop answerable for 193 2
SALISBURY 18 May 1297 to 7 Aug. 1297	347 17 2½	347 17 2½		
ELY 28 Mar. 1298 to 13 Oct. 1299	4,745 2 10½	2,704 19 6		John of Brittany 1,333 6 / King's Gascon creditors 494 10
YORK 16 Aug. 1299 to 30 Apr. 1300	1,350 14 4½	83 15 0½		Earl of Cornwall 1,206 14
LINCOLN 16 Nov. 1299 to 18 Mar. 1300	561 11 7½			Walter of Gloucester 540 5
WORCESTER 30 Jan. 1302 to 4 Feb. 1303	850 18 8³	256 13 4		Amadeus of Savoy 621 11

[1] A further £447.10.2 is allowed to the archbishop in compensation for the seizure goods of this value from certain lay fees of the archbishopric by the sheriff, and the bishop then left with a debt of £723.15.10½; Pipe R. 142, m.5d.

[2] The debt is simply restated on Pipe R. 144, m.7.

[3] The accountant has £27.6.5 'de superplusagio'.

EDWARD I (*continued*)

Bishopric and Period	Net Receipts			In Thesauro			In Garderoba			Large Payments Elsewhere			
	£	s.	d.	£	s.	d.	£	s.	d.		£	s.	d.
Y Mar. 1302 to July 1302	763	7	2¼	740	0	0							
TH AND WELLS June 1302 to Sep. 1302	557	1	5½	296	13	4				Amadeus of Savoy	260	8	1½
Y July 1302 to 'eb. 1303	1,955	2	0½[1]							Amadeus of Savoy	1,983	6	8
NDON)ec. 1303 to une 1304	506	19	3¼							(Amadeus of Savoy	450	0	0[2])
RK)ct. 1304 to Mar. 1306	3,301	6	6¼	2,983	3	7				King's valets	266	13	4
NCHESTER)ec. 1304 to Mar. 1305	1,094	18	1½	11	16	10				Amadeus of Savoy	1,066	13	4
ICHESTER Feb. 1305 to July 1305	370	11	5	308	11	7½							

[1] The accountant has £28.4.7½ 'de superplusagio'.

[2] This is only a probability. The receipts on this account are classed with other debts and t treated separately, but by a mandate of 22 Nov. 1305 the barons of exchequer were lered to allow the keeper £450 in his account for the issues of this vacant bishopric since had paid that sum, by the king's order, to Amadeus of Savoy (*Cal. Close R., 1302–07*, p. 357).

Index

Note: In entries relating to vacancies the terminal date is that of the restitution of the temporalities (where that is known). In entries relating to bishops, the initial date of the episcopate is that of the bishop's accession to the see, as given in the *Handbook of Chronology.* *s.v.*=sede vacante.

Abbeys, royal custody of, *abbatia vacante*, 5–6, 8–12, 22–3, 50 n., 172 n.; special provision for monks of, 14–15; custody in vacancy by convent, 110 n., 149

Abbotsham, John of, 178

Abbrebury, Thomas de, 181 n.

Abetot, Urse d', sheriff of Worcester, possibly keeper of Worcester *s.v.*, 7

Abingdon, abbey of, vacancy in, 6, 8, 9; *donum* paid from lands of, 43 n.; chronicle of, 5 n.; on vacancy in 1097, 6 n., 9

Abingdon, Richard of, keeper *s.v.* Ely, 89, 180 n.

Accounts of keepers of vacant bishoprics, rendered at exchequer, 44, 64, 98–109; proportion entered on Pipe Rolls, 98–101; official character of, 104, 120–1; falsification of, 107–9, 119; rolls of particulars subsidiary to, 102–3

Adderbury, Oxon., church of, 176 n.; manor of, 137 n., 138 n.

Aids, feudal, for marriage of Mathilda, daughter of Henry II, 40–2, 212; levied on vacant bishoprics by king, 26–8, 110 n.; levied *see* Tallage; *mutatio domini*, 17–18, 136–7; relation to recognitions, 137. *See* individual bishoprics

Aigueblanche, Peter d', keeper of wardrobe, 156; bishop of Hereford (1240–68), 137

Aimericy, Peter de, king's clerk, 177 n.

Airmyn, Richard, king's clerk, 174 n.; keeper *s.v.* Winchester, 64 n.; accused of peculation, 107–8

Airmyn (Ayremynne), William, king's clerk, 174 n., 196 n.

Aldington, Kent, church of, 177 n.

Alexander III, pope, 31

Alexander IV, pope, disputes with Henry III over patronage, 190

Allertonshire, subdivision of bishopric of Durham, 81 n.

Alresford, Hants, manor and borough of, 138 n.

Amadeus of Savoy, *see* Savoy

Amatus, Tegrus, merchant, 160 n.

Amundevill, John, keeper *s.v.* Durham, 25 and n.

Andrew, prior of St. Swithins, Winchester, bishop elect of Winchester, 230 n., 239

Angeli, Henry del, abbot of Peterborough, 18

Anglicus, Thomas, witness for monks of Durham, 129, 135 n.

Anglo Saxon Chronicle, on oppression by William Rufus, 21

Anketil, keeper *s.v.* Salisbury, 86

Anselm, archbishop of Canterbury (1093–1109), protests on abuses *s.v.*, 12, 31

Apulia, 155

Arundel, Roger, keeper *s.v.* York, 36

Ashridge, Roger of, king's clerk, 173 n.

Assized rents, 45, 52, 115, 117 and n.

Aston, Adam de, keeper *s.v.* Chichester, 100 n.

Attenoke, Richard, bailiff, 83 n.

Aucklandshire, subdivision of bishopric of Durham, 81 n.

Auxerre, province of, 60 n.

Avener, Ralph le, king's sergeant, 198

S

(i/p E/m)

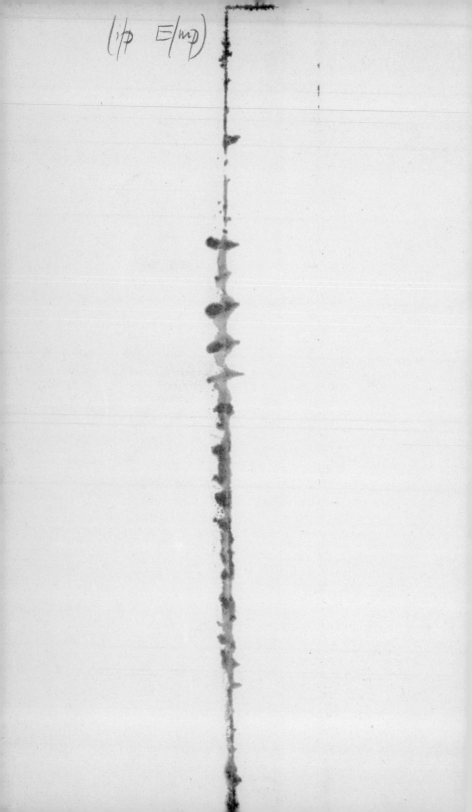